A FREE WILL BAPTIST
HANDBOOK

HERITAGE, BELIEFS, AND MINISTRIES

J. Matthew Pinson

Randall House Publications
114 Bush Road, P.O. Box 17306
Nashville, Tennessee 37217
www.randallhouse.com

Cover Design: Joy Simpkins
Copy Editing: Harrold Harrison, Larry Hampton,
David Kilgore, Dianne Sargent, Keith Fletcher

A Free Will Baptist Handbook:
Heritage, Beliefs, and Ministries

Copyright © 1998
Randall House Publications
Nashville, Tennessee 37217
Printed in the United States of America.

ISBN 089265-6883

This book is lovingly dedicated

to my grandparents,

The Reverend and Mrs. L.V. Pinson,

who taught me to

seek the old paths and walk therein.

Table of Contents

Foreword

Melvin Leroy Worthington, Th.D., Ed.D., CMP
Executive Secretary
National Association of Free Will Baptists

The writer of Ecclesiastes declares, "And further by these, my son, be admonished: of making many books there is no end; and much study is a weariness of the flesh" (Ecclesiastes 12:12). Some books are just that–books that take up shelf space. That is not the case with this work, *A Free Will Baptist Handbook: Heritage, Beliefs, and Ministries* by J. Matthew Pinson. The author captures denominational distinctives, deportment, and doctrines clearly, concisely, and correctly. He conveys with compassion and consistency the historical and organizational development as well as the divisions that have taken place during the denomination's existence.

Three elements distinguish this book as a work of significant value to denominational constituents. The first element is the *information* which is accumulated. The information in Brother Pinson's book provides an objective overview of the National Association of Free Will Baptists, Inc. He includes an accurate and authentic analysis of the history and heritage of Free Will Baptists. The documentation, doctrinal statements, denominational structure, and detailed analysis of the Free Will Baptist Church Covenant make this an indispensable tool for Free Will Baptists.

The second element that makes this work of significant value is the author's *insight.* Reverend Pinson does more than simply read, record, or recite historical facts and figures. He writes perceptively, positively, and practically. His attention to detail and his unique perception are evident both in the writing style and substance. The author's insight sets this book apart from other works written on the subject.

The third element that makes this work of significant value is the *inclusion* of articles that matter. This one volume includes an overview of the entire National Association of Free Will Baptists. The inclusion of the history, beliefs, analysis of the Free Will Baptist Church Covenant, *Treatise,* and a brief historical summary of national ministries and state associations provide an excellent research tool.

This work suggests that the writer is familiar with Free Will Baptists, focuses on Free Will Baptists, and is unapologetically committed to Free Will Baptists. The information, insight, and inclusive nature of this work commend it to every Free Will Baptist. Browsing this book will be a rich and rewarding educational experience. In my opinion, this book belongs in the library of every Free Will Baptist.

Preface

The idea for this book originated while I was interim pastor at a small church in south Alabama. When new members would come into the church and want to know more about Free Will Baptists, or when long-time members wanted more information about their denomination, I found it difficult to get them all the information they needed. This problem did not occur because there was not enough information about Free Will Baptists, but because there was so much! While there was a great deal of material published by Randall House and the various national departments, it seemed to take a wheelbarrow to deliver it to the interested individual.

Thus, I decided to combine information from the existing materials into a handy, one-volume reference book–a "Free Will Baptist handbook." As I mulled over the idea in my mind and discussed it with others, the shape of the book came together: I would discuss our history, doctrine, and various ministries in a way that was readable and helpful to the average layman. Reprints of the confessions of faith used by our forefathers, as well as a complete copy of our *Treatise* would be included.

The result is a handy book that introduces who we are, where we came from, what we believe, what God has done through us in the past, and what He is doing through us today. The book is written in plain language so as to be an understandable source of information to the average person in the pew, yet it is also a thorough and up-to-date study. The book is ideal for use with new church members, prospective members, or as a "refresher course" for seasoned Free Will Baptist church members or pastors.

Chapter one, "Our Heritage: Free Will Baptist History," gives a brief survey of our origin and history. Chapter two, "Our Beliefs: Free Will Baptist Doctrinal Distinctives," gives an overview of what we believe, particularly the distinctive doctrines that set us apart from other denominations. Chapter three, "United With the Church: Being a Free Will Baptist Church Member," is an introduction to church membership, including a discussion of the Free Will Baptist Church Covenant. Chapter four, "Our Historic Confessions of Faith," contains a reprint of three of the four most important confessions of faith in our history; while chapter five, "A Treatise of the Faith and Practices of Free Will Baptists" reprints the fourth confession of faith, our *Treatise*.

Chapter six, "The National Association of Free Will Baptists: Its Origin and Ministries," summarizes the founding and early history of the National Association as well as its ministries, including all of the national departments, agencies, and commissions. Chapter seven, "Free Will Baptist Ministries on the State and Local Levels," describes such local and state Free Will Baptist ministries as colleges and family-care homes. Chapter eight, "Unaffiliated Arminian Baptist Groups" tells about groups which share our doctrine but not aligned with the National Association of Free Will Baptists.

For the best understanding of the book, it is recommended that the reader first read through chapter one, the chapter on our heritage. Reading this chapter will set many other things in context and enable the reader to understand the other chapters better. Each chapter is, however, a self-standing unit and can be read independently of others. For this reason, there is some repetition of the themes discussed.

This book is also designed to be a handbook–a usable, hands-on reference guide for the National Association of Free Will Baptists. Thus, it is not designed to replace the excellent books, pamphlets, and promotional brochures published by the National Association. It is rather meant to be an *introduction* to the information in these materials, so that the reader may be urged to read more of the helpful material already in print. It is hoped that this book will be used to give glory to God as it helps His people understand more about their faith and their united efforts to carry the gospel to the uttermost parts of the earth.

Acknowledgments

I would like to thank the Historical Committee of the Florida State Association of Free Will Baptists for permission to adapt sections of chapters one and two from articles printed in their publication, *The Historical Review,* volumes I-III. I would also like to thank *Contact,* the official magazine of the National Association of Free Will Baptists, for their permission to adapt sections of chapters one and two from articles printed therein.

There are many individuals to thank, without whom I could not have completed this work. First and foremost, I extend my warmest gratitude to my wife, Melinda, who proofread, edited, and commented on the entire book and offered her love and encouragement, without which this book could not have come to fruition. I thank F. Leroy Forlines for standing behind me and for reading and offering helpful comments on the manuscript. Thanks also to Steve Ashby and Joel Hampton, both of whom read and offered needed insight on portions of the manuscript. I also wish to thank Dr. Alton Loveless for his vision, creativity, and dedication to the work of God as well as the Board of Trustees of Randall House Publications for making this work possible. I express thanks to my parents for modeling the Christian faith before me and lovingly equipping me with the tools with which to perform this kind of labor, and my beloved church family at Colquitt Free Will Baptist Church for serving as a receptive and encouraging sounding board for my ideas. Finally, I thank God for revealing to humanity His Truth which always and alone sets us free.

CHAPTER ONE

Our Heritage: Free Will Baptist History

THE ENGLISH GENERAL BAPTISTS, FOREFATHERS IN GREAT BRITAIN

Most Free Will Baptists can trace their heritage back to Paul Palmer, who in 1727 founded the first known Free Will Baptist church in America.[1] Paul Palmer married into the Laker family, English General Baptists who had moved to America. Fully convinced of the General Baptist faith, he established a General Baptist church in Chowan County, North Carolina, in 1727.[2] Though the early churches did not use the title "Free Will Baptist," they were commonly known as "Free-willers" and would begin to call themselves Free Will Baptists in the late 1700s.[3] The *1660 English General Baptist Confession of Faith* was used by Free Will Baptists in the South until it was condensed and revised in a new confession in 1812 (later called the *1812 Former Articles*).[4] The *1812 Former Articles* were used in the South until well into the twentieth century. Though Free Will Baptists from a few regions had spontaneous beginnings (for example, the Randall Movement of Freewill Baptists[5] in the North), the majority of Free Will Baptists today can trace their heritage, either by direct link or influence, to the Palmer Movement of the Carolinas. Since the Palmer Movement originated with General Baptist settlers from England in the late 1600s, our English General Baptist forefathers will be discussed here. It must also be noted that the Randall Movement of Freewill Baptists in the North had extensive contact with the General Baptists of

England in the 1800s, even to the point of exchanging representatives. Thus our English General Baptist heritage is instructive for all Free Will Baptists.

Smyth and Helwys in England

The General Baptists began with John Smyth and Thomas Helwys in England in the early 1600s. John Smyth (1570-1612) was a graduate of Cambridge University and taught there for a time.[6] Originally, he had been a priest in the Church of England[7] but had become dissatisfied with the unbiblical practices in that church. He went from being an Anglican priest to being a Puritan (one who remained in the Church of England but wished to purify it) to being a Separatist (one who wished to separate entirely from the Church of England). All the while, Smyth was a Calvinist as well as a paedobaptist (infant baptizer). Smyth had begun to pastor a small Separatist congregation who, like other Separatists, were being persecuted because of their lack of allegiance to the Church of England. King James I had "threatened to harrie them out of the land unless they conformed to the state church."[8] In an attempt to escape persecution and imprisonment, the small congregation exiled itself to Holland, where it settled in Amsterdam in 1607.[9]

Smyth and Thomas Helwys, a lawyer and lay-leader in the congregation, began to consider the Scriptural teaching on the subject of baptism and came to reject infant baptism in favor of believer's baptism. It is possible that this change in doctrine came about as a result of the congregation's contact with the Dutch Waterlander Mennonites.[10] This change made Smyth dissatisfied with his own "baptism" (he had been sprinkled as an infant in the Church of England). So, having no properly baptized person to baptize him, Smyth baptized himself (the so-called se-baptism) and then baptized the rest of his congregation.[11] Later, in a book entitled *The Character of the Beast*, which condemned the Anglican Church for being too close to the Roman Catholic Church, he said, ". . . all that shall in time to come separate from [the Church of] England must separate from the baptism of [the Church of] England, and if they will not separate from baptism there is no reason why they should separate from [the Church of] England as from a false church. . . ."[12]

While in Holland, Smyth and Helwys apparently came into contact with the thinking of Jacobus Arminius, the father of Arminianism. As McBeth says, the General Baptists were less influenced by John Calvin and "more influenced by the Dutch theologian Jacob Arminius, whose theology made room for free will. The General Baptists also, like other Arminians, taught the possibility of 'falling from grace.'"[13] At this time Smyth and Helwys made the transition from Calvinism to Arminianism.[14] Altogether then, the transition had been made from Anglican to Puritan to Separatist to anti-pedobaptist to Free Will Baptist.[15]

The baptism question continued to plague Smyth. His se-baptism was a real source of controversy among the other Separatists, and he began to entertain the erroneous notion that it was necessary to have some sort of succession in baptism (that he needed to be baptized by someone who had been baptized by someone who had been baptized, and so forth, all the way back to the early church). At this time, Smyth began to draw much closer to the Dutch Mennonites and soon took up Mennonite views. Mennonites believed that all war and self-defense are wrong, that Christians should not be personally involved in government or politics (or even vote), that capital punishment is immoral, and that Christians should not swear oaths in courts.

Helwys's Break With Smyth

This shift was too much for Thomas Helwys, who believed the Mennonite positions were unscriptural. He and his followers were convinced of the necessity of individual Christian participation in government. But if that were not enough, Smyth also began to teach an unorthodox view of

Christ which denied His true humanity. He also taught that Adam's sin was not imputed to the human race and that Christ's righteousness alone is not what justifies the believer, but rather a mixture of Christ's righteousness and the individual's own righteousness. Helwys and part of the small congregation went back to England shortly after Helwys had published the first Baptist confession of faith, *A Declaration of Faith of English People Remaining at Amsterdam*, in 1611.[16]

Back in England in 1612, Helwys wrote *A Short Declaration of the Mistery of Iniquity*, the first book in the English language to contend for full religious liberty for all people. That same year he established the first Baptist church on English soil in 1612. The congregation located at Spitalfield just outside of London. These first Baptists were General or Arminian Baptists. They were referred to as General Baptists because they taught that the atonement of Christ was a general atonement (that Christ died for all) rather than a particular atonement (that Christ died only for the elect, as the Calvinists said). From their beginnings the General Baptists were known as "Free-willers."[17]

Not until a generation later did the first Calvinistic Baptist church begin.[18] The Calvinistic Baptists were called Particular Baptists, because they taught a particular atonement. Hence the first Baptists were General or Free Will Baptists.

The Growth of the General Baptist Movement

By the 1640s, the English General Baptists had begun to establish numerous churches in England, and soon local associations began to spring up. Growth was steady, and by the 1650s, a "national association" of General Baptists was formed. The 1650s also saw the appearance of several General Baptist confessions of faith, doctrinal statements drawn up by local associations. In his book, *Baptist Confessions of Faith*, William L. Lumpkin states: "The Baptist confessions of faith which appeared during the period of the Commonwealth (1650-1659) were closely connected with the association movement, and they often served as its unifying instruments."[19] Such local doctrinal confessions as *The Faith and Practice of Thirty Congregations* (1651) and *The True Gospel Faith* (1654) served to give stability to the General Baptist associations by offering a unified set of doctrinal beliefs.

The *1660 English General Baptist Confession of Faith*, however, was to become for General Baptists the most widely used confession in England. Later known as the *Standard Confession of 1660*, this confession was used by the Free Will Baptists in the American South until 1812, when it was condensed and revised. Thomas Grantham was the most outstanding leader of the English General Baptists during the middle and later 1600s, and he delivered the *1660 Confession* to King Charles II on July 26, 1660.[20] Grantham was the most able theologian of the General Baptists, having written numerous books and tracts, primarily on believer's baptism. His most extensive work was entitled *Christianismus Primitivus Or the Ancient Christian Religion*. In this book, Grantham outlined the theology of the English General Baptists, especially as it relates to the doctrine of the church. Grantham reprinted the 1663 edition of the *Confession* in *Christianismus Primitivus*, along with quotations from early Christian fathers, to prove that it contained nothing novel. Besides outlining the doctrinal beliefs of the English General Baptists, the *1660 Confession* attempted to halt the persecution that the General Baptists had suffered at the hands of the Anglican Church and the English government by affirming their loyalty to England.

The *Confession* was signed mostly by men in and around London, but representatives from other areas of England were also present to sign the document. One such representative was William Jeffrey of Kent. Jeffrey and the General Baptists of Kent were the most insistent of all the General Baptists on maintaining the doctrine of feet washing as an ordinance. Jeffrey, says Lumpkin, "though a young man, was author of a remarkable doctrinal work, *The Whole Faith of Man*, which by 1660 was already a standard work of reference and appeal for General Baptists."[21]

The English General Baptists went through many changes in the late 1600s and early 1700s. Many General Baptists left behind their traditional theology—some opting for mild Calvinism and others for unorthodox ideas. Not until later in the 1700s would the movement experience doctrinal cohesion and growth. Despite this period of doctrinal controversy and decline, the General Baptist faith and practice that had been articulated in the 1660 Confession was proclaimed and preserved in the New World by General Baptists who migrated to the American colonies.

AMERICA'S FIRST FREE WILL BAPTISTS: THE PALMER MOVEMENT OF SOUTHERN FREE WILL BAPTISTS, 1685-1865

Southern Free Will Baptists have generally traced their ancestry back to the ministry of Paul Palmer, who in 1727 established the first known Free Will Baptist church in America in Chowan County, North Carolina.[22]

The Earliest General Baptists in North Carolina

America's first Free Will Baptists were called, like their English brethren, General Baptists. *General* stood for "general atonement," their strong belief in the universality of the atonement—that Christ died for all men—and its attending doctrines. Both the General Baptists in England and America were nicknamed "Freewillers," and the name caught on and began to be officially used by southern Free Will Baptists in the late 1700s. Though there were General (Free Will) Baptists in North Carolina as early as 1685, the first organized church was not begun until around 1727, under the ministry of Paul Palmer.[23] A variety of theories have been proposed concerning Paul Palmer's origins. It is not known whether Palmer himself came directly from England or not.[24] It is known, however, that Palmer married into an English General Baptist family. Palmer's father-in-law, Benjamin Laker, had been an active General Baptist layman who had apparently established an informal gathering of General Baptists in the Perquimans Precinct of North Carolina.[25]

Benjamin Laker

A look at Laker tells us a great deal about the early American Free Will Baptists and their ties with the English General Baptists. He had emigrated to Carolina from England, where he had been an active General Baptist who signed the 1663 edition of the *1660 English General Baptist Confession of Faith*.[26] A local political leader and prosperous farmer, Laker had lived in Perquimans as early as 1685. It is known from Laker's will that he owned many English General Baptist books. Among the books he left in his will was a book called *Christianismus Primitivus*.[27] This was the standard doctrinal text for the English General Baptists and was written by Thomas Grantham, the foremost leader of the English General Baptists in the 1600s. Grantham's book out-lined the doctrine of the English General Baptists, who taught, among other things, that Christ died for the sins of all mankind; that, though the sin of Adam had been imputed to man, he could be set free and saved by the righteousness of Jesus Christ which could be obtained by faith alone; that a saved person could renounce his faith in Christ and hence come out of union with Christ, never to be redeemed again; that believer's baptism was the only way to constitute a local church; that local churches should be self-governing; that God granted everyone liberty of conscience, and thus the king should allow every individual the freedom to practice his religion without fear of persecution and that individual Christians had the right to be involved in government and to keep and bear arms for the protection of family and freedom.

These doctrines had been stated in the *1660 English General Baptist Confession of Faith,* which was used by Laker and Palmer, and in turn the Southern Free Will Baptists until 1812, when it was condensed into the *1812 Former Articles.*[28]

With regard to Laker and his General Baptist influence in Eastern North Carolina in the late 1600s and early 1700s, Davidson says:

> The will of Benjamin Laker has provided the first evidence that the earliest Baptists in North Carolina included those of a General [Baptist] persuasion.
>
> It has been agreed that the records have not supported the presence of an organized General Baptist church in North Carolina before 1727 [the year Palmer's church was organized], but Laker's important social and political status would have given him a unique opportunity to spread his General Baptist faith. It should be remembered that when Paul Palmer began to preach in 1726, he found an eager audience for his General Baptist doctrine. It also should be remembered that all the Baptist churches in North Carolina before 1755 were of the General [Baptist] persuasion. These factors surely would imply that there had been a General Baptist flavor in the state before Palmer began to preach.[29]

After Laker's death, the small, unorganized band of worshipers of which he had been the leader wrote to the English General Baptists for help, in the form of either a minister or some much needed books.[30] Though the English brethren were unable to provide them with a minister and could only give them books, God had set His hand upon a man suited for the work: Paul Palmer.

Paul Palmer and His Followers

Little is known about Palmer. By 1720 he had settled in Perquimans Precinct, where by 1729 he had an estate of 964 acres.[31] Sometime before 1720, he had married Johanna Peterson, Benjamin Laker's step-daughter and the widow of a Thomas Peterson. Palmer became a respected landowner and political figure in Perquimans Precinct. His influence allowed him a hearing to proclaim his General Baptist doctrine, and he began evangelistic work in 1726. In 1727 he established a General Baptist Church in Chowan County.[32]

A few early followers were to be of great importance to the young American Free Will Baptist movement. William Sojourner, Josiah Hart, and Joseph Parker were instrumental in establishing and pastoring the first few churches that were established. Sojourner (also spelled "Surginer") was an English General Baptist from Virginia who moved to North Carolina in 1742 and became involved in the Palmer work. Hart, a physician, was greatly influenced by Sojourner and became a successful evangelist for the early Free Will Baptists, planting churches in Craven and Beaufort counties in North Carolina. Parker was born into a General Baptist family in 1705. In 1730, Parker and his wife, Sarah, went into Indian Territory in North Carolina to establish General Baptist works. These early ministers and their followers labored at a time when it was difficult to be a Baptist dissenter from the Anglican (Episcopal) Church, the established church. Their work was made easier by the Act of Toleration. A 1738 court document states:

> Permission is hereby granted to Paul Palmer of Edenton, a Protestant minister, to teach or preach the Word of God in any part of the said province (he having qualified himself as such) pursuant to an Act of Parliament made in the first year of King William and Queen Mary entitled an "Act of Tolerating Protestant Dissenters."

In a span of 25 years, these men established 20 or more General Baptist churches, and the movement grew rapidly.[33]

The Coming of the Calvinists

This growth, however, would not last long. In the 1750s, the Calvinists intruded.[34] The Particular (Calvinistic) Baptists, also called "New Lights," felt that the General Baptists needed reforming, which basically meant that they needed to be converted from Arminianism to Calvinism.[35] These

Calvinistic Baptists criticized the Free Will Baptists for not requiring what they called an "experience of grace" as a basis for baptism and church membership. What they meant by this was not simply conversion or a personal experience of the grace of God in one's life, but rather a "long and often ridiculous account of how one came to know he was elected to grace and was one of the sheep."[36] The General Baptists, on the other hand, simply required repentance and faith in Christ as the only requirement for baptism and membership in the church. In addition to this, the Calvinists claimed that the General Baptist churches were worldly and lax in their discipline. There is no way, however, to know whether this was the case or not. Old-fashioned strict Calvinists held such a low view of Arminianism that they tended to associate it with heresy or unorthodox doctrine.

Thus the Calvinistic Particular Baptists took it upon themselves to raid these early General Baptists and attempt to proselytize as many of the ministers and members to Calvinism as they could. While they were successful in converting a good many of the ministers to Calvinism, they had less success with the actual members of these early Free Will Baptist churches. A case in point is the Pasquotank Church, which had around 200 members before it was reorganized as a Calvinist Baptist church and only 12 members after. Nothing is known about what happened to these 188 former members. Since the historical records from this time are so sparse, it cannot be known for certain what they did. Some no doubt joined the churches that remained Free Will Baptist, while others doubtless gathered for worship in private homes. Some perhaps dropped out of church altogether.

Needless to say, this experience took a great toll on the growing movement, and with the majority of its churches taken over by the Calvinists, the young movement was forced to begin again, as it were, from the ground up. William Parker, the only early minister still living, together with a few others, trudged forward in the Free Will Baptist cause and continued doing what had been done before: evangelizing and planting churches. But the next 50 years were extremely difficult for the struggling movement, and growth did not begin again substantially until the early 1800s.

By the 1830s, total membership in the churches in Eastern North Carolina, not to mention Western North Carolina and South Carolina, exceeded 2,000. Thus the denomination had grown to at least more than five times the size it had been 75 years earlier, after the Calvinists had done their proselytizing.

A New Name, a New Confession of Faith, and a New Era

At the turn of the century and in the early 1800s, the name "Free Will Baptist" began to be used to designate the denomination, though "General Baptist" and "Free Will Baptist" were still used interchangeably.[37] A symbol of a new era and increasing growth among the Free Will Baptists of the Carolinas was the publication of a confession of faith which has come to be known as the *1812 Former Articles*. This confession of faith, as we noted before, was a condensed and revised version of the *1660 English General Baptist Confession of Faith*, which had been used by the Free Will Baptists up until that time. The full title of the confession was *An Abstract of the Former Articles of Faith Confessed by the Original Baptist Church Holding the Doctrine of General Provision with a Proper Code of Discipline*. The title says a great deal: First, the confession was an "abstract" (a summary) of the "former articles of faith" (the *1660 English General Baptist Confession of Faith*). Second, it is noted that this is a confession of the original Baptists of North Carolina—the General (Free Will) Baptists. And third, the distinctive doctrinal stance of the Free Will Baptists is general provision: the universal provision of the grace of God and the possibility of salvation for all who would "come and take of the water of life freely." The *1812 Former Articles* taught basically the same orthodox General

Baptist doctrines that were taught in the *1660 Confession*. One difference, however, is quite apparent.

Article ten is surprising. In its original form in the 1812 version, it teaches eternal security. The Free Will Baptists of the South defined themselves theologically in debate and interaction with Calvinistic Baptists rather than with other types of Arminians. The tendency among General Baptists in England and America for the first 250 years of their existence was, if they erred, to err on the side of Calvinism rather than on the side of extreme Arminianism, such as Wesleyanism or Campbellism. Thus it can be understood why the Free Will Baptists may have, for a few years, had questions about the doctrine of apostasy. But these questions did not last long, and in the 1830s, the statement teaching eternal security was deleted. Thus the Free Will Baptists retained their former General Baptist belief that had been outlined in their earlier confession: that those who are true believers may turn aside from faith and become as withered branches, cast into the fire and burned (John 15).

This confession of faith, as was mentioned above, was identical to the *1660 Confession* of the English brethren in some articles, but some changes were made in the interest of brevity and clarification. The confession (as amended in the 1830s) was used in the Southeastern United States until well into the twentieth century.

Growth and Challenge, 1830-1867

As noted above, Free Will Baptists in the Carolinas experienced tremendous growth in the first few decades of the 1800s and by the 1830s had over 2,000 members in their churches. The annual conference of North Carolina Free Will Baptists had grown to the extent that they voluntarily split into two conferences, called the Bethel Conference and the Shiloh Conference.[38] Tragedy struck again in 1839, when another group encroached upon the Free Will Baptists, attempting to convert Free Will Baptist ministers and church members to another doctrinal position. This time the inter-lopers were the Campbellites.[39] They believed in a works-oriented view of salvation and in baptismal regeneration (the belief that one must be baptized in order to be saved), as opposed to the faith alone teachings of the Free Will Baptists. Campbellites also believed in the abolition of all confessions of faith or treatises.[40]

This new denomination was begun by proselytizing from Baptist, Methodist, and Presbyterian churches, and the Free Will Baptists were affected as well. T. J. Latham, a school teacher and influential minister in the Bethel Conference, was the first minister to go over to the Disciples (Campbellites), and he took some other ministers and churches with him. The loss was great, with around 600 of the members leaving. This left the membership of the North Carolina Free Will Baptists at a little over 1,400. "However, recovery was rapid and in four years there were 2,563 members and 58 ministers."[41]

In 1847, a controversy arose concerning membership in secret societies. At first, the conference had a majority vote that church members should not be allowed to be members of groups like the Freemasons. But, upon reflection, the conference changed its mind and voted that each church be allowed to make the decision on its own if members could join these lodges. Davidson states,

> Article IX of the constitution of the Annual Conference stated simply that "all matters shall be decided by a majority," and on that basis, the conference resolved "that we believe the Rules of Discipline gives to each individual Church its own key—the privilege of transacting its own business.[42]

Some churches whose pastors and church members were angry over the vote to leave the decision up to the self-governing local church left the Free Will Baptists—yet another set-back. Despite these set-backs, Free Will Baptists experienced steady growth and expansion over the next few years until the onset of the War Between the States in 1861. The War took a great toll on the churches, especially in South Carolina. In the 1850s, average new baptisms (and hence new memberships) in the Annual Conference were between 150 and 200 per year. In 1861, however, only 125 new baptisms were reported, and in 1862, there were only 53—a significant drop.[43] Yet toward the end of the War, new memberships began to increase, nearly doubling those of the 1850s. In 1864, 425 new members were reported; in 1865, 275; in 1866, about 300; and in 1867, 315.[44] This kind of growth continued through the latter half of the 1800s.

The Expansion of the Palmer Movement

While Free Will Baptist strength in the South at this time centered in the Carolinas, Southern Free Will Baptists could be found in such states as Georgia, Alabama, Florida, and Tennessee. These areas came under Free Will Baptist influence as Free Will Baptists from the Carolinas began to migrate south and west into frontier territory. Some of the Free Will Baptists outside of the Carolinas had independent origins (e.g., Separate Baptists who became Free Will Baptists in Tennessee), and others had been established by Free Will Baptists from the Carolinas who had migrated to the frontier, or by direct influence with the Southern Free Will Baptists on the Eastern Seaboard.[45] And even these groups that had Separate Baptist origins were most likely influenced by Free Will Baptists who had moved west from Carolina.[46] At any rate, these groups of diverse beginnings eventually identified themselves with the Free Will Baptists of the Carolinas, using articles of faith, hymnals, and other publications from the North Carolina Free Will Baptists.

The Culture of the Free Will Baptists

It will be instructive to understand the culture of the early General Baptist settlers and their descendants in the 1800s. The early Free Will Baptists were, like most religious dissenters (those not in the Anglican or Episcopal Church) of the day, probably first-generation settlers who had come directly from England, or second- or third-generation Americans who had been converted by the General Baptists. Most of the early General Baptists were hard-working farmers whose economic and educational advantages were few. This is not to imply that the early Free Will Baptists were "anti-intellectual"; rather they had not had the educational opportunities that would have been available to the English gentry class in the Southern colonies.[47] While it is certain that they did not have the money or opportunities to take advantage of higher education (Baptists, as dissenters from the established churches in America, were not allowed to attend the higher educational institutions which had been established by the New England Puritans and the Anglicans [Episcopalians] of the South until the late 1700s), it is interesting to note that many of them could read and write at a time when the illiteracy rates in England and France were close to 50 percent, and in Southern Europe and Eastern Europe between 90 and 95 percent. This is demonstrated by the surprising fact that the two earliest records we have of General Baptists in North Carolina deal with books obtained (no doubt at great expense) from England. Benjamin Laker, though perhaps more wealthy and influential than the majority of early Free Will Baptists, valued book learning so highly that he left Christian books in his will to friends and family members. The struggling group of General Baptist worshipers left behind after Laker's death wrote the General Baptists in England requesting books that they might educate themselves in Christian doctrine. In their cultural context, this would indicate that these people were far from anti-intellectual, while, if they are judged by twentieth-century standards of "intellectuality," which would not seem historically responsible, they may fall short.

Another interesting factor is that, while the Free Will Baptists of the southeastern United States seem not to have had the great monetary resources necessary for an educational structure in the 1700s and 1800s (and though this had the undesirable side-effect of the development of pockets of "anti-education" sentiments in the 1800s), they never openly denounced education in the way it was denounced among the early Freewill Baptists of the North. It is also noteworthy that obituaries of Free Will Baptist ministers in the Carolinas, which appeared in the conference *Minutes* during the 1800s, many times *lamented* the fact that ministers were unable to avail themselves of education. In addition, the few written records we have from the early 1800s reveal a rhetorical literacy and a linguistic beauty that is hard to find in our own day.

Despite the poverty of many of the early Free Will Baptists in the South, who were usually farmers, there were always local political leaders, significant land owners, school teachers, and merchants scattered here and there in the churches. Free Will Baptists in the South never attained to the great wealth and influence of some in other Protestant denominations but were examples of the average, small farmer, what historian Frank Lawrence Owsley called "the plain folk of the South."[48]

Like other common folk in the South, Free Will Baptists took part in such rich cultural practices as singing schools, camp meetings and revival meetings, porch-front picking and singing, barn-raisings, quilting-bees, outdoor sports like swimming, hunting, fishing, trapping, and "contests of marksmanship and horsemanship such as 'snuffing the candle,' 'driving the nail,' and the 'gander pull.'"[49] Then, of course, certain less wholesome cultural practices, such as horse racing, gambling, and cock fights, were strictly prohibited.

Music played a large role in the culture and worship of the Free Will Baptists of the South. The Free Will Baptists of the 1700s sang the popular evangelical hymns of their day written by such illustrious hymn writers as Charles Wesley ("Love Divine, All Loves Excelling"), Isaac Watts ("Alas! and Did

My Saviour Bleed"), and John Newton ("Amazing Grace").
The Free Will Baptists of the South, as far as is known, did not
publish their own hymnbooks until the 1800s. The first hymnal to be published was *The Free Will Baptist Hymnbook,* edited by William Lumpkin and Enoch Cobb in 1831.[50] In 1832,
Jesse Heath, the most prominent minister from the early
1800s, and Elias Hutchins (a visitor from New England) published a hymnal entitled *Psalms, Hymns, and Spiritual Songs,
Selected for the United Churches of Christ, Commonly Called Free
Will Baptists, in North Carolina; and for Saints in All Denominations.*[51] These two hymnals were used by the Free Will
Baptists of the Carolinas until the 1850s. In 1854, R.K.
Hearn, Joseph Bell, and Jesse Randolph published a Free
Will Baptist hymnbook entitled *Zion's Hymns,* which
remained in use through the latter half of the century.[52] These
early hymnals included the popular English hymns,
American gospel hymns, and folk hymns, as well as hymns
written on distinctive topics like feet washing. These hymnals, like most all hymnals of that day, were without notes, so
the words of the hymns which were printed in the pocket-
size, hard-back books could be put to a variety of different
tunes.

Another song book used by southern Free Will Baptists of
the last century did have notes. It was called the *Sacred Harp.*[53]
Sacred Harp singing became very popular in the 1800s and is
still sung today by Free Will Baptists in some parts of the
South. *Sacred Harp* songs such as "Brethren, We Have Met to
Worship" and "When I Can Read My Title Clear" became
Free Will Baptist favorites and made their way into Free Will
Baptist hymn books. *Sacred Harp* singing was a valuable tool
of music education; since the notes were printed in shapes, it
was easier for the ordinary person to learn to read notes.
Frank Owsley discusses shaped-note singing and singing
schools in his book *Plain Folk of the Old South.* A lengthy
excerpt from this book is illustrative of the role *Sacred Harp*
music played in the culture of the Old South.

The singing schools and the community, or all day, singings were among the most enjoyable of the social institutions of the Southern folk. Every summer usually in one of the neighborhood churches, a singing master would hold a school, which lasted ten days or two weeks. Sometimes two or three singing schools would be held, especially where there were rival singing masters. The business of learning to sing by note was direct and simple; and anyone with any musical talent could, under a competent leader, learn to read notes and to sing by note by the time the school ended. The seven-shaped note system or the [four-shaped] note system of the Sacred Harp was used. The names and relative positions of these shaped notes were first learned; then followed in rapid succession note values, sharps and flats, rests, repeats, majors and minors, crescendo and diminuendo, and the four traditional parts. . . .

Learning these elementary principles, however, was only one phase and not the most enjoyable one of a singing school. A good portion of the day would therefore be taken up with singing well known sacred and popular songs, and enjoying prolonged recesses devoted to courting, and having a generally sociable time. In the general singing, and even in the teaching, the benches were drawn up in a square with the master in the center and those singing bass, alto, soprano, and tenor in separate sections.

The singing school, though an end in itself, was also the chief means of teaching the people to sing, a thing which they did often and long. At church, prayer meetings, the Sunday-afternoon singings of the younger people, and the all-day singings with dinner on the grounds, people met and sang together.[54]

Free Will Baptist Worship and Practice

The early Free Will Baptists of the South, like their General Baptist forefathers in England, took the New Testament pattern for the church very seriously. Thus, as in New Testament churches, simplicity characterized their worship and practice. A letter from Elias Hutchins, a visitor from the New England Freewill Baptists, gives us insight into the way that Free Will Baptists in the Carolinas worshiped. As Davidson says,

Hutchins especially was impressed with the reverence that was evident in the worship service of the Free Will Baptists. He spoke often of the well-behaved, solemn, attentive audiences. In one of his let-

ters, he described a baptism service held at the Pungo Free Will
Baptist Church in May, 1830, in which twenty persons were baptized.

Hutchins recounts:

> The scene was solemn and impressive, well calculated to animate the
> Christian, and fill the minds of sinners with sensations of a favorable
> character; and the large congregation that witnessed the perfor-
> mance by a commendable decorum evinced great respect for the
> ordinance.[55]

The southern Free Will Baptists placed great stress on the
value of the Christian ordinances. They retained the emphasis on feet washing as an ordinance that had characterized the
Kent Association of General Baptists in England. In fact, the
1812 Former Articles was the first Arminian Baptist confession
of faith to explicitly list feet washing as an ordinance. The
Free Will Baptists of the 1800s continued this practice, seeing
themselves as walking in the "old paths" of their forefathers
in following the commands of Christ. In speaking of the early
General Baptists in North Carolina, R.K. Hearn stated:

> We bear the same name, we have the same book of discipline, we
> preach the old doctrine, we receive members the same way without
> an experience of grace, we commemorate the Lord's Supper in the
> same way, we wash the saints' feet the same way. . . .[56]

Free Will Baptist church government in the South was simple and democratic. Though it seems that the church polity of
the early General Baptists of North Carolina was a bit more
complex, the self-government of the local church was still valued. A great deal more emphasis on the self-government of
the local church, while still retaining the importance of associational relationships, was witnessed in the 1800s. The fact
that great emphasis was placed on the local church is demonstrated by the "localism" of the Free Will Baptists, who hesi-
tated to form large associations. When a conference became

very large, the conference would voluntarily split into two conferences to make travel easier and to facilitate more efficient conference business. This measure, however, tended to have the effect of detracting from a sense of denominational unity.

Several conferences arose in North Carolina, South Carolina, and Georgia; Free Will Baptist families migrated west to states like Tennessee and Alabama; and ministers who moved to other states planted churches there. But these Free Will Baptists scattered across the South never formed a denominational structure because of the "localist" emphasis.

This phenomenon contributed to the lack of sufficient financial support of educational institutions, foreign mission works, and other ministries, which would have been established had the Free Will Baptists of the South had a more cohesive denominational structure. To say this is not to demean the self-government of the local church, local association, or conference, but the lack of a denominational organization among southern Free Will Baptists did negatively affect denominational growth and effectiveness. Free Will Baptists would have to wait until the latter part of the 1800s before they would witness efforts to bring all the Free Will Baptists of the South into one unified organization.

The Randall Movement of Freewill Baptists in the North and West

Some historians have questioned the need or relevance of recounting the history of the Randall Movement of Freewill Baptists, since that denomination merged with the Northern Baptist Convention in 1911. (The Randall group commonly combined the words *free* and *will* when referring to its movement.) However, a definite need to survey the history of the Randall Movement, since almost one-fourth of our present churches, primarily among those in the Midwest and Southwest, owe their origin to the Randall Movement, having descended from churches that were planted as home mission efforts of the Randall Movement in the 1800s. Most of the churches in Ohio and Missouri are descendants, in some way or another, of the Randall Movement; while in states such as Oklahoma, Texas, California, Illinois, and Arkansas, the origins of Free Will Baptists were a mixture of influences from the Randall and Palmer Movements. Thus, a summary of the history of the Randall Movement will be most helpful in telling the story of the National Association of Free Will Baptists.

Benjamin Randall

The Northern Freewill Baptist movement began about a century after the advent of Free Will Baptists in North Carolina, with the religious experience of a man named Benjamin Randall (1749-1808).[57] Born in New Castle, New Hampshire, Randall spent all of his life in New Hampshire, aside from his "off and on" stints as a sailor on his father's ship and a short term in the Army during the Revolutionary War.[58] During childhood and early adulthood, Randall moved through a series of stages in his religious development, which Davidson refers to as (1) the period of unconverted piety, (2) the period of converted Congregationalism, (3) the period in the Calvinistic Baptist tradition, and (4) the period of Freewill Baptist sentiment.[59]

The turning point in Randall's religious development was the death of George Whitefield, the famous Methodist evangelist. Earlier, he had heard Whitefield preach but had ignored him. On hearing of Whitefield's death, Randall recalled Whitefield's sermon and converted to Christianity. Randall joined a Congregational church in 1773 only to leave two years later because of his disagreement with the Congregational practice of infant baptism. He and some close friends withdrew from the Congregationalists in May of 1775 and joined the Baptist church at Berwick, Maine, in October of 1776.[60] The church at Berwick, like most Baptist churches in New England at that time, was Calvinistic. Randall soon began to question the predestinarianism he encountered there, and began to speak not only about man's free will in matters of salvation but also about his belief in the universality of Christ's atonement.[61] He came under harsh criticism and was soon excommunicated by the Berwick church for his adherence to Arminian principles. From there he was invited by a group of Baptists to New Durham, New Hampshire, where he went in March of 1778 and eventually established the first Freewill Baptist church in the North in 1780.[62]

Randall began preaching his free will doctrine throughout New Hampshire and Maine, and soon other Freewill Baptist churches were established.[63] Several quarterly conferences were organized, and soon churches were established in Vermont, Massachusetts, and other areas of New England.[64]

The Growth of the Movement

The growth of the northern Freewill Baptist movement in the nineteenth century was phenomenal. In 1827, at the first General Conference, 25 quarterly conferences were represented, with nearly 300 churches and a total membership of over 16,000. The Freewill Baptists moved west, expanding rapidly, preaching their gospel of free grace, free salvation, free will, and free communion. By the 1830s, the Freewill Baptist General Conference supported two schools, a printing establishment, and a national periodical, the *Morning Star*. The 1830s was also a time of interest in missions endeavors, with the Foreign Mission Society established in 1833 and the Home Mission Society established in 1834. The denomination grew rapidly during the 1830s. By 1835, the number of churches in the General Conference had grown to 434, with a total membership of 33,876.[65] The 1840s and 1850s saw great growth and expansion as well, especially in the area of higher education. In 1844, two institutions of higher learning were founded: Hillsdale College in Hillsdale, Michigan, and Geauga Seminary in Ohio. Ten years later, Bates College was established in Lewiston, Maine.[66]

The northern Freewill Baptists continued to prosper throughout the nineteenth century, with a thriving mission work at home and abroad, an aggressive publishing program, a large work among the freed slaves, and numerous educational institutions. Storer College was founded in 1867 at Harper's Ferry, West Virginia, for the purpose of educating freed slaves. Rio Grande College was founded in 1876 in southern Ohio, and in 1890 Keuka College was established in New York.[67]

The Northern Freewill Baptists and Revivalism

The Freewill Baptists of the North were intimately involved in the revivalism and social reform that characterized the Second Great Awakening. From the earliest times, the northern Freewill Baptists were active in such ventures as Sabbath schools, temperance, the abolition of slavery, and a host of other concerns. They were very much a part of the revivalism of the Second Great Awakening in America, being closely identified with the Western Revival tradition led by the father of American revivalism, Charles G. Finney. The *Morning Star,* the official organ of the Northern Freewill Baptist denomination, was among the first to reprint Finney's *Revival Lectures,* and was instrumental in establishing his prominence in New England. Theodore Dwight Weld, Finney's follower and the foremost leader of the evangelical offense against slavery, hailed the northern Freewill Baptists as perhaps contributing more than any other single denomination to the anti-slavery cause. It is also interesting to note that David Marks, the foremost evangelist of the Freewill Baptists in New England, died at Oberlin College, the leading bastion of evangelical revivalism and social reform. Charles Finney himself, then president of Oberlin, preached Marks' funeral, hailing him as one of the greatest evangelists and reformers of the day. Northern Freewill Baptists in the middle part of the nineteenth century were indeed identified with and involved in the "Finneyesque" revivalistic climate of the day.

The Decline and Demise of the Randall Movement

The Randall Movement of Freewill Baptists in the North was more prosperous than the Palmer Movement in the South. One reason for this is the early desire to join together in a General Conference, so that the organization could afford to extend its ministries further than if it had remained in smaller associations. Because of the strong denominational network that had been forged by the middle part of the 1800s, the Randall Movement began to have enough financial resources to fund colleges and other institutions of higher education. The movement underwent what historian Ruth Bordin has called the "sect to denomination" process.[68] Yet this process was not without its problems. The northern Freewill Baptists soon began to centralize the power of the denomination into the hands of a clergy-elite of the General Conference. With the over-centralization of denominational funds came the over-centralization of the ministries of the denomination—everything from missions to education. Soon the elite power brokers of the denomination began to succumb to the Modernism (religious liberalism) that was beginning to permeate the old-line American denominations. This imbibing of Modernist ideas transformed their earlier social conscience and zeal for Christian social reform into a new "Social Gospel," which tended to emphasize the need for social salvation at the expense of personal salvation and world evangelization.

These new ideas led the leaders of the northern Freewill Baptists to initiate merger talks with denominations such as the Disciples of Christ, the Congregationalists, and the Northern Baptists.[69] Denominational leaders like Alfred Williams Anthony were at the forefront of the Ecumenical Movement, and led the northern Freewill Baptists into the Federal Council of Churches (now the National Council of

Churches). By 1911 the Freewill Baptist General Conference in the North merged with the Northern Baptist Convention. With the merger, all the property of the denomination–schools, colleges, mission boards, publishing houses, and so forth–went as well.[70]

Opposition to the Merger

There was, however, a minority opposition to the merger. This opposition primarily resided in the Midwest (Ohio, Nebraska) and the Southwest (Missouri, Texas). Men like T.C. Ferguson (Missouri) and John Wolfe (Nebraska) fought to stem the tide of Modernism and to keep the General Conference of the North from merging with the Northern Baptists.[71] They were unsuccessful. Though the majority of the northern Freewill Baptist churches participated in the merger, a minority in the Midwest and Southwest remained Freewill Baptist and would soon initiate merger talks and eventually merge with the Free Will Baptist General Conference (Palmer Movement) of the Southeast.

The Remnant of the Randall Movement

The churches that dissented from the merger with the Northern Baptists and remained true to their heritage were located as far apart as Texas and Ohio. The remnant that remained in the Southwestern United States formed a new association called the Co-operative General Association, while the remnant in the area of Southern Ohio was involved in what was called the Triennial General Conference of Free Will Baptists.

Ohio Freewill Baptists and the Triennial General Conference

Certain Free Will Baptists in Ohio had long been skeptical about the desire of the northern Freewill Baptists to merge with other denominations. Among these was Thomas E. Peden. A graduate of Hillsdale College in Michigan, Peden was a leading minister in Southern Ohio. Like his fellow northern Freewill Baptists in the General Conference of the North, he was also interested in uniting with other Christian groups, but he wished to bring all the Free Will Baptists–both North and South–together, rather than uniting with denominations which had Modernist leanings or with whom the northern Freewill Baptists had little in common doctrinally. Peden figured prominently in the founding of a short-lived conference of Free Will Baptists called the Triennial General Conference.[72] This conference, which came together in 1896, comprised Free Will Baptists as far southeast as South Carolina and as far Northwest as North Dakota, also including representatives from Tennessee, North Carolina, and Arkansas.

This conference involved the efforts of Peden and others like him among the northern Freewill Baptists to find a denominational home, since they were quickly becoming dissatisfied with the Modernism and ecumenism of the Randall Movement. They wished to remain true to their heritage; so they found it best to try to unite with a group that was close to them in doctrine and polity: the Free Will Baptists of the South. Thus much mutual interaction began taking place in the late 1800s and early 1900s, especially between southern Free Will Baptists and the Freewill Baptists of Southern Ohio. This fraternal interaction eventually resulted in the naming of Peden as principal of Ayden Seminary, the Free Will Baptist educational institution in Ayden, North Carolina, in 1898. The Triennial Conference only lasted about a decade, giving way to more local organizations. It would be another ten years before most of these Free Will Baptists would reunite in the General Conference of the South.[73]

The Southwestern Convention and the Co-operative General Association

The Southwestern Convention was an organization of Free Will Baptists primarily in Texas and Oklahoma. Though this association joined the General Conference of northern Freewill Baptists in 1907, it was much more like the Free Will Baptists of the Southeast in polity and church government.[74] The Southwestern Convention was wary of the merger at first, but eventually, around 1913, many of the churches joined in with the merger with the Northern Baptists. There were many who had been involved in the Southwestern Convention that stayed out of the merger and would subsequently have a great impact on the remaining Free Will Baptists of the Southwest. Among these were I.W. Yandell, who had at one time served as president of the Southwestern Convention and became a leading figure in the remnant group of the Southwest. Another was Rev. Mrs. Lizzy McAdams, who was heavily involved in the efforts to unite the Free Will Baptists east and west of the Mississippi into the National Association of Free Will Baptists in 1935.[75]

What might be called the successor association to the Southwestern Convention was the Co-operative General Association. This association was the main vehicle of organization for the remnant group in the Southwest and would eventually merge with the General Conference of the South (Palmer Movement) to form the National Association. The Co-operative General Association was led primarily by men and women whose churches had in some way been affiliated with the Randall Movement of northern Freewill Baptists, but the Free Will Baptists involved in the association had come from diverse beginnings, some from the Randall Movement and some from the Palmer Movement. The primary function of the Co-operative General Association was that of an organization for the union of those Free Will Baptists who had stayed out of the merger in 1911. The Co-operative General Association had such illustrious leaders as T.C. Ferguson of

Missouri and John H. Wolfe of Nebraska—the two most out-
spoken opponents of the merger with the Northern Baptists
in 1911. These men provided much-needed leadership for the
new association. The Co-operative General Association first
met in Pattonsburg, Missouri, in the year 1916.[76] At this meeting, there were delegates from Nebraska, Missouri, Kansas,
Oklahoma, and Texas. In 1916, the Co-operative Association
founded the *New Morning Star,* a publication that was envisioned as the successor to the old *Morning Star* magazine of
the northern Freewill Baptist General Conference.[77]

Tecumseh College

In 1917, property was bought at Tecumseh, Oklahoma, for
the establishment of a college, Tecumseh College.[78] Tecumseh
College was to be the nerve center of the southwestern Free
Will Baptists for the next ten years. Tecumseh was established
as a college that could educate pastors to serve as leaders of
the struggling group, but the college valued a strong liberal
arts preparation and also prepared students for jobs in the
secular marketplace. Courses were offered in such fields as
biblical studies, systematic theology, sacred history, apolo-
getics, history, Greek, Latin, mathematics, physics, biology,
and chemistry. By 1921 Tecumseh was offering three degrees:
the B.A. (Bachelor of Arts), the B.Litt. (Bachelor of Letters),
and the Bachelor of Christian Letters. The bachelor's degrees
required a classical course of study which comprised studies
in religion, Greek, Latin, literature, history, philosophy,
mathematics, and the natural sciences. Tecumseh College
educated numerous men for the ministry and prepared the
leadership that would subsequently lead the Co-operative
General Association into the National Association of Free
Will Baptists. Tecumseh burned to the ground in the year
1927, ten years after its founding, but its legacy would continue to be felt among Free Will Baptists for years to come.[79]

SOUTHERN FREE WILL BAPTISTS IN THE LATE NINETEENTH AND EARLY TWENTIETH CENTURIES

The decades following the War between the States (1861-1865) witnessed tremendous growth among Southern Free Will Baptists. Two denominational centers were prominent among Free Will Baptists in the South: North Carolina and Tennessee. North Carolina, having been the birthplace of southern Free Will Baptists, was where they looked for Sunday school literature, hymnals, and other denominational helps, while Tennessee became the leader in efforts to unite all southern Free Will Baptists. With more and more cooperation from Free Will Baptists across the South, opportunities that would not have been financially possible before began to show themselves. One such possibility was that of an educational institution. A discussion of the three things mentioned above—publishing, efforts for denominational cooperation and union, and education—will help show the development of Free Will Baptists in the South in the latter part of the 1800s and the early part of the 1900s.

Publishing Among the Southern Free Will Baptists

Damon C. Dodd asserts that there were Sunday schools among Free Will Baptists in the South as early as the 1780s.[80] We do not know exactly when the Free Will Baptists of the Carolinas began to publish Sunday school literature, but we do know that by the 1870s, they had a publishing program which printed "Sabbath school" literature designed specifically for use in Free Will Baptist Sabbath schools. North Carolina, having been the birthplace of American Free Will Baptists, remained the center of publishing and education efforts, providing Free Will Baptist churches in other Southern states with hymnals, confessions of faith, books and pamphlets, and Sunday school literature.

This literature was published by the Free Will Baptist Press. The Free Will Baptist Press was founded in 1873, when the North Carolina Free Will Baptists finally solidified plans to publish a weekly magazine. The magazine and the Press struggled at first, but by the 1890s, the Press was strong and was providing Free Will Baptists across the South with all kinds of literature, as well as weekly subscriptions to the magazine, entitled *The Free Will Baptist.* When the Press was founded in 1873, the magazine was first entitled *The Free Will Baptist Advocate.* Soon, however, the name was shortened to just *The Free Will Baptist,* and many times was referred to as simply *The Baptist.* The Free Will Baptist Press and *The Free Will Baptist* magazine would prove to have a great effect on the development of Free Will Baptists in the late 1800s and the first half of the twentieth century, and would help move the scattered Free Will Baptist churches to a more cohesive denominational network, culminating in the founding of the National Association of Free Will Baptists in 1935.

**Rufus K. Hearn and His Vision
for Publishing and Education**

One initial director of the Free Will Baptist Press and *The Free Will Baptist* magazine was Rufus K. Hearn. Hearn was one of the leading Free Will Baptist ministers in North Carolina. Born in 1819, he was ordained to the ministry in 1853. Hearn was one of the ministers who could remember what the denomination was like in the early 1800s, and he served as a conserving influence in the denomination until his death in 1894. Having served as clerk of the North Carolina Annual Conference for decades, he was the driving influence behind publishing and educational efforts among Free Will Baptists in the South. Hearn was not only an illustrious farmer-preacher, but also a journalist and publisher, serving as editor and publisher of *The Free Will Baptist* and as executive director of the Free Will Baptist Press from 1880-1889. An articulate writer as well as an able historian, he wrote a short history called *Origin of the Free Will Baptist Church of North Carolina.*[81] It might well be said that Hearn

was the single most important figure in the educational program Southern Free Will Baptists envisioned in the late
1800s. This vision continued into the twentieth century and
would be invaluable to the founding of the National
Association and the continuing of Free Will Baptist ministry
and service into our own day.[82]

Ayden Seminary and Eureka College

After decades of discussion and longing for the establishment of a Free Will Baptist institution of higher education in
the South, the Free Will Baptist Seminary at Ayden, North
Carolina, was founded in 1896. Later renamed Eureka
College, this school trained Free Will Baptist men and
women from North Carolina and other parts of the South in
Christian ministry as well as the liberal arts. Students could
choose from a variety of majors, called "courses." The
Classical Course consisted of intense study of Latin and Greek,
classical literature, history, and several courses in higher
mathematics, the natural sciences, and religious studies. The
Scientific Course involved training in physics, chemistry, biology, and other sciences, as well as a staple of classical language and literature, religious studies, history, and mathematics. The *Commercial Course* required a concentration in
commerce or business, accompanied by basic courses in literature, history, religious studies, science, and mathematics.
The *Biblical Course,* primarily for ministers, concentrated on
biblical and theological studies with several required courses
in classical language and literature, history, natural science,
and higher mathematics. All students received a thoroughly
Christian education. While students in the non-biblical courses of study were not required to major in religious studies,
they were still required to take a staple of biblical and theological courses. Most importantly, Christianity was the foundation of every course. Many of the graduates of the Biblical
Course would serve as bi-vocational ministers, serving one or
more smaller churches while teaching in public schools. In

1929, only three years after the school changed its name to Eureka College, the school closed its doors under the financial hardship of the Depression Era, and in 1931, it burned to the ground. But the hopes and dreams of Free Will Baptist higher education did not burn with it. Ayden Seminary and Eureka College were the fulfillment of years of hopes and dreams for a denominational college, and they would serve as a sure foundation for Free Will Baptist higher education in the twentieth century.[83]

The Role of Tennessee in the Late Nineteenth and Early Twentieth Century

Tennessee Free Will Baptists were always at the forefront of efforts for uniting all Free Will Baptists into one denominational organization. Some Free Will Baptists of Tennessee had expressed interest in a loose relationship with the Northern Free Baptists, but such interest waned because of differences on feet washing and other matters. In 1890 the Committee on Literature and Union of the Cumberland Association of Tennessee—

> expressed thanks for increasing favor for a "union of all white Liberal* [Free Will] Baptists of the South" and named delegates to represent in "the coming General Association." The 1896 minutes also named delegates to the "General Association," as did those of 1897, indicating that said meeting would be "at Nashville, Tenn., Oct. 28, 1897."[84]

Tennessee Free Will Baptists also had a leadership role in the southern General Conference, which met at Ayden, North Carolina, in 1898. This Conference met at Cofer's Chapel Free Will Baptist Church in Nashville, Tennessee, in 1901 and again in 1907.[85] Though this General Conference's

---

*The word liberal here is the older usage of the word, which is synonymous for "free" or "liberty." It was often used as a synonym for "free will."

last meeting was held in 1910, the Tennessee Free Will Baptists did not abandon their desire for a national denominational structure.

Tennessee was not only geographically between the Southeastern Free Will Baptists (the Southern General Conference) and the Southwestern Free Will Baptists (the Cooperative General Association, remnants of the Randall Movement), but it may also be said that Tennessee had perhaps the decisive role in uniting the two bodies. In fact, John L. Welch was commissioned as a representative to the Cooperative General Association in the West as early as 1917. These overtures would lead to the year 1935, when the eastern and western segments of twentieth-century Free Will Baptists would become the National Association of Free Will Baptists.[86]

Notes for Chapter One

---

[1] More will be said about the Palmer Movement in the section of this chapter entitled "America's First Free Will Baptists."

[2] William F. Davidson, *The Free Will Baptists in America, 1727-1984* (Nashville: Randall House Publications, 1985), pp. 29, 47-48. It should be noted here that the English General Baptists, from whom southern Free Will Baptists have descended, bear no direct relationship to the present-day General Baptist denomination in America. This Arminian Baptist group arose spontaneously in the Midwest in the 1800s (Ollie Latch, *History of the General Baptists* [Poplar Bluff, Missouri: General Baptist Press, 1954], pp. 125-26). American General Baptist historian Ollie Latch says that Benoni Stinson, the founder of the American General Baptists, was influenced by the early General (Free Will) Baptists of North Carolina (Ibid.).

[3] Elizabeth Smith, "The Former Articles of Faith of the North Carolina Free Will Baptists," *The Free Will Baptist* (July 27, 1960), p. 10.

[4] Davidson, pp. 124-25. The *1812 Former Articles* were in turn used throughout the Southeast until well into the twentieth century. Both the *1660 English General Baptist Confession of Faith* and the *1812 Former Articles* are reprinted in chapter three.

[5] In this book, the name "*Freewill* Baptist" will be used to refer to the Randall Movement in the North, while "*Free Will* Baptist" will be used for the Palmer Movement in the South, since these are the ways the two groups have historically used their names.

[6] B.R. White, *The English Separatist Tradition: From The Marian Martyrs to the Pilgrim Fathers* (London: Oxford University Press, 1971), p. 116.

[7] Also called the Anglican or Episcopal Church.

[8] H. Leon McBeth, *The Baptist Heritage: Four Centuries of Baptist Witness* (Nashville: Broadman Press, 1987) p. 33.

[9] William R. Estep, *The Anabaptist Story* (Grand Rapids, Michigan: Wm. B. Eerdmans Publishing Company, 1975), p. 219.

[10] Walter H. Burgess, *John Smyth the Se-Baptist, Thomas Helwys, and The First Baptist Church in England* (London: James Clarke and Company, 1911), p. 147.

[11] Ibid., pp. 153-156; Davidson, pp. 16-17.

[12] Quoted in Davidson, p. 17.

[13] McBeth, p. 21.

[14] "Arminianism" is used here to signify anti-Calvinism in general rather than the specific thought of Jacobus Arminius. Smyth was influenced by the anti-Calvinism of the Waterlander Mennonites, whereas Helwys was more influenced by Arminius and less by the Mennonites. For a defense of this view, see J. Matthew Pinson, "The Soteriology of John Smyth and Thomas Helwys" (unpublished paper, 1997).

[15] For purposes of convenience and understanding, "Free Will Baptist" will be used interchangeably with "General Baptists" when discussing the English General Baptists and their immediate descendants in the American colonies. It must be

remembered that neither of these titles were officially used by Smyth, Helwys, and the early General Baptists.

[16]This confession of faith is reprinted in chapter four.

[17]Davidson, p. 19.

[18]McBeth, p. 39.

[19]William L. Lumpkin, *Baptist Confessions of Faith* (Valley Forge, Pennsylvania: Judson Press, 1959), pp. 171-72.

[20]Ibid., p. 223.

[21]Ibid., p. 221.

[22]While some have mistakenly held the view that Benjamin Randall, the founder of the Freewill Baptists in the North, was the "founding father of Free Will Baptists," the advent of Free Will Baptists in North Carolina, as will be shown in this chapter, predates the founding of Randall's church in 1780 by about a century.

[23]The names "General Baptist" and "Free Will Baptist" will hereafter be used interchangeably when discussing the early Free Will Baptists of North Carolina.

[24]Davidson, pp. 37-40. Davidson's doctoral dissertation was first published by Randall House Publications in 1974 as *An Early History of Free Will Baptists, 1727-1830,* and was later incorporated into his comprehensive history cited above.

[25]Ibid., pp. 38, 47-48; see George Stevenson, "Laker, Benjamin," in Dictionary of North Carolina Biography, vol. 4, ed. William S. Powell (Chapel Hill, North Carolina: University of North Carolina Press, 1991), pp. 3-5. Johanna Taylor Jeffreys Peterson, Palmer's wife, was Benjamin Laker's step-daughter.

[26]Stevenson, pp. 3-4.

[27]Thomas Grantham, *Christianismus Primitivus, Or the Ancient Christian Religion* (London: Francis Smith, 1678). See Stevenson, p. 4.

[28]The *1660 English General Baptist Confession of Faith* and its successor, the *1812 Former Articles,* are reprinted in chapter four.

[29]Davidson, p. 49.

[30]Michael R. Pelt identifies the English General Baptists to whom the Laker group wrote as the General Association of General Baptists which met in London on June 3-5, 1702 (Michael R. Pelt, *A History of Original Free Will Baptists* (Mount Olive, North Carolina: Mount Olive College Press, 1996), p. 24. This association was the orthodox group which had separated from the General Assembly of General Baptists due to doctrinal differences on the person of Christ. The General *Association* insisted that the General *Assembly* deal with those in their midst who were guilty of heresy on the person of Christ (e.g., that Christ's flesh was "heavenly flesh" or that Christ is not fully God in the same sense that God the Father is fully God).

[31]Damon C. Dodd, *The Free Will Baptist Story* (Nashville: Executive Department of the National Association of Free Will Baptists, 1956), p. 37.

[32]Ibid., p. 39.

[33]See Pelt, pp. 48-55.

[34]For a more detailed sketch of the intrusion, the reader is referred to R.K. Hearn's "Origin of the Free Will Baptist Church of North Carolina," written in the late 1800s and reprinted in *The Historical Review* (Summer 1994), a publication of the Historical Committee of the Florida State Association of Free Will Baptists.

[35]The Particular Baptists, like their brethren in England, were referred to as "particular" because of their belief in a limited atonement–a "particular" atonement–which was available only to the elect whom God had chosen irresistibly without regard to the free choice of the individual.

[36]Latch, p. 118.

[37]Davidson, pp. 196-98.

[38]Pelt, p. 117.

[39]*Campbellites* is a word used to describe the "Disciples of Christ" or the "Churches of Christ," whose founders were Thomas and Alexander Campbell. This group started in the early 1800s.

[40]See the essay by R.K. Hearn referred to above.

[41]Dodd, p. 54.

[42]*Minutes of the North Carolina General Conference of Free Will Baptists* (1853), p. 4; cited in Davidson, p. 244.

[43]T.F. Harrison and J.M. Barfield, *History of the Free Will Baptists of North Carolina* (Ayden, North Carolina: Free Will Baptist Press, 1898, vol. 2, reprinted 1959), pp. 211, 214.

[44]Ibid., pp. 217-21.

[45]With reference to the first known Free Will Baptists of East Tennessee, Robert Picirilli has reminded us that "the recounting of this information does not, in fact, tell how the 'free will' doctrine came to be the faith of these three pioneer Baptist men [Moses Peterson, John Wheeler, and William Bonaparte Woolsey] [;] what sources of influence shaped their thinking we do not know. If there were other men who taught (or baptized) them in this doctrine–as there may have been–we do not know their names or whence they came to the Great Smoky Mountains" (*The History of Tennessee Free Will Baptists.* [Nashville: Historical Commission of the Tennessee State Association of Free Will Baptists, 1985], p. 10). Our lack of information on the influences on and origins of the Free Will Baptists of Tennessee and other states underscores the need for more research.

[46]Frontier migration patterns is a fruitful area of future research in the history of the Free Will Baptists of the South. Some have assumed that new areas of Free Will Baptist work outside of the Carolinas were always spontaneous movements and unconnected with other Free Will Baptists. This view, however, does not take account of a few things: First, it is too coincidental that new Free Will Baptists who had formerly been, for the most part, Calvinistic Baptists would just happen to make the transition, not only from Calvinism to a full-blown Arminianism, but also begin to practice both open communion and feet washing–all with no influence from other Free Will Baptists. What is even more coincidental is that they almost immediately took on the name *Free Will Baptist.* It stretches the limits of

credulity to think that all this is merely coincidence. It seems much more reasonable that Free Will Baptists from the Carolinas influenced these people with their doctrine and practice. A second and perhaps more crucial fact that is not recognized by the "spontaneous appearance" theories is that myriads of Free Will Baptists from the Carolinas migrated to other southern states in the 1800s. These Free Will Baptists had to go somewhere; they did not disappear. Yet theories which over-emphasize the diversity and multiple origins of southern Free Will Baptists do not account for them. (The perspective outlined here is shared by G. W. Million in his *History of Free Will Baptists* [Nashville: Board of Publications and Literature, National Association of Free Will Baptists, 1958], p. 125.)

[47]The term "anti-intellectual" has been over-used and, indeed, abused in some historical circles. Historian Richard Hofstadter's *Anti-Intellectualism in American Life*, which tends to define "intellectualism" and "anti-intellectualism" from a twentieth-century cultural perspective rather than viewing the earlier generations of Americans in their cultural and economic contexts, comparing American literacy rates with those of the European countries, and so forth, has informed the consensus of American historical scholarship, but stands in need of correction at many points.

[48]For a greater understanding of the cultural context of the common people of the Old South, and hence of southern Free Will Baptists, particularly in the late 1700s and early 1800s, it would be beneficial to consult Frank Lawrence Owsley's masterful book, *Plain Folk of the Old South* (Baton Rouge, Louisiana: Louisiana State University Press, 1949, 1982). Owsley has a great discussion of camp meetings in the Old South.

[49]Ibid.

[50]Davidson, p. 248.

[51]Ibid.

[52]Ibid.

[53]Other song books which used "Sacred Harp" music were *Southern Harmony, Christian Harmony, The Colored Sacred Harp,* and *The Social Harp.*

[54]Owsley, pp. 124-25.

[55]Davidson, p. 212.

[56]R.K. Hearn, p. 48.

[57]This account of the Randall Movement is adapted from my M.A. thesis, "Religious Social Reform in the Antebellum North: Abolition and Temperance Reform among the Northern Freewill Baptists, 1800-1860" (University of West Florida, 1993).

[58]I.D. Stewart, *The History of the Freewill Baptists for Half a Century* (Dover, New Hampshire: Freewill Baptist Printing Establishment, 1862), p. 32; Dodd, p. 69.

[59]Davidson, pp. 168-72.

[60]Ibid, p. 170.

[61]Stewart, 44-45.

[62]"Randall, Rev. Benjamin," *Free Baptist Cyclopaedia* (Chicago: Free Baptist Cyclopaedia Company, 1889), pp. 558-59.

[63]Million, pp. 59-60.

[64]Ibid.

[65]Davidson, p. 205.

[66]Norman Allen Baxter, *History of the Freewill Baptists* (Rochester, New York: American Baptist Historical Society, 1957), pp. 138-40.

[67]Steven Hasty, "Did They Survive?" *Contact.* July 1988, pp. 12-13.

[68]Ruth B. Bordin, "The Sect to Denomination Process in America: the Freewill Baptist Experience." *Church History* 34 [March 1965].

[69]Baxter, p. 165.

[70]Ibid., 178-80.

[71]Dodd, p. 107.

[72]Davidson, pp. 335-40.

[73]Ibid.

[74]Ibid., p. 340.

[75]Ibid.

[76]Ibid., p. 341; Dodd, p. 111; Million, p. 127.

[77]Ibid.

[78]Davidson, pp. 304-05.

[79]Ibid., pp. 304-07.

[80]Dodd, p. 160.

[81]This history was published in the 1860s and later reprinted in D.B. Montgomery's *General Baptist History* (1882). This history has been reprinted in *The Historical Review*, volume II [Summer 1994].

[82]The benefit of Free Will Baptist Press, which eventually located at Ayden, North Carolina, was lost to the National Association in 1962, when the North Carolina State Convention of Free Will Baptists separated from the National Association. This separation will be discussed more fully in chapter eight. The reader who wishes to continue on to the history of our present National Association is asked to consult chapter six.

[83]For a more detailed introduction to Ayden Seminary and Eureka College, see Michael Pelt, *A History of Ayden Seminary and Eureka College* (Mount Olive, North Carolina: Mount Olive College Press, 1983).

[84]Picirilli, *The History of Tennessee Free Will Baptists*, p. 34.

[85]Ibid., p. 35.

[86]For a survey of the origin of the National Association, the reader is asked to turn to chapter six.

CHAPTER TWO

Our Beliefs: Free Will Baptist Doctrinal Distinctives

Free Will Baptists share with other evangelical Protestants
the fundamental doctrines of the Christian faith. These
include the belief that the Bible is without error in all that it
affirms; that God is three persons in one Godhead—Father,
Son, and Holy Spirit; that Christ was born of a virgin and is
both God and man in the same person; that Christ rose bodily from the dead; that He will return bodily; and that there
will be a final judgment and a resurrection to either eternal
life or eternal damnation.[1] Free Will Baptists differ, however,
with other Christians on the doctrines of soteriology (the doctrine of salvation) and ecclesiology (the doctrine of the
church). Our differences with other Christians in our interpretation of Holy Scripture are summed up in our name: *Free
Will Baptist.* "Free Will" signifies our Arminian belief that the
human will is free to resist and reject God's gracious gift of
salvation. "Baptist" signifies our Baptistic beliefs in the baptism of believers only by immersion, congregational church
government, and other distinctively Baptist beliefs.[2] An
understanding of Free Will Baptist views on the doctrines of
salvation and the church will enable us to see what makes
Free Will Baptists distinct from other Christian denominations.

THE DOCTRINE OF SALVATION

Free Will Baptists are Arminian in their doctrine of salvation. The term "Arminian" comes from the Dutch theologian

Jacobus Arminius (1560-1609) who opposed the rigid Calvinism of his day. Calvinism (the theology of the followers of the Genevan theologian John Calvin [1509-1564]) taught (and teaches) that God, in eternity past, elected or chose some individuals for eternal salvation and the rest for eternal damnation, without regard to the individual's free will or choice. Calvinists teach that God must decide who will respond to the gospel, since human beings are so sinful that they could never choose to say "yes" to God. Calvinistic doctrine is summarized in the dogmas of the *Synod of Dort*, the convention of Calvinists that came together in Holland in 1618 to condemn Arminius's teachings. The five doctrines which were enunciated at the Synod of Dort, popularly called "The Five Points of Calvinism," have been historically remembered by the acrostic TULIP:

T = Total depravity
U = Unconditional election
L = Limited atonement
I = Irresistible grace
P = Perseverance of the Saints

These are the points on which Arminians and Calvinists disagreed then, and disagree now, and an understanding of the Free Will Baptist view of salvation may be gained from an examination of these points. As has been said, Free Will Baptists take the Arminian approach. This is not to say, however, that Free Will Baptists believe the same things as all Arminians. Most Arminians are the spiritual descendants of John Wesley. His followers held a view of salvation that differed significantly from that of Jacobus Arminius. Rather than following Arminius's doctrine, Wesleyans have historically tended toward the teachings of some non-Calvinists who came after Arminius yet differed significantly from him in their interpretation of Scripture.[3] In the following section, we will explain the Free Will Baptist view of sin, election and grace, atonement and justification, and perseverance, and describe how Free Will Baptists differ from Calvinists on the one hand, and from other Arminians on the other hand.[4]

Sin and Depravity

Free Will Baptists believe in total depravity. Depravity is man's utter sinfulness. We believe that everyone born into the human race is by nature, totally sinful and guilty before God.

Original Sin

Man's sinfulness and guilt can be traced back to the sinfulness and guilt of our first parents, Adam and Eve. Adam and Eve were originally sinless. In their original state in the Garden of Eden, they were upright. As our *Treatise* says, "They naturally preferred and desired to obey their Creator, and had no preference or desire to transgress His will. . . . the only tendency of their nature was to do righteousness."[5] However, by their choice to disobey God's law and revolt against Him, they fell into a state of sin and guilt before God. The *1812 Former Articles,* a confession of faith used by Free Will Baptists in the South until well into the twentieth century, said that "in the beginning God made man upright, and placed him in a state of glory without the least mixture of misery, from which he voluntarily, by transgression, fell, and by that means brought upon himself a miserable and mortal state, subject to death."[6] The penalty for the sin and guilt of our first parents was eternal death.

Adam and Eve were not the only ones who were affected by their sin and fall. As Arminius said,

> The whole of this sin, however, is not peculiar to our first parents, but is common to the entire race and to all their posterity, who, at the time when this sin was committed, were in their loins, and who have since descended from them by the natural mode of propagation.[7]

The sin of Adam affected every individual born into the human race. Adam's sin was "imputed" or "credited" to everyone. The imputation of Adam's sin to the human race entails that we are just as sinful and guilty as Adam himself. We all sinned in Adam. Romans 5:12 teaches that "through one man [Adam] sin entered the world, and death through sin, and thus death spread to all men, because all sinned" (NKJV). F. Leroy Forlines states, "If we understand that death passed upon all men because all men sinned at some time in the past, death would pass upon all because all sinned in Adam."[8] As J.D. O'Donnell said, "Free Will Baptists believe in the total depravity of man. Because of the unity of the race in Adam, . . . Adam's sin is imputed to his posterity. The nature which Adam's posterity possesses is like the nature of Adam after the fall."[9]

As we saw in chapter one, Free Will Baptists originated with the English General Baptists in the 1600s. Our denominational forefathers in England taught the same doctrine of original sin that Arminius taught. General Baptist theology found its first expression when Thomas Helwys left John Smyth and went back to England with his congregation. In the first Baptist confession of faith, the 1611 *Declaration of Faith of English People Remaining at Amsterdam* (Helwys's congregation), Helwys outlined a few basic disagreements he had with Smyth. In his summary of the errors Smyth held, Helwys *criticized* Smyth for teaching "that Adam's sin was not imputed unto any of his posterity, and that all men are in the estate of Adam in his innocency before they commit actual sin, and therefore infants were not redeemed by Christ, but as the angels and other creatures."[10] Helwys believed that Adam's sin was imputed to every individual born into the human race, and that Christ's righteousness was imputed to every individual born into God's family by faith. He believed that those dying in infancy would go to Heaven because they were taken care of by Christ's death and righteousness, rather than simply because they were "as the angels and other creatures." The English General Baptist Thomas Grantham, one

of the first Free Will Baptist[11] theologians, said the following
about the sinfulness of man in his massive book
Christianismus Primitivus:

> The sin of mankind is either *original* or *actual*. The first is come upon
> all, even the very infant state of mankind lie under it; of whom that
> saying is true (Romans 5), "They have not sinned after the similitude
> [similarity] of Adam's transgression." Yet death reigning over them
> proves the transgression of Adam to be upon them. This is that root
> sin, called *the sin of the world* (John 1:29) whereof none are free. Nor
> is it convenient to extenuate or lessen this sin, either in its nature or
> the punishment it brings with it; it being the . . . leading thread to all
> other iniquities, mankind being hereby corrupt. . . . And hence we
> find David, when complaining of his sinful state, looks back to his
> corrupt Original (Psalm 51:5): "Behold, I was shapen in iniquity, and
> in sin did my mother conceive me."[12]

These views on original sin (the effect of Adam's original
sin on the human race) are not shared by many Arminians.
Forlines correctly states that "another view that is frequently
referred to as the Arminian view does not believe that the
race is charged with the guilt of Adam's sin. . . . While it is
true that some Arminians have advocated this view, it is by
no means unanimous and should not be called the Arminian
view."[13]

Infant Salvation

In connection with the question of original sin arises the
fate of infants or children dying before they reach an age of
moral responsibility. If they are imputed with Adam's guilt,
how can they inherit eternal life? The solution to this problem need not be a denial of the imputation of Adam's sin to
the race. Free Will Baptists believe that children will go to
Heaven who die before they have reached the age at which
they can understand (and be responsible for) right and wrong
and God's requirements for salvation. The *1812 Former*

Articles say that, though children dying in infancy are recipients of the guilt of Adam's sin, "not one of them dying in that state shall suffer punishment in Hell by the guilt of Adam's sin."[14] The question that remains is: If all human beings are sinners and are guilty of Adam's sin, how can infants go to Heaven?

When the founding father of Free Will Baptists, Thomas Helwys, left John Smyth to return to England, one of his disagreements with Smyth was Smyth's view of original sin and infant safety. Smyth thought it was necessary to do away with the doctrine of original sin—that Adam's sin was imputed to all humanity—in order to ensure that infants would not be damned. Helwys differed strongly from Smyth on this point. Helwys believed that the doctrine of infant salvation and the doctrine of original sin must both be held; to deny either one was to veer from Scripture. As was mentioned above, Helwys criticized Smyth for holding to "infant safety"—that infants were safe, "as the angels and other creatures." Helwys insisted that Christ would take care of infants—that they would be "saved" rather than merely "safe." Helwys wished to teach a doctrine of infant salvation while safeguarding the doctrine of the sinfulness of all humanity. A generation later, English General Baptist theologian Thomas Grantham said that infants "are justified by our Lord Jesus Christ from the wrath to come."[15]

The teaching of Helwys and Grantham on infant salvation has persisted down to this day.[16] There are five basic reasons why Free Will Baptists hold to the doctrine of infant salvation. First, there is no teaching in Holy Scripture that infants will be damned. Surely the Holy Spirit would have taught us that infants would be damned if this were really the case. Second, the only reference we have in Scripture to the state of an infant after death is 2 Samuel 12:23, where David says that he will see his deceased infant in Heaven.

Third, infants are not capable of moral decisions. As Forlines says,

The requirement of the condition of faith is God's way of dealing with us as persons—those who have wills. God will not transgress our personality or our will. In requiring faith, God treats us as persons and requires a response from us. Failure to require a response in which we choose Christ would be a failure to treat us as persons. This problem does not exist with the infant. *He is a person* but is not fully developed so he can exercise all the rights and privileges and assume all the responsibilities of being a person. . . . he is not capable of saying either yes or no.[17]

Fourth, the atonement of Christ, which extends to all human beings, and the grace of God, which is co-extensive with that atonement—cannot be resisted by the infant; thus the infant cannot be said to have resisted the grace of God and hence will not perish but will have everlasting life. The point in reasons three and four above is that God cannot deal with infants in the same way He deals with those of us who have reached an age of moral and spiritual accountability and responsibility. Thus, the notion of infant damnation is irrelevant, since damnation is designed only as a punishment of those who are individually morally and spiritually accountable and responsible (as is made clear in Scripture). And since there is no such thing as Purgatory, but only Heaven and Hell, the only rationally defensible position one can take based on Scripture is that God has made a place for infants in Heaven through the work of His Son, Jesus Christ.

Fifth, Jesus said in the Gospel of Matthew 19:14, "Suffer little children, and forbid them not, to come unto me: for of such is the kingdom of heaven," and in Matthew 18:10 "take heed that ye despise not one of these little ones; for I say unto you, that in heaven their angels do always behold the face of my father which is in heaven." As theologian E.Y. Mullins once said, "Infants dying in infancy cannot repent, or believe, or perform works of any kind, good or bad. We do not know how the grace of God operates in them. But we are fully assured that Christ provided for them, and that they are created anew in him and saved."[18]

Human Inability

Since man is utterly sinful from birth, Free Will Baptists believe, with Arminius, that men and women have no ability to seek God or turn to Him unless they are affected by His grace. Many interpreters have assumed that Arminius held a doctrine of free will which makes individuals totally able to choose God on their own without any divine assistance. However, Arminius's view of human freedom does not mean freedom to choose God on one's own, without the aid of divine grace. Arminius states that:

> The free will of man towards the true good is not only wounded, maimed, infirm, bent, and weakened; but it is also imprisoned, destroyed, and lost: And its powers are not only debilitated and useless unless they be assisted by grace, but it has no powers whatever except such are excited by divine grace.[19]

Free Will Baptists agree with Arminius that man is totally unable to respond to God without the assistance of God's grace. Many times Calvinists caricature Arminians as believing that man's will is free to the point that he can *naturally* choose God and salvation *all by himself.* And many Arminians verge on this. Free Will Baptists, however, deny this. For example, Forlines states: "Frequently a weaker view of depravity than I adhere to is advocated by Arminians. Some have an over-simplified view of freedom of the will. . . . The drawing power required and the drawing power supplied by the Holy Spirit would be stronger in my view than many Arminians."[20] Free Will Baptists believe that man is totally unable, in and of himself, to choose God, unless he is drawn or called by divine grace. We believe that God the Holy Spirit convicts and calls all men to salvation through the work of Christ on the cross. The *Treatise* states that "the call of the gospel is co-extensive with the atonement to all men, both by the word and strivings of the Spirit."[21] The *1812 Former Articles* state:

> We believe that sinners are drawn to God, the Father, by the Holy
> Ghost, through Christ his Son, and the Holy Ghost offers His divine
> aid to all the human family; so as they all might be happy, would
> they give place to His divine teaching.[22]

Thus, we teach that man is so totally depraved that he is
unable to save himself–to get to God on his own. Yet God in
His grace reaches out to man and draws him–convicts him,
and "excites him by divine grace." However, man *has the free
will to resist and reject this grace.*

To say that man is totally depraved is not to say that every
man is as sinful as he could be, nor that sinners do not know
right from wrong in their God-given consciences. Because of
the image of God in them, human beings are capable of making certain right moral choices. Man is a moral person. As a
result of the image of God in humanity, human beings have
a moral constitution. People have the ability to tell right from
wrong and even choose to do things that are right and avoid
wrong actions. Yet, any good deeds that man can do will
never provide acceptance before God nor will they meet a
human being's most deeply felt needs. Man is not, as Forlines
says, a "moral blank." "If fallen man were a moral blank, or
had the categories of right and wrong reversed, there would
be no point of contact for the gospel. There would be no
grounds for conviction of sin."[23]

The question arises, if both Calvinists and Arminians
believe in the total depravity of man, then what distinguishes
Calvinism from Arminianism in this area? Calvinists say that
man is so sinful that he cannot respond to God without the
drawing of divine grace. Free Will Baptists agree wholeheart-
edly. The difference is that Free Will Baptists believe this
divine drawing–conviction and calling–extends with Christ's
death to *all men,* whereas Calvinists believe that Christ died
only for those whom God had chosen to faith beforehand.
The rest are consigned to eternal damnation. This leads us to
our next topic: election and grace.

Election and Grace

Election

Free Will Baptists differ with Calvinists in their doctrines of election and grace, agreeing rather with the view of Jacobus Arminius.[24] Calvinists have typically taught that, in eternity past, God elected or chose some to faith and hence to salvation, and reprobated the rest to Hell; this election and reprobation have no conditions to be met on the part of the person who is elected or reprobated. Thus, God chose the eternal destiny of each individual without regard to the individual's choice or will.

Free Will Baptists disagree with this notion and concur with Arminius, who stated that it is God's will for all men to be saved, and that God extends His grace to all, but that men have the freedom to resist and reject the grace of God, which results in eternal punishment. Arminius saw election as God's choice to save those whom He foreknew *in Christ Jesus.*[25] The main difference between Calvinism and Arminianism on the doctrine of election is this: Calvinists believe that God, in His secret will, picks who will be saved and who will be damned, giving them no choice in the matter. Arminians, on the contrary, believe that God gives people the free will to resist His grace which goes out to all people. This is why we are called *Free Will Baptists*: because we believe in man's free will.

An understanding of the Free Will Baptist doctrine of election can be gained by looking at the doctrine of our forefathers, the English General Baptists. The General Baptists held to an election *conditioned* on union with Christ, as opposed to the *unconditional* election taught by the Calvinists.[26] The General Baptists taught that "God hath even before the foundation of the world chosen (or elected) to eternal life such as believe and so are in Christ."[27]

In Calvinism, since God had already chosen some for salvation and some for damnation, Christ was sent into the world to die only for those whom God had chosen or elected (the "elect"). Our forefathers said, like Arminius, that Christ died for every individual in the human race, so that every individual has a chance to come to Him in faith. (More will be said about the extent of the atonement in the next section.) The General Baptist understanding of election and grace is summed up well in Helwys's 1611 *Declaration of Faith of English People Remaining at Amsterdam*:

> . . . this is the election and reprobation spoken of in the Scriptures, concerning salvation and condemnation, and not that God hath predestinated men to be wicked and so to be damned, but that men being wicked shall be damned; for God would have all men saved, and come to the knowledge of the truth (I Tim. 2:4) and would have no man perish, but would have all men come to repentance (II Pet. 3:9).[28]

Article nine of the "Articles of Faith" included in our *Treatise* states that "God determined from the beginning to save all who should comply with the conditions of salvation. Hence by faith in Christ men become His elect."

Free Will Baptists believe the scriptural basis of election is revealed in Ephesians 1:4, which states that God chose us in Christ before the creation of the world. This is the foundation of the Free Will Baptist view of election. God's choice of certain individuals for salvation cannot be understood outside of a consideration of Christ. It is *in Christ* that we are elected. Romans 8:29 states, "For whom he did foreknow, he also did predestinate. . . ." "Foreknow" here carries with it the idea of intimate, close knowledge of an individual—not just that God knew something, but that God knew someone. How did God know us? In Christ! Union with Christ, according to the New Testament, is the ground or basis for our election or God's choice of us for salvation. We come into union with Christ through faith alone. Thus, Free Will Baptists believe that God's choice of people for salvation is based on their union with Christ which is conditioned on faith in Him.

Grace

The Free Will Baptist doctrine of God's grace is closely tied to the doctrine of election. Calvinists insist that God's grace is *irresistible* (that is, when God decides someone will be saved, that person will be irresistibly drawn to God by the Holy Spirit without regard to the person's choice or will). Free Will Baptists insist that God has endowed human beings with free will, and hence the grace of God is *resistible*. Scripture explicitly states that it is God's will that all should come to Him (2 Peter 3:9; 1 Timothy 2:4), but not all do come. If God wills that all should be saved but not all are saved, then it is clear that men can resist the will of God. We teach that God in His grace calls all men, universally, to be saved. Unlike the Calvinists, we believe that the Gospel Call goes out to all humanity—that God extends his divine grace to all men. Jesus said twice in the Gospel of Matthew that "many are called but few are chosen"—that is, all who hear the call of God will not respond and become one of God's chosen people (the "elect"); some will resist this grace. Christ also taught clearly that men can resist the grace of God: "How often would I have gathered thy children together, even as a hen gathereth her chickens under *her* wings, and ye would not!" (Matthew 23:37).

Thus, Free Will Baptists believe it is most consistent with Holy Scripture to teach that God extends His divine grace to all people, that God gives people the free will to resist and reject this grace, and those who do not reject the grace of God, but who respond in true faith to the unmerited grace offered to them, will come into union with Christ and thus receive salvation. God knew this before the formation of the world and thus decided to bring salvation to all who would not reject His wonderful grace.

Atonement and Justification

The Extent of the Atonement and General Provision[29]

> As Free Will Baptists, we glory in the full, free, and universal [offer
> of the] salvation of Christ to all men–the rich, the poor, the great, the
> small; Salvation is offered to all. The psalmist says, "As the heaven is
> high above the earth, so great is [God's] mercy toward them that fear
> Him." The boundless extent of heaven's blue field is a faint emblem
> of redeeming love. . . . Wherever man may stray on the remote fron-
> tier and far-off corners of the earth, the deep blue heavens bend over
> him; so the boundless blue sky of free salvation is offered to all by
> Christ Who bends over the human race, beaming with the stars of
> promise and hope, seeming to say, "Free salvation is offered to all."
> As there is room in the broad ocean for all the ships of the world to
> freely float and never crowd each other, so there is free and ample
> room in the Kingdom of Christ for all men. As all the armies of the
> world can freely wash, bathe, and cleanse themselves in the ocean,
> so in the red sea of Christ's shed blood, the world's vast population
> may freely wash and be purified as white as snow.[30]

Free Will Baptists believe that Christ died for all, for everyone born into the human race. Our forefathers, the English
General Baptists, emphasized the fact that Christ died for the
sins of the whole world, not just the elect. They were referred
to as *General* Baptists because they taught that the atonement
of Christ was a *general* atonement (that Christ died for all)
rather than a *particular* atonement (that Christ died only for
the elect, as the Calvinists said).[31] The *1660 Confession of Faith*
stated with Scripture that:

> God is not willing that any should perish, but that all should come to
> repentance (II Peter 3:9) and the knowledge of the truth, that they
> might be saved (I Timothy 2:4). For which end Christ hath com-
> manded, that the Gospel (to wit, the glad tidings of remission of sins)
> should be preached to every creature (Mark 16:15). . . .[32]

Free Will Baptists rely on numerous passages from
Scripture for their doctrine of general or unlimited atone-

ment. The confession above makes reference to 2 Peter 3:9. Free Will Baptists believe that God wishes that everyone would accept the divine offer of salvation and that He has made it possible for everyone to do so by the death of His Son on the cross. It would make little sense if God, whose will is that none should perish but that all should come to Him, sent His Son to die for but a few.

Another passage cited in the *1660 Confession*, 1 Timothy 2:4, says that it is God's will for "all men to be saved, and to come unto the knowledge of the truth." W. Stanley Outlaw comments that "Paul's statement here as well as Peter's similar declaration (2 Pet. 3:9) must, of necessity, refer to God's permissive will, which can be successfully resisted, else the Scripture would teach the doctrine of universalism. Though it is true that all men will not be saved, . . . it is also true that it is God's desire for all men to be saved."[33]

Hebrews 2:9 states clearly that Christ "tasted death for every man." Everyone agrees that, by using the word "taste" in this passage, the author of Hebrews meant that Christ fully experienced death on the cross. But unanimous agreement is not found in regard to the phrase "for every man." This phrase is said by Calvinists to refer, not to all mankind, but only to the elect. They view this passage, beginning with verse 5, as discussing not the world, but only the elect. But, as Milton Crowson has said, the Greek word for "every man," *pantos*, which literally means "everyone," is inclusive and not exclusive, and to view this passage in limited, exclusive terms, as the Calvinists do, is to do extreme injustice to the passage.[34] Another passage which clearly speaks of the universal extent of Christ's atonement is 1 John 2:2, which states that Christ "is the propitiation for our sins: and not for ours only, but also for *the sins of* the whole world."

Free Will Baptists see these and other passages as clearly establishing the doctrine of unlimited atonement and general provision. We believe that Christ's unlimited death for all humanity is the reason for the numerous scriptural commands to preach to all people, and to call all people to repentance (Matthew 24:14, 28:19; Mark 16:15; Luke 24:47; Acts 17:30). This doctrine of the extent of the atonement confirms for us the belief in the general provision of the grace of God to all people–that all have an opportunity to receive Christ in faith. Hence, our *Treatise* states that "salvation is rendered equally possible to all; and if any fail of eternal life, the fault is wholly his own."[35] This has been our belief for centuries, and was expressed in both our *1660 Confession* and *1812 Former Articles* thusly:

> We believe that no man shall suffer in Hell for want of a Christ who died for him, but, as the Scripture has said, for denying the Lord that bought him (II Peter 2:1), because he believed not in the name of the only begotten Son of God (John 3:18). Unbelief, therefore, being the cause why the just and righteous God of Heaven will condemn the children of men, it follows against all contradiction that all men, at one time or another, are found in such a capacity as that, through the grace of God, they may be eternally saved ([John 1:7]; Acts 17:30; Mark 6:6; Hebrews 3:10, [18, 19]; 1 John 5:10; [John 3:17]).[36]

E.L. St. Claire (1866-1916), a Free Will Baptist minister and educator from Georgia, summarized the Free Will Baptist view of the extent of the atonement and general provision in his sermon, "What Free Will Baptists Believe and Why":

> "Whosoever will may come." Again our Lord taught the doctrine of free will when He commanded His apostles to go into all the world and preach the gospel to every creature–because all were sinners, all have sinned. All needed redemption–salvation. [God is] calling on all to believe on the Lord Jesus Christ–believe on the only begotten Son of God, as the only means of salvation, calling all the world to repentance–not part of it. . . . not calling on some, but all. Why call if all cannot hear? Why die for all if all cannot be saved? Is not His blood sufficient? Is not the sacrifice of Christ ample?
>
> Anything short of a full, free salvation from sin is anti-Christian [and] savors not of a loving, dying Christ, but smells of the slums of religion. [God is] calling all men to repent–everywhere. Anything short of this is beneath a loving God, and only finds place in the shal-

low minds of men. . . . All come—great and small, rich and poor, all come—everyman, everywhere. Come, the sacrifice is offered; the sword is removed before the gates of the spiritual Eden, the church. Come in, every kindred, every tribe, every nation, come in! And yet there is room—room for all. Christ died for all. Jesus Christ tasted death for every man.[37]

The Nature of Atonement

Free Will Baptists have historically differed from most Arminians in their doctrines of the nature of atonement and justification. Wesleyans, Anabaptists, and other Arminian-minded groups (e.g., Disciples of Christ, Churches of Christ, etc.) have traditionally advanced the governmental view of atonement and the view of justification that issues from it. While disagreeing strongly with the Calvinist view of the *limitedness* of atonement, Free Will Baptists have traditionally agreed with the Reformed tradition on the doctrines of the nature of atonement and justification.

Before a discussion of the Free Will Baptist position on these doctrines, a brief review of the position of most Arminians will be beneficial. As said above, most Arminians adhere to the governmental view of atonement and the view of justification that results from it. This doctrine of atonement was first formulated by Hugo Grotius (1583-1645). Grotius was a follower of Arminius but clearly differed with him on a number of doctrines. Even though Grotius was the first to formulate a well-argued governmental theory of atonement and justification, similar views had been advocated by some Anabaptists and others before Grotius. According to the governmental view of atonement, Jesus Christ was sent by God to die on the cross as a substitute for the penalty that sin deserves. When an individual has faith in Christ, God the Father *sets aside* the penalty of sin as a governor who might freely pardon a criminal without any punishment. Therefore, in this view, Christ in His death does not pay the sin debt. Christ does not take on man's punishment; thus, He does not pay the penalty for man's sin. A fundamental assumption of the governmental view is that it is not absolutely necessary for man's sin to be punished.

Free Will Baptists believe the *penal satisfaction* view of atonement. This view, held by most evangelical Protestants, says that God sent His Son to die on the cross *to pay our penalty for sin.* Christ *is our* substitute. Christ actually takes our place on the cross. The death that we deserved because of our sin is dealt out to Christ on the cross. This differs from the governmental view in that God the Father demands punishment for sin; so He cannot let man dwell eternally with Him unless the debt of sin is actually paid. In the governmental view, we remember that God waives our punishment in lieu of our faith in Christ's death. In the penal satisfaction view, God, because of His holiness, could never waive our punishment. Sin must be punished. So this is the plan of God: God becomes man in the person of His Son, Jesus Christ, so that He may live a life as the only sinless man in history. After perfectly fulfilling the demands of God's holy law in His life, Christ took our sin on Himself–He "bore our sins in his own body on the tree" (1 Peter 2:24). Christ has "redeemed us from the curse of the law, being made a curse for us" (Galatians 3:13). Christ, who knew no sin, was made "sin for us" (2 Corinthians 5:21).

Thus, the name *penal satisfaction* view of atonement: *Penal* refers to punishment–God has dealt out the punishment for our sin on Jesus. *Satisfaction* refers to Jesus Christ satisfying God's holy Law–Christ was the only man ever to obey the law perfectly, and in His righteous life and death He satisfied the just demands of a Holy God. *We could not do this for ourselves.* Man is sinful and thus has failed to meet God's requirement of absolute righteousness or holiness. Hence, man must be punished because of his sin. God in His absolute holiness cannot dwell with sin. As Marie T. Hyatt has said, "We must see sin as the Bible depicts it, as something which brings wrath, condemnation, and eternal ruin in its train. We must see it as guilt that needs expiation. . . . The sinfulness of man

constitutes the fact that the atonement is a necessity."[38] God
had to choose one of two possible courses of action: (1) He
could have let all humanity suffer the eternal punishment
(Hell) due for their sin; or (2) He could provide a better way
for man's sin debt to be paid. God provided the better way.
He died on the cross, the only one worthy to take man's punishment on Himself. When we have faith in Christ, His death
and righteousness, in God's sight, become our own death and
righteousness.[39]

In the doctrine of atonement, Free Will Baptists have historically tended toward the view of Arminius himself rather
than accepting the view of later "Arminians." Arminius
believed that God must punish sin with eternal punishment
unless one meets the requirement of total righteousness
before Him. So God is portrayed as a judge who must sentence individuals to eternal death if they do not meet His
requirements. Arminius employed the analogy of "a judge
making an estimate in his own mind of the deed and of the
author of [the deed], and according to that estimate forming
a judgment and pronouncing sentence."[40] The sentence pronounced on the sinner who cannot meet the requirements of
God's justice is eternal death. Yet, since no one has the righteousness which satisfies God's holiness, it must come from
someone else. It can only come from the God-man, Jesus
Christ. Christ pays the penalty for sin on the cross—He pays,
as Arminius says, "the price of redemption for sins by suffering the punishment due to them."[41]

For Arminius, this emphasis on justice does not mitigate
God's mercy, as some later Arminians held. God *never had* to
offer Christ for the redemption of man in the first place.[42] If
God had not made a way of satisfaction for His justice
(through mercy), *then,* Arminius says, is when humanity
would have truly been judged according to God's "severe
and rigid estimation."[43] God cannot let sin go unpunished.
Thus, the only way for man to escape eternal punishment for

sin is for the perfect God-man, Jesus Christ, to take the sinner's place, to take the sinner's sin on Himself and suffer the punishment due that sin.

Arminius's view is summarized in the Free Will Baptist *Treatise.* In the chapter on "The Atonement and Mediation of Christ," the *Treatise* states:

> As sin cannot be pardoned without a sacrifice, and the blood of beasts could never wash away sin, Christ gave Himself a sacrifice for the sins of the world, and thus made salvation possible for all men. He died for us, suffering in our stead, to make known the righteousness of God, that He might be just in justifying sinners who believe in His Son. . . . The atonement for sin was necessary. For present and future obedience can no more blot out our past sins than past obedience can remove the guilt of present and future sins. If God pardoned the sins of men without satisfaction for the violation of his law, it would follow that transgression might go on with impunity; government would be abrogated, and the obligation of obedience to God would be, in effect, removed.[44]

The *Treatise* states that Christ "died for us, suffering in our stead." This statement stresses the substitutionary nature of Christ's death. Christ's death was *vicarious.* The word "vicarious" comes from the word "vicar" which means substitute. Christ is the vicar or substitute who takes our place on the cross and receives our penalty for us. O'Donnell, in commenting on this statement in the *Treatise,* aptly says that "Jesus stepped between God's wrath and man. . . . This was God receiving the stroke of His own penalty against sin, the judge paying the penalty for the condemned."[45] The *Treatise* further says that Christ's sacrifice for us was done so that God "would be just in justifying sinners who believe on His son." The only way God could have maintained His justice and holiness would be for the penalty for sin to be paid. God could not simply forgive man without inflicting punishment for sin; so God Himself, in the person of Jesus Christ, takes on the punishment for sin. Hence, God can maintain His justice while providing a way for us to spend eternity with Him.

The *Treatise* goes on to say that our own attempts at obedience to God's law could never blot out our guilt before God. Furthermore, God cannot merely pardon "the sins of men without satisfaction for the violation of his law." Unlike the governmental view, the *Treatise* says that God cannot merely pardon an individual as a governor would pardon a convicted criminal. If so, "transgression would go on with impunity"; that is, sin would continue to go unpunished. Thus, God in His infinite wisdom paid our penalty—our sin debt—on the cross through His Son Jesus Christ. If we have faith and continue in faith in Him, we will not have to pay this penalty—the penalty of eternal death. He has paid it for us.

Justification

The Free Will Baptist view of justification follows from our penal satisfaction view of the atonement. As with our view of the nature of the atonement, Free Will Baptists disagree with most modern Arminians, whose doctrine of justification results from the governmental view of the atonement. An understanding of the view that Free Will Baptists disagree with—the governmental view of justification—will set the stage for a discussion of our view of the nature of justification.

Most Arminians disagree with Jacobus Arminius, who held that, when the sinner has faith, Christ's righteousness is imputed or credited to him, and that is what provides his justification before God. Rather, they believe that we are not justified by the imputed righteousness of Jesus Christ. Since Christ does not take our penalty for sin upon Himself, that payment for the penalty is not credited to the believing sinner. In view of one's faith, God sets aside the penalty for sin and pardons the sinner as a governor would pardon a criminal. The penalty for sin is not paid, and the believer does not stand righteous before God clothed in the righteousness of Christ, but the penalty is *set aside* in view of personal faith.

Free Will Baptist doctrine differs strongly from this theory of justification. We believe that Christ paid the penalty for sin on the cross, and that God in His absolute holiness must take sin so seriously that He cannot merely set aside the penalty and pardon us like a governor would pardon a criminal. We can only be justified in God's sight when the penalty for our sin has been paid and when we can stand righteous before God, clothed in the absolute righteousness of Christ, which is imputed or credited to us through faith. This is the absolute righteousness that God requires of us.

Thus, Free Will Baptists believe that when the sinner first places his faith in Christ, he comes into union with Christ, and Christ's death—the payment of the penalty for sin—is imputed or credited to him. It is as though Christ's death is the sinner's own death. Another result of union with Christ is that His righteousness is imputed to us (Romans 4:6); we are clothed in his righteousness, and our sins are laid on Him. Paul speaks of this union on more than one occasion. He says in his letter to the Romans, "There is therefore now no condemnation to them which are in [union with] Christ Jesus" (Romans 8:1), that we are "baptized into Christ's death" (Romans 6:3), that we are "planted [or grafted] together with Christ" (Romans 6:5), and that we have "died with Christ" (Romans 6:6).[46]

In this intimate union with Christ, His history (His righteousness and death) becomes our history, and our history (our sin) becomes His history. It is clear from Scripture that we cannot ourselves obtain the righteousness that God requires for us to stand just before Him. So He provides us with a God-provided righteousness: the righteousness of Jesus Christ imputed or credited to us through faith. Paul speaks of this imputation of righteousness on numerous occasions (2 Corinthians 5:21; Philippians 3:9; Romans 3:21; 4:6). Forlines sums up our view of justification in the following statement: "On the condition of faith, we are placed in union with Christ. Based on that union we receive His death and righteousness. Based on the fact that Christ's death and righteousness became our death and righteousness, God as Judge declares us righteous."[47]

This has been the view of Free Will Baptists for centuries and the view of our theological forebear, Jacobus Arminius. Arminius believed that justification takes place when God as Judge pronounces the believing sinner just or righteous because he has been imputed with the righteousness of Christ, which is his through faith. Arminius distinguished sharply between imputed righteousness and inherent (our own) righteousness, saying that the righteousness by which we are justified is in no way inherent (or within us) but is Christ's righteousness which is "made ours by gracious imputation."[48]

We spoke earlier of the serious disagreements between Thomas Helwys, our English founder, and John Smyth, which eventually led Helwys and his flock to leave Smyth and his group in Holland and return to England. One of the disagreements centered around the doctrine of justification. Smyth had begun to teach that we are justified, not by Christ's righteousness alone, but by our own righteousness as well. Helwys taught, on the contrary, that "man is justified *only* by the righteousness of Christ, apprehended by faith."[49] This has been the Free Will Baptist doctrine of justification ever since. Thomas Grantham echoed this doctrine in his book *Christianismus Primitivus.* He stated: "That God imputes righteousness to men without works, is so plain, that it can never be denied. What is thus imputed, is not acted by us, but expressly reckoned as a matter of free gift, or Grace; and this can be the righteousness of none but Christ."[50]

This was also the teaching of the American Free Will Baptists in their *1812 Former Articles,* a condensed and revised version of the *1660 Confession* of their ancestors, the English General Baptists:

> We believe that no man has any warrant in the Holy Scriptures for justification before God through his own works, power, or ability

which he has in and of himself; only as he by grace is made able to come to God, through Jesus Christ; believing the righteousness of Jesus Christ to be imputed to all believers for their eternal acceptance with God (Romans 4:24; Acts 8:20-21).[51]

Thus, it can be seen that Free Will Baptists believe according to Scripture that justification is the act whereby God views the sinner as righteous on the basis of the righteousness and death of Christ, which has been imputed to him and has become his own through personal faith in Christ.

Perseverance and Falling Away

The scriptural doctrine of justification by the imputed righteousness of Christ, apprehended by faith, has great implications for the Christian life and for our doctrine of perseverance and falling away. As long as a person has faith in the Lord Jesus Christ, the righteousness of Christ is his because he is in union with Christ, and as long as he is in union with Christ, he is saved.

The Resistibility of Grace After Conversion

Free Will Baptists believe that it is possible for a believer to cease to believe in Jesus Christ and hence to fall away from grace and forfeit his salvation. As stated earlier, Free Will Baptists agree with Arminius that the grace of God can be resisted, whereas traditional Calvinists say that the grace of God is irresistible. If one is a consistent Calvinist and believes that the grace of God is irresistible before conversion, then it makes sense that it would be irresistible after conversion and the believer would not have the free will to resist God's grace and lose his salvation.

It is ironic that most modern-day believers in eternal security (or "once-saved-always-saved") believe that man has free will prior to conversion—that the grace of God is resistible *prior* to conversion. In this, they differ from their strict Calvinist forefathers. Yet somehow, they believe that *after* conversion, grace suddenly becomes irresistible and the Christian no longer has the free will to resist the grace of God, stop having faith, and lose his salvation. It makes little sense that one's free will would suddenly cease after conversion when, before conversion, he had the free will to reject God's gracious gift of salvation. If man can reject God's gift of salvation prior to conversion, why can he not reject God's gift after conversion?

Free Will Baptists are consistent in their belief that the grace of God is resistible–before and after conversion. Thus, a Christian can cease to have faith–he can make shipwreck of his faith–and hence be taken out of union with Christ. When this occurs, he is no longer imputed with the righteousness of Jesus Christ, which alone can save him, and his salvation is lost forever.

This has been the Free Will Baptist doctrine of the perseverance of the saints from our beginning, when Thomas Helwys said that "men may fall away from the grace of God (Hebrews 12:15) and from the truth which they have received and acknowledged (Hebrews 10:26), and after they have tasted of the heavenly gift and been made partakers of the Holy Ghost (Hebrews 6:4, 5)."[52]

The Assurance of Salvation and the Possibility of Apostasy

A look at the chapter on "The Perseverance of the Saints" in our *Treatise* will help us understand the Free Will Baptist view of perseverance and falling away. The *Treatise* opens with a statement about the assurance of salvation: "There are strong grounds to hope that the truly regenerate will persevere unto the end, and be saved, through the power of divine grace which is pledged for their support. . . ."[53] This statement testifies to the assurance that we will receive a crown of righteousness in Heaven if we persevere in faith to the end of our lives (Revelation 2:10). The *1660 Confession* says the same basic thing in the second part of its statement on perseverance:

But such who add unto their faith virtue, and unto virtue knowledge, and unto knowledge temperance, etc. (II Peter 1:5-7), such shall never fall (II Peter 1:8-10), 'tis impossible for all the false Christs and false prophets that are, and are to come, to deceive such, for they are kept by the power of God, through faith unto salvation (I Peter 1:5).[54]

The confession quotes from 1 Peter 1:5, which says that we as Christians are kept by the power of God through faith unto salvation. We may be assured that we are kept by the power of God—the divine power which is pledged for our support. But notice that the verse says that we are kept by the power of God *through faith.* Only *through faith* will we continue to be kept by God. Without faith it is impossible to please God (Hebrews 11:6). Only as long as we continue in faith (and thus in Christ) will we be saved; but if we cease to have faith, we will no longer be kept by God and will forfeit our salvation.

The second sentence in the *Treatise* statement says that the Christian's "future obedience and final salvation are neither determined nor certain, since through infirmity and manifold temptation they are in danger of falling; and they ought, therefore, to watch and pray lest they make shipwreck of their faith and be lost."[55] This sentence states that if we are not careful to keep abiding in Christ, we are in serious danger of falling from grace. We should be careful to stay close to God lest we make shipwreck of our faith. When one makes shipwreck of his faith—when he ceases to have faith—he is again lost irreparably. Picirilli comments on the last clause in the *Treatise* statement, noting that it—

. . . makes very clear that the loss of *faith* is what is finally involved in the shipwreck of a Christian life. We must see this point clearly if we are to understand the basis for our doctrine of perseverance. It would not do to word our statements of doctrine so as to give the impression that salvation is based on a man's own works. The Bible specifically declares that salvation is *not* of works. This declaration, in Ephesians 2:8 and 9, applies just as strongly to *keeping* salvation as it does to *getting* it. We will never obtain Heaven by virtue of our works. First, last, and always, the condition man must meet is *faith.*[56]

The Apostle Peter says in 2 Peter 2:20 that if one loses his salvation, "the latter end is worse with [him] than the beginning." This verse shows us the gravity and seriousness of apostasy. The only way the latter end could be worse than the beginning is if a person could never be saved again. Before conversion (the beginning), one is not a child of God but has the chance to become a child of God if he will come to Christ in faith. How could the latter end (after a person loses his salvation) be worse than this? There is only one way this could be so. The latter end (loss of salvation) is worse than the beginning (not yet being saved before conversion) because the one who has lost his salvation can *never be saved again.*

This is a very serious situation. Let us stress here that when Free Will Baptists speak of "losing one's salvation," they are not referring to "lose" in the way one does who loses a pocket knife or a safety pin and who might find it again. Rather, Free Will Baptists teach that it is not that easy to lose one's salvation, and as long as one remains in faith, and hence in Christ, he will not lose his salvation. If a person is in Christ when he dies, he will go to Heaven. As Picirilli says,

> Sometimes you also meet people who feel very unsure whether they are going to make it, or whether they're going to hold out. They seem to carry their salvation around like a fragile glass in their hands, taking every step gently on tiptoe, afraid that at any moment they will unwillingly drop the priceless possession and smash it to smithereens. Such folk live in constant doubt and fear about gaining Heaven. Now it is probably better to be overly cautious than overly careless, but it sure is miserable to live in daily despair about salvation, fearful that the slightest misstep will plunge one into Hell. And this is *not* the scriptural teaching nor the Free Will Baptist doctrine. . . . You can be sure, then, that you will not "accidentally" fall short of the kingdom of God. If you leave the Lord, it will be because you will to do so. Are you a child of God by faith in Christ? Then you can walk in the peaceful confidence of I Thessalonians 5:9: "For

God hath not appointed us to wrath, but to obtain salvation by our Lord Jesus Christ."[57]

When Free Will Baptists speak of "losing salvation," we refer to Webster's primary definitions of *lose:* "to destroy," "to suffer deprivation of," "to fail to keep or maintain," "to get rid of."

The Scriptural Teaching on Apostasy

Our belief in the possibility of apostasy or the loss of salvation is based on numerous passages of Scripture which teach the resistibility of grace before and after conversion. Though numerous passages of Scripture teach the possibility of apostasy, we will look at only a few as cases in point. The clearest passage warning the believer of the possibility of falling away is Hebrews 6:4-6:

> For it is impossible for those who were once enlightened, and have tasted of the heavenly gift, and were made partakers of the Holy Ghost, and have tasted the good word of God, and the powers of the world to come, if they shall fall away, to renew them again unto repentance; seeing they crucify to themselves the Son of God afresh, and put him to an open shame.

This passage describes the fate of those who were once Christians and fell away. One would be hard put to consider those described here as anything less than regenerate, saved, Christian people. They are described as "enlightened," which means "illuminated" or "enlighten[ed] spiritually, imbu[ed] with saving knowledge."[58]

These people are also said to have *tasted* three things: the heavenly gift of salvation, the good word of God, and the powers of the future Kingdom of God. Some Calvinists have said that the word *taste* just means that they lightly tasted salvation, but did not "eat of it;" in other words, they were at the door of salvation and may have had some kind of experience with God, but they did not go through the door and have a conversion experience through faith. This explanation, however, makes little sense, since the same Greek word for taste is used to describe Jesus's death on the cross in Hebrews 2:9, where the writer says that Christ tasted death for every man. Surely the Calvinists would not say that Jesus just lightly tasted of what it might have been like to die, but did not actually die; surely they would not say that Jesus came to the door of death, but did not go through. Thus, it must be said that the people described in Hebrews 6 were indeed Christians, since they tasted salvation in the same way Christ tasted death.

These people are also described as "partakers of the Holy Ghost." How can an unbeliever be a partaker of the Holy Ghost? It must also be noted that they had repented; the only way one cannot be "renewed unto repentance" is if they have already repented. Since repentance is a condition of salvation, these individuals must have been saved. Only a strained reading of the passage will result in the conclusion that these were unbelievers. The most natural reading of the passage establishes that those described here were full-fledged believers.

This passage was written to Jews who were in danger of leaving Christ and retreating into Judaism. The author of Hebrews was writing to keep Jewish readers from making that mistake.[59] The people the author describes in this passage—those whom the author is holding up as an exemplary warning to his readers—had fallen away. The passage further states that having fallen away, it is impossible "to renew them again unto repentance" (Hebrews 6:6).

The Permanence of Apostasy

Once a person falls away, it is impossible for him to be saved again, since repentance is involved in the initial act of salvation. An even stronger statement is made in Hebrews 10, where the author says that there "remaineth no more sacrifice for sins" for the one who has fallen away, for he has "trodden under foot the Son of God, and hath counted the blood of the covenant, wherewith he was sanctified, an unholy thing." It is clear that the person described here was once a Christian, for only a Christian can be sanctified by Christ's blood. As 2 Peter 2:20 says, if one falls from grace, the latter end is worse than the beginning. Both writers state unequivocally that once a person loses his salvation or falls away, he can never be saved again.

This has been the historic belief of Free Will Baptists for centuries. In his *Christianismus Primitivus*, Thomas Grantham referred to those who had lost their salvation, saying that their state was "irrevocable—whom Jude calls *Trees twice dead, plucked up by the Roots*: and consequently uncapable of bearing fruit in God's vineyard for ever." He goes on to say:

> Of the same force are these two places, Hebrews 6:4-6 and Hebrews 10:26-30. For when Men have *destroyed a state of Faith* (in respect of themselves) trodden under foot the Son of God; counted the blood of the Covenant wherewith they were sanctified an unholy thing, and thus doing despite to the Spirit of Grace; These Men cannot (As *Chrysostom* notes upon the place) be twice made Christians; and there being but one Sacrifice for Sin, there remains no more for such. . . .[60]

The *1660 Confession* is just as strong on the irrevocable nature of apostasy. Citing John 15:6 as an example of this, the *Confession* states that those who do not abide (remain) in Christ will be "cast into the fire and burned."[61]

The Cause of Apostasy

What causes one to lose his salvation? Failure to continue in faith. Losing salvation may be looked at as the opposite thing that happens when one is converted to Christ. When one is converted, his faith brings him into union with Christ, and as a result of this union, he is imputed or credited with Christ's righteousness. On the basis of Christ's righteousness, he is justified—he stands just before God. When one ceases to have faith, the opposite happens. He is *taken out of* union with

Christ and no longer has Christ's righteousness, and hence
no longer stands just before God. Thus, the way one loses salvation is to cease having faith. If one has faith, then one has
Christ's righteousness. If one ceases to have faith, he no
longer has Christ's righteousness and is lost forever.

Some might say, "Well, if I have Christ's righteousness,
then my own righteousness doesn't matter." *This is not the case.*
Though Scripture is clear that we can never be justified in the
sight of God based on *our own* works, merit, ability, or righteousness, it is just as clear about the *devastating* effects of sin
on the Christian life. Unlike some eternal securitists who
teach the doctrine (called "antinomianism"[62]) that since one is
justified by faith he may persist in a life of sin, Free Will
Baptists cry out, *One cannot persist in a life of sin and expect his
relationship with God to continue.*

How does this harmonize with the doctrine of justification
through faith alone? This is how: Sin has damaging effects on
the Christian's relationship with God. The author of Hebrews
warns us not to be hardened by sin (Hebrews 3:13).
Unrepentant sin has the effect of hardening us against the
wooing and conviction of the Holy Spirit and puts a tremendous strain on our relationship with God. Even one unrepentant sin can place a great deal of tension on our relationship
with Him. When a Christian regresses into a condition in
which he is guilty of much unrepentant sin (or has slidden
back in his walk with God), his relationship with Christ
becomes more and more strained. The Holy Spirit's voice of
conviction becomes more and more faint; his heart becomes
harder and harder, and he becomes calloused toward the
Word of God and the preaching of the Word. When this happens, the Christian has placed himself into the extremely
dangerous condition whereby he might fully and finally
renounce his faith in Christ and be lost. Forlines says more
about this:

[Tampering with sin] can lead to a spirit of defeat and place one under the chastising hand of God (Hebrews 12:7-11). In the determination that God has, that His people will be holy, He places His people under chastisement. God's determination to make His people holy will bring a Christian to a point that he will either have to repent or forsake God altogether. If he should turn from God this will mean turning from faith. He will make shipwreck of faith (I Timothy 1:18-19).[63]

Some Arminians teach that if a person loses his salvation, he must work really hard in order to get it back again. But this is not the biblical doctrine of loss of salvation. Our doctrine is much stronger than this. If one falls away from God's grace—if one loses his salvation—he can *never* be restored again into the favor of God. It is too late for him. He is lost forever. This is *much stronger* than saying that one can lose his salvation and get it back again, over and over. Our doctrine makes unrepentant sin in the Christian's life a *much more serious* matter. If one continues in sin he is liable to renounce faith in Christ; and when this happens, salvation is irrevocably lost, and this lost condition can never be remedied. This doctrine should instill in us the grave importance of "adding to our faith virtue, and to virtue knowledge, and to knowledge temperance," since losing our salvation is a permanent state. Yet Peter says that if we keep our faith strong and lively by doing these things, we will never fall (2 Peter 1:5-10).

THE DOCTRINE OF THE CHURCH

Free Will Baptists have their name because they believe in free will and because they are Baptists. The Free Will Baptist concept of the church is distinctive. We have always sought to base our doctrine of the church, and our practice in the church, solely on the New Testament pattern. A discussion of the Free Will Baptist doctrine of the church will include six basic topics: the nature of the church, the mission of the church, the offices of the church, the government of the church, the ordinances of the church, and the worship of the church. Our beliefs on these matters are part and parcel of who we are—not simply doctrinal appendages, but rather an outworking of what we believe about the free salvation offered through Jesus Christ.

The Nature and Mission of the Church

The Nature of the Church

Our *Treatise* describes two usages of the word "church." One usage refers to what Christians have traditionally called the invisible church, or the universal church. The *Treatise* states: "The Church of God, or members of the body of Christ, is the whole body of Christians throughout the world, and none but the regenerate are its members."[64] O'Donnell says the invisible church "consists of all those who have become the children of God by faith in Jesus Christ."[65] While some Baptists, such as the Landmark Baptists, have taken a negative view of other denominations, insisting that they are the only true church, Free Will Baptists have always recognized that while they believe their doctrine of the church is the biblical doctrine, they are not the only true church. This concept is involved in our belief in open communion—that all true Christians, regardless of baptism or denomination, may come to the Lord's table. (This concept will be discussed later in the section on the Lord's Supper.)

The most basic usage of the word "church" is that employed to refer to the local church. The *Treatise* says, "A Christian church is an organized body of believers in Christ who statedly assemble to worship God, and who sustain the ordinances of the Gospel according to the Scriptures." The local church is often referred to as the *visible church.* In their doctrine of the church, Free Will Baptists distinguish themselves from churches that baptize infants, insisting that the church is an organized body of *believers only.* This concept has been called the believers' church or gathered church.

Thomas Helwys, the founder of the first General (Free Will) Baptist Church (and the first Baptist church) on English soil, said that–

> the church of Christ is a company of faithful people (I Corinthians 1:2; Ephesians 1:1) separated from the world by the word and Spirit of God (II Corinthians 6:17) being knit together unto the Lord and unto one another, by baptism (I Corinthians 12:13) upon their own confession of faith (Acts 8:37) and sins (Matthew 3:6).[66]

The *1660 Confession* concurred with Helwys's statement in its Article II: "That the right and only way of gathering churches (according to Christ's appointment) (Matthew 28:19-20) is first to teach or preach the gospel (Mark 16:16) to the sons and daughters of men; and then to baptize (that is in English to dip) in the name of the Father, Son, and Holy Spirit. . . ."[67]

This has been the teaching of Free Will Baptists from their beginning when Helwys and the English General Baptists adopted the Anabaptist doctrine of the gathered church. Most churches of that time were state churches; that is, when one was born into a particular geographical region, he would be baptized as an infant and become a member of the church of that region, whether it was Catholic, Lutheran, Reformed, or Anglican. The Anabaptists, and the Baptists after them, rejected this practice as unbiblical, stating that the Scriptures teach that only believers are to be baptized and become members of the church. Thus they were dubbed "Anabaptists" (re-baptizers), because they began to baptize adults who had been baptized as infants. The doctrine of the gathered church is based upon this model–believer's baptism as opposed to infant baptism. (More will be said about this in the section on baptism.)

Our forefathers insisted, as we do, that the only churches in the New Testament were churches of believers who had separated from the world and had covenanted together to perpetuate the worship of God, the preaching of the Word, the ordinances, and the spread of the gospel. Any concept of the church which is based on heredity is foreign to the New Testament. This belief arises from the importance of freedom in Free Will Baptist thought. We believe that no one can coerce or force one to be a Christian. Neither God nor man can force faith or Christianity; it must be a free decision on the part of the individual. Thus our scriptural doctrine of the church is that the church is made up of *freely gathered* believers who in their free will have chosen not to reject God's grace, have chosen to be baptized as a symbol of their death with Christ, and have chosen to covenant themselves together with other free believers, as the Holy Scripture instructs. This is the New Testament concept of the church—an *ekklesia* (Greek for "church" or an assembly of called-out believers). This is the only way the New Testament refers to churches (see Acts 8:1; 1 Corinthians 1:2; 2 Corinthians 1:1; Galatians 1:2; 1 Thessalonians 1:1; 2 Thessalonians 1:1).

The second part of the *Treatise* statement on the church is: "Believers in Christ are admitted to this church on giving evidence of faith in Christ, obtaining consent of the body, being baptized, and receiving the right hand of fellowship."[68] Helwys said in 1611 that:

> Every church is to receive in all their members by baptism upon the confession of their faith and sins wrought by the preaching of the Gospel, according to the primitive institution (Matthew 28:19) and practice (Acts 2:41). And therefore churches after any other manner, or of any other persons are not according to Christ's testament.[69]

Thus, only those who have confessed faith and have been baptized by immersion are to be received into the fellowship of the body by vote and the right hand of fellowship.

The Mission of the Church

The mission of the church is to carry out the Great Commission: "Go ye therefore, and teach all nations, baptizing them in the name of the Father, and of the Son, and of the

Holy Ghost: Teaching them to observe all things whatsoever I have commanded you: and, lo, I am with you alway, even unto the end of the world" (Matthew 28:19, 20).

Carrying out the Great Commission involves three things: evangelism, edification, and education. These, in summary, comprise the mission of the church. The first clause of the Great Commission is: "Go ye therefore, and teach all nations." This is an instruction to evangelize, to spread the gospel, to make disciples of all nations. Thus, Free Will Baptists believe that it is necessary for the local church to be involved in the ministry of evangelism and discipleship. Evangelism not only involves personal evangelism and evangelism in the church community, but also providing the means to evangelize the world. Thus, Free Will Baptists place great emphasis on world missions.

The second clause of the Great Commission is: "baptizing them in the name of the Father, and of the Son, and of the Holy Ghost." This is a command to incorporate into the life of the church those who respond in faith to the gospel instruction to covenant together with other believers into a local body. We might infer from this that all the gospel ordinances are important in carrying out the Great Commission. This is where edification comes in. To *edify* is to build up the Christian in his personal and spiritual life. Through baptizing the believer and incorporating him into the life of the local church, we begin the life-long process of edification, building up the believer in his personal and spiritual life through communal relationships with his brothers and sisters in Christ.

The third clause of the Great Commission is: "teaching them to observe all things whatsoever I have commanded you." This is a command to educate the people of God. Education involves preaching and teaching the Word of God and the principles of the Word to His people. This involves instruction on every aspect of the Christian's life, not just "spiritual" matters, but also instruction on the Christian's everyday life—on relationships, on society, on family—to take every thought captive to the obedience of Christ (2 Corinthians 10:5). Implicit in this command is the need for educational institutions to extend the education of God's people in the Christian view of the world and of life. This is why Free Will Baptists have seen the need to band together in support of ministerial training institutions, Christian schools, Bible colleges, liberal arts colleges, and graduate schools of theology—so that they may provide the people of God with every opportunity to be educated in a thoroughly Christian world and life view.

This is the mission of the church: to spread the gospel to all the world, to incorporate believers into the life of the church and to build them up in their personal and spiritual lives, and to educate them in the Christian world and life view.

The Ministry and Government of the Church

The Officers of the Church
Free Will Baptists believe that the New Testament teaches that there are two primary officers in the local church: ministers and deacons. These are the spiritual officers in the church. We also believe that there may be other officers who assist the church in her teaching, worship, and administrative capacities, such as trustees, clerks, treasurers, Sunday school superintendents, teachers, music ministers, youth directors, and so forth. This discussion, however, will be taken up with the ministry of ministers and deacons.

Three words are used in the New Testament to describe ministers in the local church: elder, pastor, and bishop. These three words all refer to the same office (Acts 20:17, 28; Titus 1:5-7; 1 Peter 5:1, 2). The word *elder*, though used interchangeably with the words *pastor* and *bishop*, was used to designate the dignity of the ministerial office in the church. The word *bishop* means "overseer" or one who looks after or cares for the church. The word *pastor* means "shepherd," one who

cares for and feeds the sheep.[70] Forlines describes the basic
function of pastors:

> The pastor, according to the New Testament, is the overseer of the
> church. The tie in with the work of a shepherd tells us that a pastor
> must exercise his leadership with loving concern for his members.
> He leads as one who has gained the respect of the people, not by
> exercising the strong arm of authority. While there can be no doubt
> that the pastor should have a ministry to the unsaved, the fact that all
> of the names of his office in the New Testament refer to a relation-
> ship to the members of the church surely means that the pastor must
> take very seriously his ministry to the needs of saints.[71]

Free Will Baptists have always made less of a clergy-laity
distinction than the Roman Catholic and many Protestant
groups. This belief is based on the doctrine of the priesthood
of all believers–that we are all priests and have direct access
to Christ. This doctrine opposes clericalism or a belief in pastoral authoritarianism, maintaining instead that pastors are
the servant-leaders of the church, looking after the spiritual
needs of their fellow believers.

Our *Treatise* states that the primary duties of ministers are
"to preach the Word, administer the ordinances of the
Gospel, visit their people, and otherwise perform the work of
faithful ministers."[72]

What qualifies one to be a minister? The *1660 Confession's*
biblically based statement on the qualifications of a minister
are instructive on the Free Will Baptist doctrine of the ministry:

> The elders or pastors which God hath appointed to oversee and feed
> his church (constituted aforesaid) are such who, first being of the
> number of disciples, shall in time appear to be vigilant, sober, of
> good behavior, given to hospitality, apt to teach, etc., not greedy of
> filthy lucre (as too many National ministers are), but patient; not a
> brawler, not covetous, etc., as such chosen to and ordained to office
> (according to the order of Scripture) (Acts 14:23). . . .[73]

This statement says several things about the church and her ministry: God has appointed (called) elders or pastors to oversee and feed His flock. Ministers must obviously be "of the number of disciples"; that is, a believer or disciple of Christ. Ministers must be "vigilant, sober, of good behavior, given to hospitality, apt to teach, not greedy, patient, covetous, or brawlers." A minister is chosen and ordained to his office. This confessional statement refers to 1 Timothy 3:1-7:

> This is a true saying, If a man desire the office of a bishop, he desireth a good work. A bishop then must be blameless, the husband of one wife, vigilant, sober, of good behaviour, given to hospitality, apt to teach; Not given to wine, no striker, not greedy of filthy lucre; but patient, not a brawler, not covetous; One that ruleth well his own house, having his children in subjection with all gravity; (For if a man know not how to rule his own house, how shall he take care of the church of God?) Not a novice, lest being lifted up with pride he fall into the condemnation of the devil. Moreover he must have a good report of them which are without; lest he fall into reproach and the snare of the devil.

Free Will Baptists take these qualifications for the Christian ministry quite seriously in their selection of ministers. These are basic qualifications for ministry in the local church. While some Free Will Baptist associations have ordained women, "most associations do not ordain women to the ministry."[74]

How is one set apart for the gospel ministry? Free Will Baptists believe that God divinely calls the minister to His service. O'Donnell says, "The minister should be *especially called of God to the work.* . . . Whatever the various experiences before one announces a call, one should have developed in his heart a continuing conviction that God has called him."[75] This call will not be the same for everyone. Some, for instance, will have a more dramatic call to the ministry than others. But all will have a deep conviction that this is what God has called them to do, that God has placed within their hearts a sincere desire to be a minister of His gospel. First

Timothy 3:1 says, "If a man desire the office of a bishop, he desireth a good work."

How is a Free Will Baptist minister ordained? This process differs from association to association. When one senses a call to ordained ministry, his local church determines whether or not to recommend him to the presbytery or ordaining council of the association of which it is a member. The local church voluntarily delegates the responsibility of examining and ordaining ministers to the presbytery or ordaining council of the association or conference. The minister must usually undergo a period of licensure for a year. To become a licensed minister, the individual must be recommended by his church and examined by the presbytery of his local association.

When his period of licensure is up, the minister will be examined again as to his theological beliefs, his competency, and his qualifications for ministry. Minimum standards for ordination vary from association to association. Some associations require formal ministerial education, while others require no such education; some associations require the ordinand to take an extensive written examination on Scripture, theology, church polity, and so forth; while others require an extensive oral examination. All associations require "sufficient materials to determine a reasonable acquaintance with the Bible, Christian doctrine, and Free Will Baptist teachings."[76] When the licentiate satisfies the presbytery or ordaining council as to his call, qualifications, and suitability for the ministry, he will be ordained in a service with laying on of hands. Being a minister of the gospel is no easy task and is a responsibility that should only be taken on with much "fear and trembling." But being a servant of the people of God carries with it great rewards. "Whosoever will be great among you, let him be your minister; and whosoever will be chief among you, let him be your servant: even as the Son came not to be ministered to, but to minister" (Matthew 20:26-28).

The other primary officer of the local church is the *deacon*. In some associations, deacons are ordained by the associations, while in others they are ordained by the local church. Our *Treatise* states that the deacons are "to minister to the congregation and exercise general spiritual leadership."[77] The deacon is to assist in the administration of the ordinances, to minister to the needs of the poor and down-trodden, and to be a source of spiritual advice to members of the flock. Helwys, in his 1611 *Declaration of Faith*, highlighted the role of deacons in seeing to the physical needs of the poor, describing deacons as "men and women who by their office relieve the necessities of the poor and impotent brethren concerning their bodies (Acts 6:1-4)." Thus, from the beginning, deacons in Free Will Baptist churches have been concerned with the needs of the poor and downcast. Deacons must meet the scriptural qualifications outlined in 1 Timothy 3:8-13.

Church Government (Polity)

Free Will Baptists have historically held to the principle of the self-government of the local church, also known as congregational church government.[78] Picirilli has defined the congregational system of church polity as that system which "teaches that the authority for government resides in the congregation of the local church."[79] This definition of congregational church government is consistent with Free Will Baptist practice which insists that local congregations, while self-governing, ought voluntarily to band together in conferences or associations for the cooperative furtherance of Christ's kingdom.[80] However, the congregational system of church polity is opposed to any form of church government which allows any body or individual outside the local church to govern or meddle in the affairs of the local church. This principle is supported by two New Testament principles: first, that each church in the New Testament was a self-governing body (see Acts 6:1-6; 15:1-2, 22; 1 Corinthians 16:1-3; 5:13; 2 Thessalonians 3:6, 14, 15); and second, that religious authority rested in the hands of the members of the congregation (see 1 Peter 5:1-3; 2 Corinthians 1:24; Acts 20:28). The self-government principle is also supported by two other important biblical truths: the priesthood of all believers and the freedom of the individual conscience.

All systems of church government, except the congregational system, fail to harmonize with these important biblical truths. Free Will Baptists have long emphasized freedom and non-coercion of religious belief—either by God or by man. God does not coerce us or force us to do His will. God will not coerce our beliefs—our conscience—and men cannot. Holy Scripture says that we are all priests and have direct access to God. Only congregational church polity, as it has been defined here, fits with these principles. For example, if a local Free Will Baptist church (body of believers) decides by majority vote to join another denomination, they have that right—they have the right to follow their own conscience. We may not want them to leave, and we may try to persuade them not to leave, but we dare not coerce their belief or practice, thereby obliterating their personal and spiritual freedom.

The association of which the local church is a member may advise, but it cannot coerce or force. If a church is errant, the association is obligated to break fellowship with the church after serious efforts are made to reclaim it; but the association must not coerce the local body of believers to do anything. We believe that the only just method of a congregation's deciding a matter is by majority vote, and that whatever a congregation decides is final and is subject to no other human authority outside itself.

Our English General Baptist forefathers taught this form of church polity. They said that the local church should be self-governed; yet they held, like we still do, to a close relationship between sister churches in local, regional, and national associations. The English General Baptists employed what might be called "roving ministers"—what they called "messengers"–who would advise the churches or serve churches who were without a pastor, and so forth.

Grantham described this system in his *Christianismus Primitivus*. He said that though the association (what he called a "general assembly") and its messengers (a "general council"–what we might call an executive committee) may give counsel to the local church, the church is not obligated to follow their advice, though they are obliged to consider the advice seriously. In a section entitled "Of the Second Question, How far Agreements made by a general Assembly do oblige the churches concerned by their Representative," Grantham states:

> To ascribe infallibility to any assembly since the Apostle's days, as to that assembly whereof they were members (Acts 15) must in no wise be allowed; for then it would follow, that the Decrees made in such Synods, must be added to the Scriptures, as the undoubted Dictates of the Holy Ghost, for so were the Decrees of that Assembly [of the Apostles], as we see (Acts 15). . . . Wherefore, though we ought to consider with great respect what is concluded by a General Council of Christ's true ministers, yet may we lawfully doubt what they deliver, unless they confirm it by the Word of the Lord."[81]

Oxford historian B.R. White describes these early "executive committees" in the days of our forefathers in the 1600s as "consultative bodies" and says that Grantham's "view of the 'authority' of messengers was that of *advisers* whose counsel must be listened to with great respect and from which a church or minister should only differ with considerable caution."[82] Helwys had lain the foundation for such a view in 1611, when he said that "no church ought to challenge any prerogative over any other."[83]

This view has been the Free Will Baptist view of the relationship between the local church and the association or conference from that time to the present. Our *Treatise* states that the association's only power over the church is "advisory" and "persuasive" and that the most an association can do, if the local church considers with great respect what is concluded by an association and still dissents, is "to withdraw fellowship from the local church as a member of the association."[84]

The Ordinances and Worship of the Church

The Ordinances of the Church

Free Will Baptists, along with other Baptists and Anabaptists, believe in *ordinances* rather than *sacraments*. The word *sacrament* was defined by the Roman Catholic Council of Trent as something presented to the senses which *conveys grace*. This definition was held onto by many Protestants, but the Anabaptists, Baptists, and many Reformed groups in the era of the Protestant Reformation (1517-1650) rejected this idea in favor of the concept of *ordinances*. This was a revival of the early Christian concept of ordinances, and was prefigured by Ulrich Zwingli (1484-1531), the Zurich reformer. This concept views the ordinances as symbols of gospel truths rather than as instruments through which grace travels. When Catholics, Episcopalians, Lutherans, and others say that the sacraments convey or carry grace, they mean, for instance, that the baptismal waters literally wash away original sin, or that Christ is literally present in the Lord's Supper in a way that is not true of His presence in other places.[85] Free Will Baptists, along with other Baptists, believe that ordinances do not convey grace but rather symbolize gospel truths and vividly remind us of Christ and His gospel.

Baptist theologian A.H. Strong defines "ordinances" more stringently as "those outward rites which Christ has appointed to be administered in his church as visible signs of the saving truth of the gospel. They are signs, in that they vividly express this truth and confirm it in the believer."[86] While this definition is somewhat limiting, it can be useful in understanding the nature of an ordinance. Free Will Baptists believe that there are three Gospel ordinances. Article 13 in the "Articles of Faith" included in our *Treatise* identifies these:

> *Baptism,* or the immersion of believers in water, and the *Lord's Supper,* are ordinances to be perpetuated under the Gospel. *Feet Washing,* an ordinance teaching humility, is of universal obligation, and is to be ministered to all true believers.[87]

We will look at these three ordinances in order.

Baptism. All Baptists believe and practice *believer's baptism.* We believe only believers should be baptized. Thus, we disagree with infant baptism or with the baptism of those who cannot understand enough to have faith. The Anabaptists of the 1600s sought to restore the church to the doctrine of its earliest times, and recovering believers' baptism was essential to this. As noted before, *Anabaptist* means "re-baptizer." The Anabaptists were called this because they would baptize people who had been baptized as infants in the state churches (Catholic, Lutheran, Reformed, Anglican). Our forefathers the English General Baptists agreed with the Anabaptists on this doctrine, insisting that baptism is the act whereby believers are immersed in water as a symbol of their death, burial, and resurrection (salvation) in and with Christ. This has been the consistent teaching of Free Will Baptists. Why do we believe what we believe about baptism? Let us look at two aspects of baptism in an attempt to understand why Free Will Baptists teach what they do about baptism: the *recipients* of baptism, and the *mode* of baptism.

Free Will Baptists believe that the only proper *recipients* of baptism are believers. We believe this for three reasons: First, it is clear from Scripture that true baptism only follows a personal decision of repentance and faith (Mark 16:16; Acts 2:38, 41; 8:12, 37; Romans 6:3-6). The New Testament knows of no instances where infants or children under the age of accountability or responsibility were baptized, and it nowhere instructs us to baptize them.

Second, we believe that the free act of faith cannot be coerced, forced, or pressured. To bring infants salvation by baptism (Catholics) or to make them members of the church (Presbyterians) is either forcing salvation or pressuring them into it. The Bible emphasizes that we are free moral agents who must use our whole personality to decide for ourselves in spiritual matters. Infant baptism is something that is done without the infant's knowledge (this would hold for baptizing children who are too young to understand as well, since they do not have a real understanding of what is happening). But this is not the way spiritual decisions like baptism are presented in the New Testament; they are shown as free decisions by rational, responsible, and morally accountable people.

Third, infant baptism did not begin until the third century A.D. Historical research has revealed that infant baptism was condemned in the early churches until the third century A.D. This point has been proven conclusively by Kurt Aland and others. The first place we see infant baptism mentioned in the early Christian writings is in the writings of Tertullian, who disagreed with the practice. He heard some were practicing infant baptism, and he strongly disapproved of the practice.[88] Thus, since Scripture teaches that only those who believe should be baptized, and since infants cannot willingly assent to baptism, and since the baptism of infants is a later addition to the doctrine of Christ and the apostles, Free Will Baptists and many others have concluded that it must be administered to believers only and not to infants.

The *mode* of baptism concerns how it is done or what procedure is used in administering it. Many Protestants and all Catholics teach that the proper mode is sprinkling. Free Will Baptists believe that the Bible teaches immersion (dipping, dunking) to be the true and proper mode of baptism. There are three reasons for this. First, the Greek word for baptism, *baptizo,* means literally "to dip or submerge." Harrison and Barfield, in their *History of the Free Will Baptists of North Carolina,* state the following: "While there are various other Greek words to express various other applications of water [such as sprinkle, wash, pour], the Bible, while using them in other connections, never once uses any of them in connection with the ordinance of baptism—using always and only *baptizo.*"[89]

Second, Free Will Baptists believe that Scripture explicitly teaches that baptism is only by immersion. Paul's description of baptism in Romans 6:3, 4 is that of a visible picture of our death, burial, and resurrection with Christ. This fits well with the other information we have about baptism in the New Testament; namely, that the word means "to dip or submerge," and that great amounts of water are always used for baptisms (John 3:23; Acts 8:37-39).

Third, sprinkling is an even later innovation than infant baptism. While Eastern Orthodox churches baptize infants, they still baptize them by immersion. The Roman Catholic Church, however, began to sprinkle rather than immerse around the fifth century, and many Protestants continued the practice after the Protestant Reformation. Ironically, though Lutherans and Calvinists by and large practice sprinkling as the mode of baptism, Martin Luther and John Calvin both acknowledged that immersion was the mode of the early Christians. Based on these observations, Free Will Baptists unequivocally believe that true baptism comes only by immersion.

The above beliefs on baptism have been historically held since the early 1600s. We have already quoted the *1660 Confession* as saying that baptism is of believers only and means "in English to dip." Grantham said:

> Certainly in this case [infant baptism] there hath been a very great mistake, which calls for some careful and speedy information, that so the purity of the use of the Gospel ordinances may be attained,

according to the usage of the first churches, in which we only find
actual believers (by profession at least) admitted . . . and not so much
as one infant in those churches any way concerned in the duties of
the New Covenant. . . .[90]

The successor confession to the *1660 Confession*, the *1812
Former Articles*, stated that "We believe that the gospel mode
of baptism is by immersion and that believers are the only
subjects for baptism."[91] And our *Treatise* maintains this conviction with its definition of baptism as "the immersion of
believers in water, in the name of the Father, the Son, and the
Holy Spirit."[92]

Baptism is a sign that we are dead, buried, and raised with
Christ. It is a symbol of our discipleship to Christ. Thus, only
believers are to be baptized, and this is to be done by immersion.

The Lord's Supper. Free Will Baptists are one with other
Baptists in their view of the nature of the Lord's Supper, but
we have historically disagreed with other Baptists on the
recipients of the Lord's Supper. Baptists have traditionally
agreed with the view of the Protestant Reformer Ulrich
Zwingli that the Lord's Supper is a symbol of the death of
Christ for our sins, to be celebrated as a memorial or remembrance of His death. Article 53 of *The Faith and Practice of
Thirty Congregations*, an early English General Baptist confession of Faith (1651), exemplifies this view:

> Jesus Christ took Bread, and the juice of the Vine, and brake, and
> gave to His disciples, to eat and drink with thanksgiving; which prac-
> tice is left upon record as a memorial of His suffering, to continue in
> the Church until he come again (I Cor. 11:23-26).[93]

Christ instituted the Supper by using unleavened bread to
symbolize His broken body and wine to symbolize His shed
blood on the Cross. He said, "This do in remembrance of
me." Thus, Free Will Baptists celebrate the Lord's Supper as

a remembrance symbolizing Christ's death. Our *Treatise* says that the Lord's Supper is "a commemoration of the death of Christ for our sins" and that it expresses the believer's "love for Christ, his faith and hope in Him, and pledges to Him perpetual fidelity."[94] Therefore, we disagree with Roman Catholics, who teach that the bread and wine literally become Christ's body and blood when they are blessed by the priest (transubstantiation). We disagree with Lutherans and Episcopalians who insist that Christ is spiritually present in the elements in a way that He is not present other places. We believe that taking the Lord's Supper does not convey special grace or "wash our souls out," as some have put it, but rather that, if we come to the Supper with the right spirit, we will be blessed by commemorating our Lord's death for us.

Free Will Baptists in their doctrine of *open communion* differ from other Baptists. The *Treatise* states that the Lord's Supper is "the privilege and duty of all who have spiritual union with Christ to commemorate His death, and no man has a right to forbid these tokens to the least of His disciples."[95] We believe that true Christians, regardless of their baptism or church membership, may come to the Lord's table. Many Baptists have taught that only those who have received scriptural baptism by immersion can come to the Lord's table. Some have even limited the Lord's Supper to members of their own denomination. We have always disagreed heartily with this view. As Harrison and Barfield said in 1897, "Communion is the Lord's Supper, and its table is His table. It follows, therefore, that all the Lord's children have alike a right to their common Father's table, and that no one of His children has any right to exclude another one of them from it."[96] Picirilli concisely sums up our doctrine of open communion:

> You will note in First Corinthians 11:28, when Paul is discussing the Lord's Supper, he says, "Let a man examine himself. . . ." We Free Will Baptists take this verse quite literally and so we do not pretend to tell anyone else whether he should or should not partake the

Lord's Supper. Therefore, when you find communion practiced in a
Free Will Baptist church, you will find that any Christian is invited
to partake with us at the Lord's Table.[97]

The Washing of the Saints' Feet. Free Will Baptists believe
that the washing of the saints' feet in connection with the
Lord's Supper is also an ordinance of the gospel. While Free
Will Baptists are among only a few Baptist groups who practice feet washing today, most Baptists used to practice the
ordinance but have gradually gotten away from the practice.[98] There are other groups that also practice the ordinance
of feet washing: Mennonites, Brethren, Church of God,
Hutterians, Primitive Baptists, and some Methodists. Most
Free Will Baptists in America have always practiced feet
washing. The practice of feet-washing was very common
among our English forefathers, the English General Baptists.
William Jeffrey, an English General Baptist minister in the
county of Kent argued that feet washing should continue to
be practiced by all the churches, contending for the ordinance as "setting out the Christ's humility, declaring the ways
of Christ are self-denying ways. [Feet washing], being a self-
denying practice serves to humble the creature, and when
performed decently and in order, tend[s] to produce affection
among the brethren."[99]

The *1812 Former Articles* name feet-washing as one of the
ordinances of the gospel, as do the associational confessions
of faith that have been used by most American Free Will
Baptists in their history. Our *Treatise* states that feet washing
is—

. . . a sacred ordinance, which teaches humility and reminds the
believer of the necessity of a daily cleansing from all sin. It was instituted by the Lord Jesus Christ, and called an "example" on the night
of His betrayal, and in connection with the institution of the Lord's
Supper. It is the duty and happy prerogative of every believer to
observe this sacred ordinance.[100]

Why do Free Will Baptists believe that feet washing is an ordinance of the Gospel? To understand this, we must look again at what an ordinance is. From a Biblical perspective, an ordinance is any rite that has been ordained by God to be practiced perpetually by the church. Feet washing clearly meets this criterion. However, even when measured against more exacting definitions, feet washing measures up. We have already referred to Strong's definition of an ordinance: "Those outward rites which Christ has appointed to be administered in his church as visible signs of the saving truth of the gospel. They are signs, in that they vividly express this truth and confirm it in the believer."[101] Does feet washing measure up to these criteria for an ordinance? We believe it does. Let us look at John 13, where Christ's washing of the disciples' feet is recounted, and see if feet washing meets these standards of an ordinance.

First we see that feet washing is an outward rite. Jesus's washing of the disciples' feet was not the practice of an ordinary custom for two reasons: (1) Though feet washing in that culture was a commonplace practice—feet were always washed when guests first came in the house—it is reasonable to assume that the disciples' feet were washed already, before Jesus washed their feet. Jesus washed the disciples' feet after supper was served, long after their feet were already washed. (2) The feet of guests were always washed by servants or hosts, not by masters or teachers or rabbis. Jesus was not the servant, but rather the master of the disciples, and He washed their feet. These two points clearly show the ritual significance of feetwashing. Jesus was not just practicing common custom but was using ritual to teach the disciples.

Second, we see that feet washing was appointed by Christ to be administered in His church. Jesus said, "If I then, your Lord and Master, have washed your feet; ye also ought to wash one another's feet. For I have given you an example, that ye should do as I have done to you" (John 13:14, 15). The Greek word for *ought* here means "bound" or "obligated."

Thus, Jesus commanded His followers to emulate the practice, saying that they were bound or obligated to do so. It is interesting to note that the command regarding feet washing is stronger and clearer than the command to perpetuate the Lord's Supper.

Third, we see that feet washing is a visible sign of the saving truth of the gospel which vividly expresses this truth and confirms it in the believer. At least four central gospel truths are expressed and confirmed by the ordinance of feet washing: humility, brotherly love, the humiliation and incarnation of Christ, and sanctification.

Humility and brotherly love are at the heart of the Christian gospel. They are the essence of Christlikeness. Paul taught us to let the mind of Christ be in us (Philippians 2:5), who came not to be served, but to serve (Matthew 20:28). Humility and service were the essence of the life and ministry of Jesus, the Suffering Servant. The humility Christ taught and modeled before us is the proof of our brotherly love. Christ taught that brotherly love was the very essence of His gospel. In Matthew 22:37-40, Christ gives us the very core of the gospel. After being asked which was the greatest commandment, He responded that the first and great commandment was: "Thou shalt love the Lord thy God with all thy heart, and with all thy soul, and with all thy mind." But He did not stop there; He mentioned a second commandment which He said was like the first: "Thou shalt love thy neighbour as thyself." And to underscore the point, He went on to add, "On these two commandments hang all the law and the prophets." This is the two-pronged gospel: a right relationship with God which radically changes our attitudes toward ourselves and others. If the second commandment is not kept, if we do not love our neighbor as ourselves, then the first is also broken.

Christ's institution of feet washing was a visible picture of this principle. As there is a two-pronged gospel, so we believe in a two-pronged communion: communion with God in

Christ in the Lord's Supper, and communion with our brothers and sisters in the washing of their feet. Only by following the command of Christ in both these ordinances can we symbolically realize the true gospel in the life of the church. Thus, Free Will Baptists celebrate their relationship with God through Christ in the Lord's Supper. And they then celebrate the outworking of this relationship by vividly symbolizing, in feet washing, the radical change that a relationship with Christ makes with their brothers and sisters.

Feet washing is also a picture of the humiliation and incarnation of Christ, the Suffering Servant, who disrobed Himself of His Heavenly garment and came to earth to bring us salvation. This is at the heart of the gospel. We see in John 13 a graphic picture of this humiliation and incarnation: Christ laid aside His garments, took a towel, girded Himself, and knelt to wash the disciples' feet. This is illustrative of Christ's laying aside the splendor of Heaven, girding Himself with humanity, and coming down to earth to save a lost world. If this is not a visible sign of the saving truth of the gospel, as Strong says, which vividly expresses the gospel and confirms it in the believer, then it can scarcely be said that anything is.

A fourth gospel truth that feet washing vividly expresses and confirms in the believer is the truth of sanctification, or growth in holiness. This truth is illustrated clearly by Jesus in the feet washing narrative. Jesus tells Peter that if He does not wash Peter's feet, Peter will have no part with Him. Then Peter asks Jesus to wash not only his feet but also his hands and his head. Jesus responds that the disciples' bodies are already clean, and do not need to be washed again, but only their feet need to be washed. (He notes in passing that one of the disciples, Judas, was not clean.) What does Jesus mean here? Jesus is telling Peter, and He is telling us, that feet washing represents the daily cleansing from sin which is a necessary part of sanctification. All the disciples except Judas, says Jesus, had had their bodies washed—this is a symbol of justification, yet they still needed to have their feet washed (sanctification).

The New Testament teaches us that justification and sanctification go hand in hand. We were justified so that we might be sanctified. As Forlines has said, sanctification is a necessary by-product of justification.[102] We were buried with Christ (justification) so that we might be raised with Christ (sanctification). This growth in Christlikeness and daily cleansing from sin are at the core of the Gospel, which says that Christ came to give us His righteousness so that we might be freed to practice personal righteousness and flee from sin. This is the object of the work of Christ in our lives. This gospel truth is most vividly expressed and confirmed in the believer in the holy ordinance of feet washing. Thus, we see that these gospel truths—humility, brotherly love, the humiliation and incarnation of Christ, and sanctification—are vividly expressed and confirmed in the believer. Therefore, Free Will Baptists believe that feet washing is a rite that was appointed by Christ to be administered in His church, and that it is a visible sign of the saving truth of the gospel which expresses and confirms that truth. Thus, it is an ordinance of the gospel.

We need no more evidence for the ordinance than the command of Christ; yet we see that the ordinance of feet washing was practiced in the early churches. First Timothy 5:10 mentions the ordinance in a discussion of godly widows. Several of the early Christian writers also discuss the ordinance. We will refer to only a few. Tertullian (A.D. 160) said:

> I must recognize Christ, both as he reclines on a couch, when he presents a basin for the feet of the disciples, and when he pours water into it from a ewer, and when he is girt about with a linen towel. . . .
> It is thus in general that I reply upon the point, admitting indeed that *we use along with others these articles* (*De Corona* 8).

Ambrose, in the third century A.D., chides the church at Rome for her failure to observe feet washing:

> We are not unaware of the fact that the Church in Rome does not
> have this custom, whose character and form we follow in all things.
> Yet it does not have the custom of washing the feet. So note: perhaps
> on account of the multitude this practice declined. Yet there are
> some who say and try to allege in excuse that this is not to be done
> in the mystery, nor in baptism nor in regeneration, but the feet are
> to be washed as for a guest. But one belongs to humility, the other to
> sanctification: "If I wash not thy feet, thou shalt have no part with
> me" (*The Sacraments* 3.5).

Augustine of Hippo as late as the fifth century referred to feet
washing, in a letter he wrote, as a regular practice. He said,
"As to the feetwashing . . . the question has arisen at what
time it is best, by literal performance of this work, to give
public instruction in the important duty which it illustrates"
(*Second Letter to Januarius* 18.33). In his *Homilies on John*,
Augustine refers to feet washing as a "sacramental sign"
which has its significance in the Lord's teaching us to forgive
one another (*Homilies on John* 59.5).

While examples like these could be multiplied, these few
will suffice to show that the conception and practice of feet
washing as an ordinance did not find its origin in the sixteenth century with the Anabaptists and that the ordinance is
not unique to Free Will Baptists, but has long precedent in
the history of Christianity, and indeed is found to be in practice among the earliest Christians.

For these reasons, Free Will Baptists take utmost joy in the
practice of this blessed ordinance, which teaches us to love
others in true humility, as did our Lord, who laid aside His
Heavenly garb and came to earth so that we might have His
absolute righteousness imputed and grow in holiness through
Him.

The Worship of the Church[103]

Free Will Baptists have always believed in freedom, simplicity, and order in worshiping God in Spirit and in Truth.
Thus we have been opposed to the employment of set forms

and liturgies as well as to undue emotionalism in worship. While some Free Will Baptists have expressed themselves in worship in a more emotional way and some in a less emotional way—and while we have given each other that freedom—we have always agreed in our belief in the freedom, simplicity, and order of Christian worship. This belief arises from our concern to be as close to the New Testament as we can. While some denominations believe it is proper to add to the New Testament picture of Christian worship, Free Will Baptists see no need and believe they are on safer ground to imitate the New Covenant worship exemplified in the ministry of Christ and His apostles.

In this, we agree with the Anabaptists, who in the sixteenth century sought to rid themselves of the accumulation of extra-biblical tradition over the centuries. Since they acknowledged that the Bible was the only rule of the faith and practice of the church, they thought that it was best, therefore, to attempt to stay as close as they could to what they saw in the New Testament about worship. Our forefathers agreed.

Free Will Baptists have hence looked to the ministry of Christ, with His unencumbered and unceremonious mode of teaching and worship, which strikes the reader of the Gospels with a singular simplicity and spontaneity. We have also looked to the ministry of the apostles and their early New Testament churches, which were characterized by a pure and simple freedom and congregational participation in worship which was balanced by a sense of sincerity and order and a lack of confusion (1 Corinthians 14:26-33).

Free Will Baptists believe it is necessary to emulate this mode of worship. Thus we have shied away from liturgical forms and appurtenances which would make worship a rote practice, hinder the free moving of the Spirit of God, and obstruct the clear communication of the Word. We find no need to improve upon scriptural teaching and example, and thus have avoided adding our own renovations or refinements to it, as has been done by the Catholic Church, as well as some Protestant churches. As Grantham said,

> It cannot be supposed that the Apostles (or however Christ Himself) would leave the churches without necessary instruction, how to perform this great duty; which they press with Greatest vehemency. . . . Yet we find no such forms or liturgies instituted by them, nor to be instituted by others in pursuance of any trust reposed in any of their successors by them.[104]

By the same token, we have avoided too much emotion. While Free Will Baptists have placed great value on the role of emotion in Christian worship, we have sought not to give it such a place that it could lead to confusion and hinder the worship of God, but have sought to worship "decently and in order," as the Apostle Paul instructed. The emphasis of the apostle was always on rationality and intelligibility in worship, allowing the unfettered Word to work, by the power of the Spirit, in the minds and hearts of worshipers. Paul saw that freedom and simplicity need not be accompanied by a feelings-based worship which would guide our raw instincts with pure emotion, but rather are most truly characterized by the Word-directed mind and heart responding in worship to God, the Creator, Redeemer, and Preserver.

Free Will Baptists also see that, even after the death of the Apostles and the writing of the New Testament, the earliest Christians worshiped in the same spirit as seen in the New Testament. We believe it further confirms the picture we see in the New Testament.

We do not always emulate the New Testament pattern of worship as we should. Yet we believe if we follow this example the Holy Spirit has put before us, we will truly be enabled to worship God in Spirit and in Truth. The results will be learning more of the grace of God in Christ, being led by the Holy Spirit, and most of all, giving glory to God almighty.

NOTES FOR CHAPTER TWO

[1]See the confessions of faith in chapters three and four for a more elaborate statement of these doctrines.

[2]Free Will Baptists have traditionally differed with most other Baptists in their belief in open communion and feet washing as an ordinance.

[3]Many Arminians are really misnamed, since their theology is so different from Arminius's own theology.

[4]Those who articulate the type of Arminianism from which Free Will Baptist theology differs are primarily Wesleyans (Methodists, Nazarenes, Holiness, Pentecostals). Other groups which tend toward the same type of soteriology, are the Anabaptists (Mennonites, Brethren, Amish) and the Restorationists (Disciples of Christ, Churches of Christ, Independent Christian Churches).

[5]*A Treatise of the Faith and Practices of Free Will Baptists,* part 2, chapter 4, section 2. This document is reprinted in chapter five.

[6]*1812 Former Articles,* article 4. It should be remembered that the *1812 Former Articles were a revision of the 1660 English General Baptist Confession of Faith,* which was used by our forefathers until it was revised in 1812. The above title is an abbreviated form of the original title, *An Abstract of the Former Articles of Faith Confessed by the Original Baptist Church Holding the Doctrine of General Provision With a Proper Code of Discipline.*

[7]Jacobus Arminius, *The Works of James Arminius.* The London Edition, translated by James Nichols and William Nichols (Grand Rapids, Michigan: Baker Book House, 1986), vol. II, p. 156.

[8]F. Leroy Forlines, *Systematics: A Study of the Christian System of Life and Thought* (Nashville: Randall House Publications, 1975), p. 124. See chapter 8 of *Systematics* for a fuller explanation of the doctrines of sin and depravity. See also F. Leroy Forlines, *Romans,* in the *Randall House Bible Commentary* (Nashville: Randall House Publications, 1987), pp.129-146.

[9]J. D. O'Donnell, *Faith for Today: A Presentation of Free Will Baptist Beliefs* (Nashville: Randall House Publications, 1974), p. 22.

[10]Cited in William J. McGlothlin, ed., *Baptist Confessions of Faith* (Philadelphia: American Baptist Publication Society, 1911), p. 93.

[11]The reader is reminded that I am using the names "Free Will Baptist" and "General Baptist" interchangeably, since we were called General Baptists when our forefathers first came from England, and since our predecessors in England were also called "Free Willers." The reader is also reminded that our forefathers, the General Baptists, are different from the present-day General Baptists in America, who arose spontaneously in the nineteenth century, though they are closer to us in doctrine and practice than other Baptists. The American General Baptist historian Ollie Latch states that Benoni Stinson, the founder of the American General Baptists in the 1820s, was evidently influenced by our General (Free Will) Baptist ancestors in North Carolina. (Ollie Latch, *History of the General Baptists* [Poplar Bluff, Missouri: General Baptist Press, 1954], pp. 125-26.)

[12]Thomas Grantham, *Christianismus Primitivus, Or the Ancient Christian Religion* (London: Francis Smith, 1678), pp. 77-78.

[13]Forlines, *Systematics*, p. 128.

[14] *1812 Former Articles*, Article 13.

[15] *Christianismus Primitivus*, book 2, chapter 1, p. 4.

[16]An example of this doctrine is found in the Articles of Faith of the Cumberland Association in Middle Tennessee, written in the latter part of the 1800s: "We believe in the justification of infants by the imputed righteousness of Jesus Christ" (article 10). Some Free Will Baptists profess a belief that is closer to the infant safety position.

[17]Forlines, *Systematics*, p. 172.

[18]E.Y. Mullins, *The Christian Religion in its Doctrinal Expression* (Philadelphia: Judson Press, 1917), p. 302.

[19]Arminius Works, II:192.

[20]Forlines, *Systematics*, pp. 207-08.

[21] *Treatise*, part 2, chapter 8.

[22] *1812 Former Articles*, article 9.

[23]Forlines, *Systematics*, pp. 120-21.

[24]In short, *elect* means "to choose for salvation." *Predestination* means "deciding one's destiny beforehand." *Grace* means "God's provision of salvation." See the articles "Elect, Election," "Grace," and "Predestination" in Walter A. Elwell, ed., *Evangelical Dictionary of Theology* (Grand Rapids, Michigan: Baker Book House, 1984), pp. 348-49, 479-92, 870-72.

[25]Arminius, II:392-93.

[26] *Conditional election* means that God elects or predestines individuals based on a condition–the condition of being *in Christ*. *Unconditional election* means that there are no conditions; the choice to elect comes from God's arbitrary will without regard to conditions met on man's part.

[27] *1660 Confession*, article 8. The confession has also been referred to as *The Standard Confession, 1660*. See also Samuel Loveday, *Personal Reprobation Reprobated: Being a Plain Exposition of the Ninth Chapter to the Romans* (London: Francis Smith, 1676).

[28] *A Declaration of Faith of English People Remaining at Amsterdam*, article 5.

[29] *General Provision* is defined as the provision of salvation to all people, if they would "take of the water of life freely" (Revelation 22:17).

[30]T.F. Harrison and J.M. Barfield, *History of the Free Will Baptists of North Carolina* (Ayden, North Carolina: Free Will Baptist Press, 1898, reprinted 1959), vol. 1, pp. 110-11.

[31]The later Calvinistic Baptists, who arose a generation after our beginning in England, were thus called "Particular Baptists."

[32] *1660 Confession*, article 4.

[33]W. Stanley Outlaw, *1 Timothy* in the *Randall House Bible Commentary* (Nashville: Randall House Publications, 1990), p. 202. Universal atonement is not to be confused with universalism. Belief in universal atonement simply means that Christ died for everyone. But this does not mean that everyone will be saved, which is universalism.

[34]Milton Crowson, *The Epistle to the Hebrews* (Nashville: Randall House Publications, 1974), p. 26.

[35]*Treatise*, part 2, chapter 8.

[36]*1660 Confession*, article 4; *1812 Former Articles*, article 6. The Scripture citations in brackets were included in the *1660 Confession* but were not included in the *1812 Former Articles*; otherwise, the statements are identical.

[37]E.L. St. Claire, *What Free Will Baptists Believe and Why* (Ayden, North Carolina: Ayden Free Will Baptist Printing Company, n.d.), p. 3.

[38]Marie T. Hyatt, *Why the Atonement was Necessary* (Nashville: Board of Publications and Literature, National Association of Free Will Baptists, 1944), p. 17.

[39]For a fuller explanation of this process, see F. Leroy Forlines, *Systematics*, pp. 149-74.

[40]Arminius, II:256.

[41]Ibid, I:419.

[42]"God requires satisfaction because he is holy, but he makes satisfaction because he is love" (Hyatt, p. 20).

[43]Arminius, II: 257.

[44]*Treatise*, part 2, chapter 6, no. 1.

[45]O'Donnell, p. 37.

[46]See Forlines, *Romans*, pp. 146-58 and 198-99 for a fuller explanation of union and identification with Christ.

[47]Forlines, *Systematics*, p. 160. See *Systematics*, pp. 149-74, for a more comprehensive treatment of our doctrine of justification.

[48]Arminius, II:257.

[49]*A Declaration of Faith of the English People Remaining at Amsterdam*, article 6.

[50]*Christianismus Primitivus*, book 2, p. 67. See also John Griffith, *God's Oracle and Christ's Doctrine, Or, The Six Principles of the Christian Religion* (London: Richard Moon, 1655), pp. 13-16.

[51]*1812 Former Articles*, article 13.

[52]*A Declaration of Faith*, article 7.

[53]*Treatise*, part 2, chapter 13.

[54]*1660 Confession*, article 18.

[55]*Treatise*, part 2, chapter 13.

[56]Robert E. Picirilli, *Perseverance* (Nashville: Randall House Publications, 1973), p. 18.

[57]Ibid., pp. 14-15.

[58]C.L. Wilibald Grimm, *Grimm's Wilke's Clavis Novi Testamenti*, translated by Joseph Henry Thayer (Grand Rapids, Michigan: Zondervan Publishing House, 1977), p. 663.

[59]Forlines, *Systematics*, p. 212.

[60]*Christianismus Primitivus*, book 2, chapter 11, p. 155.

[61] *1660 Confession,* article 18.

[62] While most "eternal securitists" today are more antinomian in doctrine, strict, consistent Calvinists (those who believe all five points of the TULIP) are usually not antinomian. Five-point Calvinists normally believe, like us, that the Christian must persevere in faith and obedience. The only difference is, they believe that God will ensure such perseverance; whereas we believe that God maintains the integrity of our free will and that we may resist His grace.

[63] Forlines, *Systematics,* p. 219.

[64] *Treatise,* part 2, chapter 15.

[65] O'Donnell, p. 70.

[66] *A Declaration of Faith,* article 10.

[67] *1660 Confession,* article 11.

[68] *Treatise,* part 2, chapter 15.

[69] *1660 Confession,* article 11.

[70] F. Leroy Forlines, *Notes on Ecclesiology* (Nashville: Free Will Baptist Bible College), p. 3.

[71] Ibid., p. 4.

[72] *Treatise,* part 2, chapter 17, no. 2.

[73] *1660 Confession,* article 15. "National ministers" refers to ministers of the Church of England. It will be remembered that our forefathers were persecuted for separating from the state church of England (also called the Anglican or Episcopal Church).

[74] *A Treatise of the Faith and Practices of Free Will Baptists,* 1974: "The Practices of Free Will Baptists," part 4, chapter 2, section 1.D. This sentence has since been deleted.

[75] O'Donnell, p. 74.

[76] *Treatise,* part 4, chapter 2, section 1, D:1.

[77] *Treatise,* part 4, chapter 1, section 4, B.

[78] It must be emphasized that we as Free Will Baptists use the term "congregational" in the sense that the church is a self-governing or self-determining body, not that the church is in isolation from other churches or the conference/association. Likewise, the term "autonomy," when applied to the local church, is used in its primary dictionary definition of "self-determining" or "self-governing" rather than "independent." Those concerned about historic Free Will Baptist polity should shy away from the use of the term "independent" when speaking of the status of a local church, since Free Will Baptists believe that the Bible teaches the association of churches one with another in conferences and associations, while at the same time recognizing the local church's right to be self-governing and even separate from a conference or association should it so choose.

[79] Robert E. Picirilli, *Church Ordinances and Government* (Nashville: Randall House Publications, 1973), p. 27.

[80] Likewise, Free Will Baptist polity has always held that ministers are subject solely to their presbytery or ordaining council. Churches voluntarily agree to this policy when joining an association or conference. Therefore, an ordaining council

has the power to revoke the ministerial credentials of any of its ministers. A local church which maintains as their minister one who has been barred by the presbytery or ordaining council of the conference or association of which that church is a member is subject to the withdrawal of fellowship by that association or conference.

[81] *Christianismus Primitivus,* Book 2, Chapter 10, p. 139.

[82] B.R. White, *The English Baptists of the Seventeenth Century* (London: The Baptist Historical Society, 1983), p. 116. Italics mine.

[83] "A Declaration of Faith," article 12.

[84] *Treatise,* part 4, chapter 3, section 4. The relationship between church and association is the same as that between local association and state association, and state association and national association (ibid.).

[85] In Roman Catholic doctrine, the bread and wine literally become the body and blood of Christ when blessed by the priest. In Lutheran and Episcopalian doctrine, Christ is actually present in the bread and the wine.

[86] A.H. Strong, *Systematic Theology* Philadelphia: Judson Press, 1907, p. 930

[87] *Treatise,* "Articles of Faith," part 3, article 13.

[88] See Kurt Aland's book *Did the Early Church Baptize Infants?* (Philadelphia: Westminster Press, 1963).

[89] Harrison and Barfield, vol. 1, p. 117.

[90] *Christianismus Primitivus,* book 2, chapter 1, p. 6.

[91] *1812 Former Articles,* article 18.

[92] *Treatise,* part 2, chapter 18, no. 1.

[93] Reprinted in Lumpkin, *Baptist Confessions of Faith,* p. 183.

[94] *Treatise,* part 2, chapter 18, no. 2.

[95] Ibid.

[96] Harrison and Barfield, vol. 1, p. 125.

[97] Picirilli, *Church Ordinances and Government,* pp. 19-20.

[98] It is interesting to note that in the Appalachian mountains, where modern culture has not impacted the culture as much as in other areas, practically all Baptists, whether Free Will Baptists, Missionary Baptists, Southern Baptists, Regular Baptists, or Primitive Baptists, still practice feet washing. (See Howard Dorgan, *Giving Glory to God in Appalachia: Worship Practices in Six Baptist Subdenominations* [Knoxville, Tennessee: University of Tennessee Press, 1987].)

[99] William Jeffrey, *The Whole Faith of Man,* p. 102.

[100] *Treatise,* part 2, chapter 8, no. 3.

[101] The selection of a standard "Baptist" definition of ordinance—of which A.H. Strong's is most representative—is clearly arbitrary. In another writing, I discuss more deeply the concept of ordinances from a Biblical perspective, asserting that any definition of ordinance which says that a practice *must* meet any criteria above being ordained by God for perpetuation is non-biblical and arbitrary. However, any rite which measures up to a definition like Strong's would of necessity fit the biblical model, since the biblical criteria are also included in Strong's definition (i.e., being ordained by God to be perpetuated in the church). See J. Matthew

Pinson, "Toward a Free Will Baptist Conceptual Framework for a Theology of the Ordinances," unpublished paper (1996).

[102]See Forlines, *Systematics,* pp. 176-180.

[103]While this section discusses primarily the mode of worship, see the section, "Growing through Worship" in chapter three for a discussion of the purpose of worship.

[104]*Christianismus Primitivus*, book 2, chapter 6, p. 76.

CHAPTER 3

United with the Church: Being a Free Will Baptist Church Member

WHAT YOUR CHURCH MEMBERSHIP MEANS

The local church is made up of people who have covenanted together with each other to worship God, live for Christ, carry out the Great Commission, and obey the commandments and ordinances of Christ. "For where two or three are gathered together in my name, there am I in the midst of them" (Matthew 18:20). But what does it *mean* to be a *member* of a local church? In Acts 2:41-47, we see a precedent for church membership. This passage says that about 3,000 individuals became members of—were "added to"—the early churches (2:41).

Requirements for Church Membership

At least three things relative to the meaning of church membership can be gleaned from the above passage. First, there is such a thing as church membership. Twice the passage describes the process of the Lord's *adding* individuals to the early churches.

Second, church membership is based upon and comes only after conversion or *salvation*. Acts 2:47 describes church members as those who were "saved." By salvation, of course, is meant that the church member is one who has first and foremost repented (turned from) his life of sin and turned to Christ in faith, receiving Christ into his life. This receiving of

Christ also involves believing the Word of God. This is implied in verse 41, which says that those who "gladly received his [Peter's preached] word" were baptized. While this verse is not the only place where this is taught, it implies that saving faith involves assent to the saving truths of the gospel. Thus conversion–repentance and faith–involves the whole person, heart, mind, and will. This spiritual conversion is necessary before one becomes a member of the local church.

Third, we see that baptism follows conversion and is a necessary prerequisite to church membership (Acts 2:41). Baptism is a symbol of, among other things, incorporation into the body of Christ by death to sin and resurrection to newness of life. The local church is the visible body of Christ. Thus, baptism is necessary for membership in the visible church. This understanding of baptism and church membership naturally excludes from church membership infants and small children who are not morally and spiritually accountable. For these reasons, Free Will Baptists believe that saving faith and baptism are the only requirements the New Testament gives for membership in the local church. Only after an individual confesses faith in Christ and receives baptism by immersion can the church receive that person into fellowship. This is done by means of majority vote and is followed by the extension of the right hand of fellowship to the new member.

Our Unique Place as Church Members

We see another glimpse of the meaning of church membership in 1 Corinthians 12. In this chapter, Paul is teaching the Corinthian Christians about spiritual gifts. He wants them to know that each Christian has unique gifts to give to the body of Christ. There is a diversity of gifts among the members of the body of Christ because there is a diversity of members. This passage can be applied either to the invisible or visible church (see chapter two), but we are here concerned with its applications to the meaning of membership in the visible, local church.

The Apostle Paul likens the church to a body (the church is elsewhere in Scripture called the body of Christ). Just as a body has several different members with different functions, so the church has several different members with different gifts to offer and roles to fill. Without each of these unique members exercising their spiritual gifts and filling their role, the local church cannot maximally operate in the way God intended. As individual church members, we should seek to identify what our special spiritual gifts are—the gifts God has provided us with which to minister—and we should exercise those gifts to the glory of God in our local church. Thus, in the church, there are, as Francis Schaeffer often said, "no little people" and "no little places." God has a place for each member of the church in His work, and God needs us to be the best we can be in the place He has put us, with the gifts He has given us. Without *you*, the church cannot function in the way it was meant to function.

Church membership means that we are Christians who have repented of our sins and received Christ by faith. It means that we have been baptized to symbolize our death, burial, and resurrection with Christ and our incorporation into His body. And it means that we as Christians have each been uniquely blessed with spiritual gifts which God believes are essential to the mission and ministry of the local church. The next section of this chapter will concern the Free Will Baptist Church Covenant, which discusses some of our duties as church members.

THE CHURCH COVENANT

Free Will Baptists have adopted a Church Covenant which serves as a guide to what being a member of a local Free Will Baptist church is about. Understanding the Church Covenant will help us better understand our role as church members, and by examining the covenant phrase-by-phrase we can gain a better understanding of its meaning and its significance for each of us.

Paragraph one reads:

Having given ourselves to God, by faith in Christ, and adopted the Word of God as our rule of faith and practice, we now give ourselves to one another by the will of God in this solemn covenant.

This first paragraph of the covenant describes our "giving" of ourselves. First, as Christians we *have given ourselves to God.* We are willing participants in the life God has for us. We acknowledge that we, as sinful people saved by divine grace, have come into a relationship with a Holy God *by faith in Christ.* Thus we realize our unworthiness before God. Only by means of the death of the sinless Son of God, who paid the penalty for our sins on the cross, can we give ourselves to God. Christ loved us and gave Himself for us; thus, we can be in union with God through Him.

God has revealed Himself and His saving plan to humanity through His Word. We realize that we owe our knowledge of God to His Word, in which He shows Himself to us. We believe that the Bible is the Word of God and thus we have *adopted the Word of God as our rule of faith and practice.* We allow the Word of God to instruct us in every area of our lives—in the faith that is at the center of our lives and in its practice in our everyday lives. We understand that the Bible has authority over us, and we bow to that authority in every area of life.

With this understanding, we *give ourselves to one another.* We agree to become one in Christ, for "by one Spirit are we all baptized into one body" (1 Corinthians 12:13). We acknowledge that we are members in the family of God. We are brothers and sisters in Christ. We belong to each other; as the Apostle Paul says, we are "members of one another" (Ephesians 4:25). Giving ourselves to one another means that we will put each other first. We will focus on the needs of our fellow members of the body of Christ, rather than focusing on our own needs. This is only a glimpse of the significance of giving ourselves to one another.

We give ourselves to one another in a *solemn covenant,* which is an agreement. Thus, by agreeing on some guidelines for our lives as Christians in a local assembly, we show that we are giving ourselves to God and to one another and allowing principles that transcend our individual selves to serve as guideposts for our lives. Notice that we do this because we believe it is *the will of God.* We acknowledge that God's will should be at the center of every decision we make, of every path we embark upon. The next six paragraphs elaborate on just what is involved in this agreement.

Paragraph two reads:

We promise by His grace to love and obey Him in all things, to avoid all appearance of evil, to abstain from all sinful amusements, and unholy conformity to the world, from all sanction of the use and sale of intoxicating beverages, and "to provide things honest in the sight of all men."

We make this *promise by God's grace.* We promise to *obey Him in all things,* realizing that true *love* for God results in a life of obedience to Him and conformity to His will. Thus we should *avoid all appearance of evil.* We should strive to live a life outwardly so that others will not be caused to fall into sin because of our example (see Romans 14 and 1 Corinthians 8). This involves *abstaining from all sinful amusements and unholy conformity to the world.* The kinds of things we do for pleasure say a great deal about what our priorities are. As children of God, we acknowledge that we must avoid sinful pleasures. As Paul said, "Be not conformed to this world, but be transformed by the renewing of your mind, that ye may prove what is that good and acceptable and perfect will of God" (Romans 12:2). Being transformed from the inside out by changing our patterns of thinking–taking every thought captive to the obedience of Christ (2 Corinthians 10:5)–will

cause us not to be conformed to the world and its entice-
ments, but to be conformed to the image of God's son, Jesus
Christ. Thus we should strive not to be conformed outwardly to this world, but be transformed inwardly by the mind of
Christ.

One of these sinful amusements is intoxication. Therefore,
the covenant reads that we ought *to abstain from all sanction of
the use and sale of intoxicating beverages.* The covenant thus takes
a stance of total abstinence from all alcoholic beverages. In
our day, this admonition would also include other intoxicants; namely, illegal drugs. Free Will Baptists all agree that
we must personally and corporately maintain a stance for
temperance in our society and stand for righteousness in all
areas of life. Avoiding sinful amusements includes not only
avoiding intoxicants but abstaining from a host of things that
can lead us away from our devotion to God. If we are striving to be conformed to Christ's image rather than to the basic
principles of the world, we will work hard to avoid sinful
amusements, laboring more diligently to be obedient to the
God we love.

The final phrase in paragraph two is a quotation from
2 Corinthians 8:21: *"to provide things honest in the sight of all
men."* This verse appears in the context of Paul's collection
for the believers in Jerusalem. Rather than merely being content to know within himself that he was honest, he wanted to
ensure that everyone else knew; so he requested that each
church appoint men to assist him in the collection. This kind
of attitude is imperative in our covenant relationship with
one another.

Paragraph three reads:

*We agree faithfully to discharge our obligations in reference to the
study of the Scriptures, secret prayer, family devotions, and social
worship; and by self-denial, faith, and good works endeavor to "grow
in grace and the knowledge of our Lord and Saviour Jesus Christ."*

This paragraph discusses several of our duties as
Christians, recognizing that they are not options but *obliga-*

tions. The first reference is to *the study of the Scriptures.* In paragraph one, we acknowledged that we have adopted the Word of God as our rule of faith and practice. Here we recognize the importance of studying God's Word. Only by probing the Scriptures to find their meaning and significance for our lives today can we realize the importance of God's speaking to us in His Word. More will be said about Bible study under the section in this chapter entitled "Growing Through Your Church."

In addition to recognizing the importance of studying the Word of God, we realize our obligations to engage in *secret prayer, family devotions, and social worship.* Prayer could be characterized as "communication with God." Family devotions and social worship are ways of describing two sides of worship, the one private, the other corporate. These important duties will also be elaborated on later in this chapter.

The next agreement in paragraph three is *to "grow in grace and the knowledge of our Lord and Saviour Jesus Christ,"* a quotation from 2 Peter 3:18. Christian faith is not just an experience tied only to human emotion, but involves the whole person—the heart (emotions), the mind (intellect), and the will. To mature in the faith is to grow in grace and in knowledge. The covenant here mentions three additional ingredients in this growth in grace and knowledge: *self-denial, faith, and good works.* These are Christian disciplines—Christian habits—that must become part and parcel of the mature Christian's life. Faith in the sense in which it is used here is not speaking of saving faith, the faith through which we are justified (see chapter 2), but rather it is speaking of maintaining a firm trust in God after we have been converted. This trust must be accompanied by self-denial (see Philippians 2) and good works, which demonstrate outwardly that we have been changed inwardly by the Holy Spirit. We are reminded here of 2 Peter 1:5-7, 10b:

And beside this, giving all diligence, add to your faith virtue; and to virtue knowledge; And to knowledge temperance; and to temperance patience; and to patience godliness; And to godliness brotherly kindness; and to brotherly kindness charity. . . . for if ye do these things, ye shall never fall.

Paragraph 4 reads:

We will not forsake the assembling of ourselves together for church conferences, public worship, and the observance of the ordinances of the Gospel, nor fail to pay according to our ability for the support of the church, of its poor, and all its benevolent work.

This section of the covenant opens up with a quotation from Hebrews 10:25, saying that *we will not forsake the assembling of ourselves together.* As Christians, we have the duty and responsibility to be involved in the life of the church of which we are a member, and this encompasses our obligation to meet regularly with our church family. The covenant mentions three types of "assembly" that we need not to forsake: church conferences (business meetings), public worship, and meetings in which ordinances of the church are observed. Committed Christians will therefore seek to attend the worship services of the church to the best of their ability.

Many who attend regular worship services, however, have for some reason been less concerned about attendance at special meetings of the church, whether spiritual (the ordinances) or administrative (business meetings). Perhaps this is due to the lack of education on the importance of these services. We must come to understand that attending services of baptism and communion (the Lord's Supper and Feet Washing), as well as other services of spiritual magnitude in the church, are vital to the life of the growing Christian. Additionally, the involved church member will not stay away from church business meetings. We must not have the idea that the business of Christ's church is "less spiritual" than the other meetings. Involvement in the *total* life of the church is no less than a necessity for the growing Christian.

This total involvement is further described in paragraph four, which states that we will not *fail to pay according to our ability for the support of the church, of its poor, and all its benevolent work*. While tithing will be discussed under the section entitled "Growing Through Giving," we must briefly mention here the significance of being involved in our church financially. This, again, implies total rather than partial involvement. The covenant mentions three areas for which we are to give financially: (1) for the support of the church, (2) for the poor of the church, and (3) for the church's benevolent ministries (giving to outside causes). And this giving–this *paying*– is described as being *according to our ability*. This phrase, of course, does not mean our ability to support the church and her ministries after we have paid for everything else we need and want, but to give according to that with which God has financially blessed us.

Paragraph five reads:

We agree to accept Christian admonition and reproof with meekness, and to watch over one another in love, endeavoring to "keep the unity of the Spirit in the bonds of peace," to be careful of one another's happiness and reputation, and seek to strengthen the weak, encourage the afflicted, admonish the erring, and as far as we are able to promote the success of the church and of the gospel.

This paragraph moves from general comments about the Christian's responsibility to his church to more specific assertions about the importance of relationships within the Christian congregation. The foundation of Christian relationships in the body of Christ, inside and outside of the local congregation, is *meekness*, which gives us the willingness to *accept Christian admonition and reproof* from fellow believers. (See 1 Thessalonians 5:12-14.) If our pride will not allow us to be accountable to other believers within the church, accepting their admonition and reproof in a spirit of love, then we have not begun to live out the mind of Christ.

In addition to being open to the "watchcare" of others in the church, we should strive to *watch over one another in love*.

But this watching over others is only possible if we are willing to have them watch over us. "Watching," if done in a truly Christian manner, will not degenerate into a spirit of distrust or judgment but will result in a concern for the best interest of other members of the family of God.

Both the concern to watch over others and the humble willingness to be watched over go hand in hand with the next phrase of the covenant: We should endeavor to *"keep the unity of the Spirit in the bonds of peace."* This phrase quotes directly from Ephesians 4:3. Concern for unity and peace in the church makes perfect sense because "There is one body, and one Spirit, even as ye are called in one hope of your calling; One Lord, one faith, one baptism, One God and Father of all, who is above all, and through all, and in you all" (Ephesians 4:4-6). Because we are all called by the same One Lord, because we have one faith, one baptism, one Father, we should exhibit a unity of spirit and mind which is outwardly visible to the world (see Philippians 2:2). This unity will not be present if the church is not characterized by peace.

The covenant goes on to list ways we can ensure that we exhibit this unity through peace. Foundational to this is a concern on our part *to be careful of one another's happiness and reputation.* This again implies a selflessness that seeks other's best interests over our own. Perhaps the decisive downfall of many Christians is the way they speak of their fellow Christians. What we say—and what we allow to be said—of our brothers and sisters in Christ directly bears on our *carefulness* to guard their happiness and reputation. The covenant then mentions three additional things concerned with unity in the body of Christ: *strengthening the weak, encouraging the afflicted,* [and] *admonishing the erring.* Finally, we are, *as far as we are able, to promote the success of the church and the Gospel.* This is a very general statement that hearkens back to the emphasis on total commitment to Christ, His gospel, and His church. The covenant does not present a low view of the church but rather a high view. The church is the embodiment of Christ in this world and the vehicle for spreading His Good News in our communities and to the world. Therefore, we are obligated to promote her success to the best of our ability.

Paragraph six reads:

We will everywhere hold Christian principle sacred and Christian obligations and enterprises supreme; counting it our chief business in life to extend the influence of Christ in society; constantly praying and toiling that the Kingdom of God may come, and His will be done on earth as it is in Heaven.

This section of the covenant speaks of the implications of the gospel of Jesus Christ for the world outside the doors of the church. The key word here is *everywhere,* which implies that the Lordship of Christ applies to every area of our lives, not merely to selected areas or "religious" areas. Thus, in both religious and non-religious areas of our lives, we are to do two things: (1) *hold Christian principle sacred* and (2) *hold Christian obligations and enterprises supreme.* The principles of Christianity (the Christian world-and-life-view) are the governing principles by which we live and should be brought to bear on every aspect of our personal lives. But these Christian principles, this Christian view of the world and of life, is not merely personal, but involves group obligations and enterprises—attempts by groups of Christians to further the cause of Christ in their world.

Because of our concern to allow the principles of Christianity to govern our personal and societal lives, we must make it *our chief business in life to extend the influence of Christ in society.* This statement implies, again, that the gospel has implications for all of society and culture. Christians are to be "salt and light" in their world (Matthew 5:13, 14). The covenant forces us to discard any individualistic notions of the Christian faith and realize the significance of the gospel for all of life, thought, and culture.

In this vein, the covenant alludes to the Lord's prayer in its next declaration: *constantly praying and toiling that the Kingdom*

of God may come, and His will be done on earth as it is in Heaven.
This refers to Christ's return, that blessed hope which we all
await. However, it also refers to the importance of extending
the principles of the Kingdom in society by winning men and
women individually to Christ and by realizing the implications of the Good News of Jesus Christ in all areas of life, personal and social.

Paragraph seven, the concluding paragraph of the
covenant, reads:

*To this end we agree to labor for the promotion of educational and
denominational enterprises, the support of Missions, the success of
Sunday schools, and evangelistic efforts for the salvation of the
World. And may the God of peace sanctify us wholly, and preserve us
blameless unto the coming of our Lord Jesus Christ.*

To this end means "in order to accomplish this goal"–the
goal being the contents of paragraph six. In other words, in
order to accomplish the goal of extending the gospel into all
areas of life and culture and of winning souls to Christ, we
agree to work to accomplish certain tasks. Then the covenant
goes on to list some of the most important *means* of reaching
this goal in which the church and her members should be
intimately involved. The attainment of this goal involves
labor, hard work. It will not come merely by wishful thinking,
but must be brought about by action.

The covenant mentions five basic things churches and
their members must be laboring to promote: First, *the promotion of educational enterprises.* Education is a basic ingredient
for attaining the goal of winning people to Christ and extending the gospel into all areas of life. Thus, we should be
involved in providing education for our young people that is
based on a Christian world-view. Then they may win people
to Christ and take the gospel into every area of life, both
sacred and secular. This is why we have colleges. Each Free
Will Baptist church member should agree to do all he can to
promote Christian educational enterprises. The most effective way to do this is through denominational channels.

Second, we agree to *promote denominational enterprises.* We have spoken in chapter five of the denominational enterprises in which Free Will Baptists are involved. These enterprises people and churches to touch individuals, communities, and the world with the gospel of Jesus Christ as effectively as possible. We should do all we can, as individuals and as congregations, to support these denominational ministries.

Third, we agree to labor in the *support of missions.* We must keep our concern for both foreign and home missions at the forefront of our minds. This is the primary reason for the existence of the National Association of Free Will Baptists. By supporting missions through prayer, financial assistance, and other means, the church member, through his local congregation, is enabled to reach out with the gospel past his own home and community to other parts of the United States and to the uttermost parts of the earth. Supporting missions allows everyone to be intimately involved in every phase of Christ's Great Commission.

Fourth, we agree to work for the *success of Sunday schools.* Each Christian should strive to support Sunday school because it is a means of educating the people of God. However, Sunday school can also be a tool for evangelism and church growth. Our National Association has a Sunday School and Church Training Board which provides our churches with quality materials for the carrying out of these goals. We should do all we can as individuals and as churches to promote the success of Sunday schools.

Fifth, the covenant sums up our reason for engaging in these enterprises. We should be committed to and involved in evangelistic efforts for the salvation of the world.

The covenant appropriately closes with the beautiful benediction of the Apostle Paul from 1 Thessalonians 5:23: *"And may the God of peace sanctify us wholly, and preserve us blameless unto the coming of our Lord Jesus Christ."*

GROWING THROUGH YOUR CHURCH

The Church Covenant outlines the need for Christian growth through the local church and gives several ways in which this can be accomplished. In what follows, we will briefly discuss six of those ways, expanding on the thoughts that were introduced in the section on the Church Covenant: worship, prayer, learning, evangelism, giving, and serving.

Growing Through Worship

While in chapter two we briefly discussed the mode of worship or the *way* we should worship, here we will consider the purpose and importance of worship and how our involvement in it is necessary to Christian growth. The English word *worship* means "worthship," implying the worthiness of someone to receive special honor or praise. Thus the purpose of worship is literally to ascribe worth to God. When we speak of worship in the context of the local church, we refer to *corporate* worship: the worship of the body of believers. This is "together-worship," the event in which a body of believers gathers together to ascribe worth to God.

Corporate worship consists of the singing of praise to God, prayer, the reading of Scripture, the preaching of the Word, and the collection of tithes and offerings. Regular worship is to be supplemented by the occasional observance of Christian ordinances. It is not as though there is anything "exciting" about these activities. In themselves, they seem rather mundane. But when the worshiping congregation comes together and offers up their sacrifice to God by observing these simple, divinely-ordained rites, they are filled with an unparalleled significance for every serious worshiper. In true Christian worship, God is glorified in every sincere and biblically based action of the worshipers. Worship is an act of reverence before God. God is glorified and revered through such humble and common things as singing, praying, reading, preaching, and giving. Yet we find that through worship

God meets us. In our day, worship is too often viewed as a "feel-good" time, when we can go to get our spiritual batteries charged. But we dare not let the focus in worship be upon ourselves; we must maintain the centrality of God in worship. Only by focusing on God can we allow Him to meet us in worship. Only by emphasizing the centrality of ascribing worth to God can we be blessed by our act of worship.

Worship is a necessary element of Christian growth. The Christian who does not join with his brothers and sisters in the corporate worship of God will find that his spiritual growth will be stunted. Twentieth-century Christianity has emphasized too much the individual aspects of Christianity. Thus, many modern Christians are very concerned about "what worship can do for me." We must get away from an individualistic approach to our faith and revive the biblical emphasis on the corporate nature of the worshiping and ministering community. This is what the church was meant to be. We have covenanted together at agreed upon times to meet with our brothers and sisters in the worship of the Lord. This is an indispensable element in our growth into mature Christians. We grow through worship.

Growing Through Study

There are numerous places in Holy Scripture in which we are commanded to study the Word of God. In John 5:39, Jesus commands us to "search the Scriptures" because "they testify of me." This verse is a command to probe deeply into the entirety of the Old Testament, and by extension the New Testament, because the Bible is a book about Jesus Christ and the redemption He brings. The Bible with its message of Christ is God's revealed Word to us and declares our only hope of eternal life. The more we study the Bible, the more we learn of Christ, and the more we are able to allow our minds and hearts to be transformed into the image of God's Son.

Another place we are told to study the Scriptures is in 2 Timothy 2:15, where Paul instructs Timothy, "Study to shew thyself approved unto God, a workman that needeth not to be ashamed, rightly dividing the word of truth." This verse means, "Be diligent to interpret the Bible properly." Like Timothy we are called on to be diligent in our interpretation of the Bible, so that we too may interpret the Scriptures accurately. The only way this can be done is by studying the Bible thoroughly and often.

Personal Bible study will help us grow as Christians (see 1 Peter 2:2, Hebrews 5:12-14), but we also need to be involved in the group study of the Bible and Christian teaching. We are afforded numerous opportunities for Christian growth in the context of the local church, whether the church is small or large. Sunday school is the most obvious example of an opportunity for Christian growth through study. Through personal study, we prepare ourselves for weekly group study of the Word. When we meet weekly with others of like mind and heart and probe the Scriptures together, we grow in the knowledge of the Word. Believer's growth in the Word in turn provides the foundation for growth in the Spirit and in increasing conformity to the image of Christ.

This group study can also take place through Church Training, Wednesday evening Bible study, and small home-group studies with other church members. The right kind of group study is always biblically based, but it can center on the study of Christian doctrine, everyday application, ethics, church history, and a host of other topics. But the aim is always Christian growth. We grow through study.

Growing Through Bible Reading and Prayer

Just as we grow through study, we also grow through Bible reading and prayer. Bible study implies the reading of Scripture, but we must be careful that our reading of Scripture is not merely to "get information" on a topic just for the sake of learning and not for application and life-transformation. We must make Bible reading and study a time of devotion to our Lord and a time when the Holy Spirit can work through the Word to change us, to help us grow.

Bible reading and prayer are like a conversation. Though we can sense the still, small voice of God through prayer, it is helpful to view reading Scripture as God communicating with us, and praying as our communicating with God. Through times of Bible reading and prayer, both personally and in groups, we can carry on a two-way conversation with God. Just as communication is an essential ingredient in marriage, it is essential to a vital, growing relationship with the triune God. Some marriages fail or are mediocre due to "small talk." We must be careful that our devotional life does not consist merely of occasional reading of snippets of God's Word and "canned" prayers. This can easily degenerate into communication with God which consists only of small talk. By keeping communication lines open and vibrant between ourselves and God, we will be able to grow in our relationship with Him.

Bible reading and prayer are not merely for the individual, however. Times of sustained prayer and Bible reading in a small group setting are also necessary to grow together in our relationships—with each other and with God. When believers gather in group devotions, the Holy Spirit uses spiritual community to build Christ's church. We grow through Bible reading and prayer.

Growing Through Evangelism

An *evangel* is someone who bears good tidings or good news. Thus when we speak of evangelism, we mean the bearing of the Good News (gospel) of Jesus Christ. Being an evangel means you take your rightful place in carrying out the Great Commission both personally and as part of your church. Sharing your faith with others keeps it from becoming stagnant. Winning souls to Christ is necessary to Christian growth.

The Christian who shares his faith is fulfilling his role as a witness to the saving grace of Jesus Christ in his own life. Acts 1:8 says, "But ye shall receive power, after that the Holy Ghost is come upon you: and ye shall be witnesses unto me both in Jerusalem, and in all Judaea, and in Samaria, and unto the uttermost part of the earth." This verse teaches that the Holy Spirit gives us the power to be witnesses for Christ in our everyday lives. Witnessing, rather than a chore or a special task, is a natural outgrowth of being indwelt by the Holy Spirit, a condition that every Christian experiences. Furthermore, this natural part of the Christian experience, sharing our faith, is to be done not only to those in our own communities but also to those in other parts of the world. As church members, we are privileged to be involved in a community of faith which bears witness to Christ through church outreach programs, evangelism training, and action programs. But we are also empowered to be witnesses to people in other parts of the world. We do this in two ways: prayer and financial support. Personal and corporate prayer for the lost in other parts of the world, and giving financially through the local church, allows our witness to reach beyond our own locality.

The dedicated church will be busy training her members to share their faith with others—personal evangelism or soul-winning—and will also be involved in community outreach as a body. Ask your pastor about ways you can grow through evangelism both personally and as a member of the larger body. You will grow through evangelism.

Growing Through Giving

Giving to God through your church is a necessary ingredient to spiritual growth. Giving in this section is used in the sense of financial giving or financial stewardship. The next section will focus on giving in non-monetary ways.

Financial giving is an outgrowth of stewardship. To be a steward is to be a caretaker of that with which God has blessed you. Christians recognize that God is the giver of all good things. Therefore, they realize the importance of being good stewards of the gifts God has given them. The way we view our money grows out of an attitude of Christian stewardship. If we are good stewards of the money and material goods God has given us, then we will seek to please Him in our financial decisions.

First and foremost among our financial decisions is our decision to give to God what He requires of us financially. The Free Will Baptist *Treatise* teaches that *tithing* is "God's financial plan for the support of His work" (*Treatise,* part 2, chapter 16). Tithing consists of contributing ten percent of one's income to the church. In Malachi 3:10a God says, "Bring ye all the tithes into the storehouse, that there may be meat in mine house." Free Will Baptists believe that God requires each Christian to give ten percent of his income back to God through the local church. Though tithing was part of the Mosaic Law, its precedent was set before the ceremonial law (Genesis 14:20; 28:22), and was confirmed by Jesus. In Matthew 23:23 Jesus says that paying tithes ought to be done. The system of tithes and offerings, by which each Christian pays ten percent of his income toward the work of the Lord and then gives free will offerings above and beyond that ten percent, is the most scriptural method for the support of the church and her ministries. Some people seem to have the idea that tithing means giving ten percent of what is left over after you've met your needs. But the biblical picture is of giving ten percent of your entire income.

You will grow by tithing to God through your church. First, you will grow spiritually because you will be fulfilling the requirements of God, striving to be a good steward of the resources with which God has blessed you. Second, you will grow by receiving added blessings from God. In Malachi 3:10b, God says, "prove me now . . . if I will not open you the windows of heaven, and pour you out a blessing, that there shall not be room enough to receive it." And third, you will

grow together with your brothers and sisters in the body of
Christ. Your cooperative efforts will bring about the furtherance of the gospel message and will promote the ministries of
your local church at home and around the world. We grow
through giving.

Growing Through Serving

   The tragedy of many local churches in our day is that such
a small percentage of church members are actually involved
in *service*. But service to God and others through the local
church is essential to Christian growth. One of the chief characteristics of Christ was the fact that He was a servant. In fact,
Philippians 2 says that He had such a servant's mind that He
was willing to be a servant even to the point of death, His
own death on the cross. Paul admonishes us in this passage to
"let this mind be in you, which was also in Christ Jesus."
Having the mind of Christ means having the mind of a servant. A servant's mind produces the attitude of service–desiring to serve others rather than to be served. Too much
Christianity in our day runs counter to the biblical attitude of
servanthood. Too many Christians focus not on how they can
be of service to others in the church, but how others in the
church can be of service to them. How often have we heard
seemingly mature Christians say something like, "We
changed churches because we wanted to be *ministered to.*"
How tragic, for the word *minister* means literally "to serve."
The attitude of the growing Christian toward his church
should be one of serving others and God through the local
church, rather than a mindset of being served. Jesus said, "Let
him who is greatest unto you be your minister [servant]."

   Service in the church is a key ingredient to spiritual
growth. You can grow by serving your church in numerous
ways. And as previously stated, God gives different people
unique gifts for service. Some Christians may be called by
God to serve in an area that the world would consider small
and insignificant, but whatever area God calls you to serve in

is important. While the list below is incomplete, it may serve as a start for identifying ways you can grow through serving in your local church (see figure 1, page 122).

This list is of necessity only a start, provided to give examples of the innumerable opportunities for Christian service within the context of the local church. Take on a servant's attitude, and you will grow.

As we have seen in this brief section, growing is not just a personal endeavor but a corporate undertaking; that is, it is a concern for the body of Christ, not merely the individual. Only through Christian community, which is ideally set in the context of the local church, can we experience true and vital growth in the grace and knowledge of our Lord and Savior Jesus Christ (2 Peter 3:18).

CHRISTIAN EDUCATION
- ❏ Superintendent/Director
- ❏ Officer
- ❏ Teacher
- ❏ Vacation Bible School

YOUTH MINISTRY
- ❏ Leader
- ❏ Asst. Leader
- ❏ Officer
- ❏ Musician

WOMEN'S ORGANIZATION
- ❏ Officer
- ❏ Committee Member
- ❏ Musician
- ❏ Prayer Leader

MUSIC MINISTRY
- ❏ Adult Choir Director
- ❏ Adult Choir/Ensemble Member
- ❏ Youth Choir Director
- ❏ Youth Choir/Ensemble Member
- ❏ Pianist
- ❏ Organist
- ❏ Help in Children's Choirs
- ❏ Laymen's Chorale

I am a . . .
- ❏ tither of my income.
- ❏ Deacon (or willing to be one).
- ❏ Trustee.
- ❏ Committee member.
- ❏ Church officer.

I will help in . . .
- ❏ audio-visual aids.
- ❏ drama.
- ❏ bulletin board arrangements.
- ❏ distributing food for the needy.
- ❏ crafts for V.B.S., etc.
- ❏ church library work.
- ❏ the church nursery.
- ❏ photography or art.
- ❏ recreation and games.
- ❏ planning social activities.
- ❏ providing refreshments for activities.
- ❏ preparing church bulletins.
- ❏ providing secretarial help.
- ❏ sending cards to visitors and absentees.
- ❏ telephoning visitors and absentees.
- ❏ transportation (getting people to church).
- ❏ the conference/association meetings by serving as a delegate.
- ❏ ushering.
- ❏ visitation for evangelism.
- ❏ visitation for pastoral care.

My special gift is:
- ❏ Singing
- ❏ Playing an instrument
- ❏ Speaking before others
- ❏ Bookkeeping
- ❏ Counseling/friendship counseling
- ❏ Greeting people before services
- ❏ Reading aloud before others
- ❏ Producing children's programs
- ❏ Visual arts
- ❏ Working with the sick and shut-in
- ❏ Praying for unsaved friends and relatives
- ❏ Praying for fellow members and pastor(s)

(Figure 1)

Our Historic Confessions of Faith: Three Important Confessions of Faith of Our History

THOMAS HELWYS'S DECLARATION, 1611

Composed in 1611, this confession of faith, entitled *A Declaration of Faith of English People Remaining at Amsterdam,* is the first Baptist confession of faith ever written. It was largely composed by Thomas Helwys after his small congregation had separated from John Smyth. Written just before this first Baptist congregation returned to England from exile in Holland, this is the first systematic summary of Arminian, Free Will Baptist beliefs.

A

DECLARATION OF FAITH

of

ENGLISH PEOPLE

Remaining at Amsterdam in Holland

We believe and confess:

1.

That there are THREE which bear record in Heaven, the FATHER, the WORD, and the SPIRIT; and these THREE are one God, in all equality (1 John 5:7; Philippians 2:5-6). By whom all things are created and preserved, in Heaven and in Earth (Genesis 1).

2.

That this GOD in the beginning created all things of nothing (Genesis 1:1) and made man of the dust of the earth (Genesis 2:7), in His own image (Genesis 1:27), in righteousness and true holiness (Ephesians 4:24): yet being tempted, fell by disobedience (Genesis 3:1-7). Through whose disobedience, all men sinned (Romans 5:12-19). His sin being imputed unto all; and so death went over all men.

3.

That by the promised seed of the woman, JESUS CHRIST, [and by] His obedience, all are made righteous (Romans 5:19). All are made alive (1 Corinthians 15:22), His righteousness being imputed unto all.

4.

That notwithstanding this Men are by nature the children of wrath (Ephesians 2:3), born in iniquity and in sin conceived (Psalm 51:5), wise to all evil, but to good they have no knowledge (Jeremiah 4:22). *The natural man perceiveth not the things of the Spirit of God* (1 Corinthians 2:14). And therefore man is not restored unto his former estate, but that as man, in his estate of innocency, having in himself all disposition unto good, and no disposition unto evil, yet being tempted might yield, or might resist: even so now being fallen, and having all disposition unto evil, and no disposition or will unto any good, yet GOD giving grace, man may receive grace, or may reject grace, according to that saying, Deuteronomy 30:19: "I call Heaven and Earth to record. This day against you, that I have set before you life and death, blessing and cursing: Therefore choose life, that both thou and thy seed may live."

5.

That GOD before the foundation of the world hath pre-destinated that all that believe in Him shall be saved (Ephesians 1:4, 12; Mark 16:16), and all that believe not shall be damned (Mark 16:16), all [of] which he knew before (Romans 8:29). And this is the election and reprobation spo-ken of in the Scriptures concerning salvation and condemna-tion; and not that GOD hath predestinated men to be wicked and so to be damned, but that men, being wicked, shall be damned; for GOD would have all men saved, and come to the knowledge of the truth (1 Timothy 2:4), and would have no man to perish, but would have all men come to repen-tance (2 Peter 3:9), and willeth not the death of him that dieth (Ezekiel 18:32). And therefore GOD is the author of no men's condemnation, according to the saying of the Prophet (Hosea 13): "Thy destruction, O Israel, is of thy self, but thy help is of me."

6.

That man is justified only by the righteousness of CHRIST, apprehended by faith (Romans 3:28; Galatians 2:16); yet faith without works is dead (James 2:17).

7.

That men may fall away from the grace of GOD (Hebrews 12:15) and from the truth, which they have received and acknowledged (Hebrews 10:26), after they have tasted of the heavenly gift, and were made partakers of the HOLY GHOST, and have tasted of the good word of GOD, and of the powers of the world to come (Hebrews 6:4-6). And after they have escaped from the filthiness of the world, may be tangled again therein and overcome (2 Peter 2:20). That a righteous man may forsake his righteousness and perish (Ezekiel 18:24, 26). And therefore let no man presume to think that because he hath, or had once, grace, therefore he shall always have grace: But let all men have assurance, that if they continue unto the end, they shall be saved: Let no man then presume; but let all work out their salvation with fear and trembling.

8.

That JESUS CHRIST, the Son of GOD, the second person or subsistence in the Trinity, in the fullness of time was manifested in the flesh, being the seed of David, and of the Israelites, according to the flesh (Romans 1:3; 8:5), the son of Mary the virgin, made of her substance (Galatians 4:4) by the power of the HOLY GHOST overshadowing her (Luke 1:35) and being thus true man, was like unto us in all thing[s], sin only excepted (Hebrews 4:15), being one person in two distinct natures, TRUE GOD, and TRUE MAN.

9.

That JESUS CHRIST is Mediator of the New Testament between GOD and Man (1 Timothy 2:5), having all power in Heaven and in Earth given unto Him (Matthew 28:18), being the only KING (Luke 1:33), PRIEST (Hebrews 7:24), and PROPHET (Acts 3:22). Of His church, He also being the only law-giver, hath in His Testament set down an absolute and perfect rule of direction, for all persons at all times, to be observed; which no prince, nor any whosoever, may add to or diminish from as they will avoid the fearful judgments denounced against them that shall so do (Revelation 22:18-19).

10.

That the church of CHRIST is a company of faithful people (1 Corinthians 1:2; Ephesians 1:1) separated from the world by the Word and Spirit of God (2 Corinthians 6:17), being knit unto the LORD, and one unto another, by Baptism (1 Corinthians 12:13), upon their own confession of the faith (Acts 8:37) and sins (Matthew 3:6).

11.

That though in respect of CHRIST, the Church be one (Ephesians 4:4), yet it consisteth of divers particular congregations, even so many as there shall be in the world, every of which congregation, though they be but two or three, have CHRIST given them, with all the means of their salvation (Matthew 18:20; Romans 8:32; 1 Corinthians 3:22), are the Body of CHRIST (1 Corinthians 12:27) and a whole Church (1 Corinthians 14:23); and therefore may and ought, when they are come together, to pray, prophesy, break bread, and administer in all the holy ordinances; although as yet they have no officers, or that their officers should be in prison, sick, or by any other means hindered from the church (1 Peter 4:10; 2:5).

12.

That as one congregation hath CHRIST, so hath all (2 Corinthians 10:7). And that the Word of GOD cometh not out from any one, neither to any one congregation in particular (1 Corinthians 14:36), but unto every particular church, as it doth unto all the world (Colossians 1:5, 6); and therefore no church ought to challenge any prerogative over any other.

13.

That every church is to receive in all their members by baptism upon the confession of their faith and sins wrought by the preaching of the Gospel, according to the primitive institution (Matthew 28:19) and practice (Acts 2:41). And therefore churches constituted after any other manner, or of any other persons are not according to CHRIST'S Testament.

14.

That Baptism, or washing with water, is the outward manifestation of dying unto sin and walking in newness of life

(Romans 6:2-4); and therefore in no wise appertaineth to infants.

15.

That the LORD'S Supper is the outward manifestation of the spiritual communion between CHRIST and the faithful mutually (1 Corinthians 10:16-17) to declare His death until He come (1 Corinthians 11:26).

16.

That the members of every church or congregation ought to know one another, that so they may perform all the duties of love one towards another, both to soul and body (Matthew 18:15; 1 Thessalonians 5:14; 1 Corinthians 12:25). And especially the elders ought to know the whole flock, whereof the HOLY GHOST hath made them overseers (Acts 20:28; 1 Peter 5:2-3). And therefore a church ought not to consist of such a multitude as cannot have particular knowledge of one another.

17.

That brethren impenitent in one sin after the admonition of the Church are to be excluded [from] the communion of the saints (Matthew 18:17; 1 Corinthians 5:4, 13) and therefore not the committing of sin doth cut off any from the church, but refusing to hear the church to reformation.

18.

That excommunicants in respect of civil society are not to be avoided (2 Thessalonians 3:15; Matthew 18:17).

19.

That every church ought (according to the example of CHRIST'S disciples and primitive churches) upon every first day of the week, being the LORD'S day, to assemble together to pray, Prophesy, praise God, and break bread, and perform all other parts of spiritual communion for the worship of GOD, their own mutual edification, and the preservation of true religion and piety in the church (John 20:19; Acts 2:42 and 20:7; 1 Corinthians 16:2), and that ought not to labor in their callings according to the equity of the moral law, which CHRIST came not to abolish, but to fulfill (Exodus 20:8, etc.).

20.

That the officers of every church or congregation are either elders, who by their office do especially feed the flock concerning their souls (Acts 20:28; 1 Peter 5:2, 3), or deacons, men and women who by their office relieve the necessities of the poor and impotent brethren concerning their bodies (Acts 6:1-4).

21.

That these officers are to be chosen when there are persons qualified according to the rules in Christ's Testament (1 Timothy 3:2-7; Titus 1:6-9; Acts 6:3, 4), by election and approbation of that church or congregation whereof they are members (Acts 6:3, 4; 14:23), with fasting, prayer, and laying on of hands (Acts 13:3; 14:23). And there being but one rule for elders, therefore but one sort of elders.

22.

That the officers of every church or congregation are tied by office only to that particular congregation whereof they are chosen (Acts 14:23; 20:17; Titus 1:5), and therefore they cannot challenge by office any authority in any other congregation except they would have an Apostleship.

23.

That the Scriptures of the Old and New Testament are written for our instruction (2 Timothy 3:16) and that we ought to search them, for they testify of CHRIST (John 5:39), and [are] therefore to be used with all reverence, as containing the Holy Word of GOD, which only is our direction in all things whatsoever.

24.

That Magistracy [government has been ordained by] God, that every soul ought to be subject to it not for fear only, but for conscience's sake. Magistrates are the ministers of God for our wealth; they bear not the sword for nought. They are ministers of GOD to take vengeance on them that do evil (Romans 13). That it is fearful sin to speak evil of them that are in dignity, and to despise government (2 Peter 2:10). We ought to pay tribute, custom, and all other duties. That we are to pray for them, for GOD would have them saved and come to the knowledge of His truth (1 Timothy 2:1-4). And therefore they may be members of the church of CHRIST, retaining their magistracy, for no holy ordinance of God debarreth any from being a member of CHRIST'S church. They bear the sword of GOD, which sword in all lawful administrations is to be defended and supported by the servants of GOD that are under their government with their lives and all that they have according as in the first institution of that holy ordinance. And whosoever holds otherwise must hold (if they understand themselves) that they are the ministers of the devil, and therefore not to be prayed for nor approved in any of their administrations,—seeing all things they do (as punishing offenders and defending their countries, states, and persons by the sword) is unlawful.

25.

That it is lawful in a just cause for the deciding of strife to take an oath by the name of the Lord (Hebrews 6:16; 2 Corinthians 1:23; Philippians 1:8).

26.

That the dead shall rise again, and the living being changed in a moment, having the same bodies in substance, though divers in qualities (1 Corinthians 15:38, 52; Job 19:15-28; Luke 24:30).

27.

That after the resurrection all men shall appear before the judgment seat of CHRIST to be judged according to their works; that the Godly shall enjoy life Eternal, the wicked, being condemned, shall be tormented everlastingly in Hell (Matthew 25:46).

THE 1660 ENGLISH GENERAL BAPTIST CONFESSION OF FAITH

The confession below, often called *The Standard Confession, 1660*, was the most widely used confession of faith of the English General Baptists of the 1600s and hence was naturally used by early Free Will Baptists in the South. Thomas Grantham, the premier theologian of the General Baptists delivered the confession to King Charles II on July 26, 1660.

A BRIEF
CONFESSION
or
DECLARATION OF FAITH

Set out by many of us, who are (falsely) called *Ana-baptists*, to inform all men (in these days of scandal and reproach) of our innocent belief and practice: for which we are not only resolved to suffer persecution and the loss of our goods, but also to life itself, rather than to decline the same.

I. We believe and are verily confident that there is but one God the Father, of Whom are all things, from everlasting to everlasting, glorious and unwordable in his attributes (1 Corinthians 8:6; Isaiah 40:28).

II. That God in the beginning made man upright, and put him into a state and condition of glory, without the least mixture of misery, from which he by transgression fell, and so came into a miserable and mortal estate, subject unto the first death (Genesis 1:31; Ecclesiastes 7:29; Genesis 2:17; Genesis 3:17-19).

III. That there is one Lord Jesus Christ, by Whom are all things, Who is the only begotten Son of God, born of the Virgin Mary; yet as truly David's Lord and David's root as David's son and David's offspring (Luke 20:44; Revelation 22:16), Whom God freely sent into the world (because of His great love unto the world) Who as freely gave Himself a ransom for all (1 Timothy 2:5, 6), tasting death for every man (Hebrews 2:9), a propitiation for our sins; and not for ours only, but also for the sins of the whole world (1 John 2:2).

IV. That God is not willing that any should perish, but that all should come to repentance (2 Peter 3:9) and the knowledge of the truth, that they might be saved (1 Timothy 2:4). For which end Christ hath commanded that the Gospel (to wit, the glad tidings of remission of sins) should be preached to every creature (Mark 16:15). So that no man shall eternally suffer in Hell (that is, the second death) for want of a Christ that died for them, but as the Scripture saith, for denying the Lord that bought them (2 Peter 2:1) or because they believe not in the name of the only begotten Son of God (John 3:18). Unbelief therefore being the cause why the just and righteous God will condemn the children of men, it follows against all contradiction that all men at one time or other are put into such a capacity as that (through the grace of God) they may be eternally saved (John 1:7; Acts 17:30; Mark 6:6; Hebrews 3:10, 18, 19; 1 John 5:10; John 3:17).

V. That such as who first orderly come into and are brought up in the schools of Christ's church, and waiting there, come to degrees of Christianity, rightly qualified and considerably gifted by God's spirit; ought to exercise their gifts not only in the church, but also (as occasion serves) to preach to the world (they being approved of by the church so to do) (Acts 11:22-24; Acts 11:19, 20), and that among such some are to be chosen by the church and ordained by fasting, prayer, and laying on of hands for the work of the ministry (Acts 13:2, 3; Acts 1:23). Such so ordained (and abiding faithful in their work) we own as ministers of the Gospel; but all such who come not first to repent of their sins, believe on the Lord Jesus, and so baptized in His name for the remission of sins, but are only brought up in the schools of humane learning, to the attaining of humane arts and variety of languages, with many vain curiosities of speech (1 Corinthians 1:19, 21; 2:1, 4, 5), seeking rather the gain of large revenues, than the gain of souls to God: such (we say) we utterly deny, being such as have need rather to be taught themselves, than fit to teach others (Romans 2:21).

VI. That the way set forth by God for men to be justified in, is by faith in Christ (Romans 5:1).

That is to say, when men shall assent to the truth of the Gospel, believing with all their hearts that there is remission of sins, and eternal life to be had in Christ.

And that Christ therefore is most worthy their constant affections and subjection to all His commandments, and therefore resolve with purpose of heart so to subject unto Him in all things, and no longer unto themselves (2 Corinthians 5:15).

And so, shall (with godly sorrow for the sins past) commit themselves to His grace, confidently depending upon Him for that which they believe is to be had in Him: such so believing are justified from all their sins, their faith shall be accounted unto them for righteousness (Romans 4:22-24; Romans 3:25, 26).

VII. That there is one Holy Spirit, the precious gift of God, freely given to such as obey Him (Ephesians 4:4; Acts 5:32), that thereby they may be thoroughly sanctified, and made able (without which they are altogether unable) to abide steadfast in the faith, and to honour the Father, and His Son Christ, the Author and Finisher of their faith (1 Corinthians 6:11). There are three that bear record in Heaven, the Father, the Word, the Holy Spirit, and these three are one; which Spirit of promise such have not yet received (though they speak much of him) that are so far out of love, peace, long-suffering, gentleness, goodness, meekness, and temperance (the fruits of the Spirit) (Galatians 5:22, 23) as that they breathe out much cruelty and great envy against the liberties and peaceable living of such as are not of their judgment, though holy as to their conversations.

VIII. That God hath even before the foundation of the world chosen (or elected) to eternal life, such as believe, and so are in Christ (John 3:16; Ephesians 1:4; 2 Thessalonians 2:13), yet confident are we, that the purpose of God according to election was not in the least arising from foreseen faith in, or works of righteousness done by the creature, but only from the mercy, goodness, and compassion dwelling in God, and so it is of him that calleth (Romans 9:11) whose purity and unwordable holiness cannot admit of any unclean person (or thing) to be in His presence, therefore His decree of mercy reaches only the godly man, whom (saith David) God hath set apart for Himself (Psalm 4:3).

IX. That men not considered simply as men, but ungodly men, were of old ordained to condemnation, considered as such, who turn the grace of God unto wantonness, and deny the only Lord God, and our Lord Jesus Christ (Jude 4). God indeed sends a strong delusion to men, that they might be damned; but we observe that they are such (as saith the apostle) that received not the love of the truth, that they might be saved (2 Thessalonians 2:10-12) and so the indignation and wrath of God is upon every soul of man that doth evil (living and dying therein) for there is no respect of persons with God (Romans 2:9-11).

X. That all children dying in infancy, having not actually transgressed against the Law of God in their own persons, are only subject to the first death, which comes upon them by the sin of the first Adam, from whence they shall be all raised by the second Adam; and not that any one of them (dying in that estate) shall suffer for Adam's sin, eternal punishment in Hell (which is the second death) for of such belongs the Kingdom of Heaven (1 Corinthians 15:22; Matthew 19:14), not daring to conclude with that uncharitable opinion of others, who, though they plead much for the bringing of children into the visible church here on earth by baptism, yet nevertheless by their doctrine that Christ died for some, shut a great part of them out of the Kingdom of Heaven forever.

XI. That the right and only way, of gathering churches (according to Christ's appointment) (Matthew 28:19, 20) is first to teach or preach the Gospel (Mark 16:16) to the sons and daughters of men; and then to baptize (that is in English to dip) in the name of the father, son, and Holy Spirit, or in the name of the Lord Jesus Christ; such only of them as profess repentance towards God and faith towards our Lord Jesus Christ (Acts 2:38; Acts 8:12; Acts 18:8). And as for all such who preach not this doctrine, but instead thereof, that Scriptureless thing of sprinkling of infants (falsely called baptism) whereby the pure Word of God is made of no effect, and the New Testament-way of bringing in members into the church by regeneration cast out; when as the bond-woman and her son, that is to say, the Old Testament-way of bringing children into the church by generation, is cast out, as saith Scripture (Galatians 4:22-24, 30; Matthew 3:8, 9), all such we utterly deny, forasmuch as we are commanded to have no fellowship with the unfruitful works of darkness, but rather to reprove them (Ephesians 5:11).

XII. That it is the duty of all such who are believers baptized, to draw nigh unto God in submission to that principle of Christ's Doctrine, to wit, prayer and laying on of hands, that they may receive the promise of the Holy Spirit (Hebrews 6:1, 2; Acts 8:12, 15, 17; Acts 19:6; 2 Timothy 1:6) whereby we may mortify the deeds of the body (Romans 8:13) and live in all things answerable to their professed intentions, and desires, even to the honour of Him, who hath called them out of darkness and into his marvellous light.

XIII. That it is the duty of such who are constituted as aforesaid, to continue steadfastly in Christ's and the apostles' doctrine, and assembling together in fellowship, in breaking of bread, and prayer (Acts 2:42).

XIV. That although we thus declare the primitive way and order of constituting churches, yet we verily believe, and also declare, that unless men so professing and practicing the form and order of Christ's doctrine shall also beautify the same with a holy and wise conversation, in all godliness and honesty, the profession of the visible form will be rendered to them of no effect; for without holiness no man shall see the Lord (Hebrews 12:14; Isaiah 1:11, 12, 15, 16).

XV. That the elders or pastors which God hath appointed to oversee and feed his Church (constituted aforesaid) are such who, first being of the number of disciples, shall in time appear to be vigilant, sober, of good behavior, given to hospitality, apt to teach, etc., not greedy of filthy lucre (as too many National[1] ministers are) but patient; not a brawler, not covetous, etc., and as such chosen and ordained to office (according to the order of Scripture) (Acts 14:23), who are to feed the flock with meat in due season and in much love to rule over them with all care, seeking after such as go astray; but as for all such who labor to feed themselves with the fat, more than to feed the flock (Ezekiel 34:2, 3), seeking more after theirs, than them, expressly contrary to the practice of the ministers of old, who said, we seek not yours, but you (2 Corinthians 12:14). All such we utterly deny, and hereby bear our continued testimony against (Ezekiel 34).

XVI. That the ministers of Christ, that have freely received from God, ought freely to minister to others (1 Corinthians 9:17), and that such who have spiritual things freely ministered unto them ought freely to communicate necessary things to the ministers (upon the account of their charge) (1 Corinthians 9:11; Galatians 6:6). And as for tithes, or any forced maintenance, we utterly deny to be the maintenance of Gospel ministers.

XVII. That the true church of Christ ought after the first and second admonition to reject all heretics (Titus 3:10, 11), and in the name of the Lord to withdraw from all such as profess the way of the Lord, but walk disorderly in their conversations (2 Thessalonians 3:6) or any ways cause divisions or offences, contrary to the doctrine (of Christ) which they have learned (Romans 16:17).

XVIII. That such are true believers, even branches in Christ the Vine, and that in His account, whom He exhorts to abide in Him (John 15:1-5), or such who have charity out of a pure heart and of a good conscience and of faith unfeigned (1 Timothy 1:5) may nevertheless for want of watchfulness swerve and turn aside from the same (John 15:6, 7), and become as withered branches, cast into the fire and burned (John 15:6). But such who add unto their faith virtue, and unto virtue knowledge, and unto knowledge temperance, etc. (2 Peter 1:5-7), such shall never fall (2 Peter 1:8-10), 'tis impossible for all the false Christs and false prophets that are, and are to come, to deceive such, for they are kept by the power of God, through faith unto salvation (1 Peter 1:5).

XIX. That the poor saints belonging to the church of Christ are to be sufficiently provided for by the churches, that they neither want food or raiment, and this by a free and voluntary contribution (and not of necessity or by the constraint or power of the magistrate) (2 Corinthians 9:7; 1 Corinthians 8:11, 12) and this through the free and voluntary help of the deacons (called overseers of the poor), being faithful men, chosen by the church and ordained by prayer and laying on of hands, to that work (Acts 6:1-6). So that there is no need in the Church of Christ of a magisterial compulsion in this case, as there is among others, who being constituted in a fleshly and generational way are necessitated to make use of a carnal sword, to compel even a small, mean, and short maintenance for their poor; when as many other members of their churches can and do part with great and large sums of money to maintain their vain fashions, gold, pearls, and costly array, which is expressly contrary to the Word of God (1 Timothy 2:9, 10; 1 Peter 3:3). Alas, what will such do when God riseth up, and when He visiteth, what will they answer him? (Job 31:14).

XX. That there shall be (through Christ Who was dead, but is alive again from the dead) a resurrection of all men from the graves of the earth (Isaiah 26:19), both the just and the unjust (Acts 24:15), that is, the fleshly bodies of men, sown into the graves of the earth, corruptible, dishonorable, weak, natural (which so considered cannot inherit the Kingdom of God), shall be raised again, incorruptible, in glory, in power, spiritual, and so considered, the bodies of the saints (united again to their spirits), which here suffer for Christ, shall inherit the Kingdom, reigning together with Christ (1 Corinthians 15:21, 22, 42, 43, 44, 49).

XXI. That there shall be after the resurrection from the graves of the earth, an eternal judgment at the appearing of Christ and His kingdom (2 Timothy 4:1; Hebrews 9:27), at which time of judgment which is unalterable and irrevocable, every man shall receive according to the things done in his body (2 Corinthians 5:10).

XXII. That the same Lord who showed Himself alive after His passion, by many infallible proofs (Acts 1:3), Which was taken up from the disciples, and carried up into Heaven (Luke 24:51), shall so come in like manner as He was seen go into Heaven (Acts 1:9-11), and when Christ Who is our life shall appear, we shall also appear with Him in glory (Colossians 3:4), for then shall He be King of Kings, and Lord of Lords (Revelation 19:16), for the Kingdom is His, and He is the Governor among the nations (Psalm 22:28) and King over all the earth (Zechariah 14:9), and we shall reign (with Him) on the earth (Revelation 5:10), the kingdoms of this world (which men so mightily strive after here to enjoy) shall become the kingdoms of our Lord, and His Christ (Revelation 11:15), for all is yours (O ye that overcome this world) for ye are Christ's, and Christ is God's (1 Corinthians 3:22, 23), for unto the saints shall be given the Kingdom, and the greatness of the Kingdom, under the whole Heaven (Daniel 7:27). Though (alas) now men be scarce content that the saints should have so much as being among them; but when Christ shall appear, then shall be their day, then shall be given unto them power over the nations, to rule them with a rod of iron (Revelation 2:26, 27), then shall they receive a crown of life, which no man shall take from them, nor they by any means turned, or overturned from it, for the oppressor shall be broken in pieces (Psalm 72:4), and their now vain rejoicings turned into mourning and bitter lamentations, as 'tis written (Job 20:5-7), the triumphing of the wicked is short, and the joy of the hypocrite but for a moment; though his excellency mount up the Heavens, and his head reach unto the clouds, yet shall he perish for ever, like his own dung; they which have seen him, shall say, where is he?

XXIII. That the Holy Scriptures is the rule whereby saints both in matters of faith and conversation are to be regulated, they being able to make men wise unto salvation, through faith in Christ Jesus, profitable for doctrine, for reproof, for instruction in righteousness, that the man of God may be perfect, throughly furnished unto all good works (2 Timothy 3:15-17; John 20:31; Isaiah 8:20).

XXIV. That it is the will and mind of God (in these Gospel times) that all men should have free liberty of their own consciences in matters of religion or worship, without the least oppression or persecution, as simply upon that account; and that for any in authority otherwise to act we confidently believe is expressly contrary to the mind of Christ, Who requires that whatsoever men would that others should do unto them, they should do unto others (Matthew 7:12), and that the tares and the wheat should grow together in the field (which is the world) until the harvest (which is the end of the world) (Matthew 13:29, 30, 38, 39).

XXV. We believe that there ought to be civil magistrates in all nations, for the punishment of evil doers, and for the praise of them that do well (1 Peter 2:14) and that all wicked lewdness and fleshly filthiness, contrary to just and whole-some (civil) laws, ought to be punished according to the nature of the offences; and this without respect of any persons, religion, or profession whatsoever; and that we and all men are obliged by Gospel rules, to be subject to the higher powers, to obey magistrates as saith 1 Peter 2:13. But in the case the civil powers do, or shall at any time, impose things about matters of religion, which we through conscience to God cannot actually obey, then we with Peter also do say, and accordingly do hereby declare our whole and holy intent and purpose, that (through the help of grace) we will not yield, not (in such cases) in the least actually obey them; yet humbly purposing (in the Lord's strength) patiently to suffer whatsoever shall be inflicted upon us, for our conscionable forebearance.

These things (O ye sons and daughters of men) we verily believe to be the Lord's will and mind, and therefore cannot but speak, and if herein we differ from many, yea from mul-titudes, from the learned, the wise, and prudent of this world we (with Peter and John) do herein make our solemn and serious appeal, namely, whether it be right in the sight of God to hearken unto men (of a contrary persuasion) more than unto God? Oh let the judicious judge righteous judgment (Acts 4:19-20).

And in the belief and practice of these things (it being the good old apostolical way), our souls have found that rest and soul peace which the world knows not and which they cannot take from us; of whom then should we be afraid? God is become our strength, our light, our salvation; therefore, we are resolved (through grace) to seal the truth of these things in way of suffering persecution, not only to the loss of our goods, freedoms, or liberties, but with our lives also (if called thereunto).

Moreover, we do utterly, and from our very hearts, in the Lord's fear, declare against all those wicked and devilish reports and reproaches falsely cast upon us, as though some of us (in and about the city of London) had lately gotten knives, hooked knives, and the like, and great store of arms besides what was given forth by order of Parliament, intending to cut the throats of such as were contrary minded to us in matters of religion, and that many such knives and arms, for the carrying on some secret design, hath been found in some of our houses by search; we say, from the truth of heart, in the Lord's fear, that we do utterly abhor and abominate thoughts thereof, and much more the actions; and do hereby challenge both city and country (in our innocency herein) as being not able to prove the things whereof they accuse us; and do for evermore declare the inventors of such reports to be liars and wicked devisers of mischief, and corrupt designs. God that is above all will justify our innocency herein, Who well knows our integrity in what we here declare, that the Lord lay it not to their charge.

In the time of building the decayed house of God, Sanballat and Tobiah (wicked counsellors) hired Shemaiah to make good Nehemiah afraid; and labored against him, that they might have matter for an evil report, that they might reproach him and hinder the building of the house of God (Nehemiah 6:12). For I have heard (saith the prophet) the defaming of many; report, say they, and we will report it (Jeremiah 20:10).

Subscribed by certain elders, deacons, and brethren met at London, in the first month (called March, 1660) in the behalf of themselves and many others unto whom they belong, in

London, and in several counties of this nation, who are of the same faith with us.

Joseph Wright	John Hammersly
William Jeffrey	William Russel
Thomas Monck	Joseph Keeich
John Hartnoll	Nicholas Newberry
Benjamine Morley	Samuel Lover
Francis Stanley	George Wright
George Hammon	John Parson, Jr.
William Smart	John Claton
John Reeve	Thomas Seele
Thomas Parrot	Michael Whiticar
John Wood	Giles Browne
Francis Smith	John Wells
Edward Jones	Stephen Torie
Humphrey Jones	Thomas Lathwel
Matthew Caffen	William Chadwell
Samuel Loveday	William Raph
John Parson, Sr.	Henry Browne
Thomas Stacy	William Paine
Edward Stanley	Richard Bowin
John Gennings	Thomas Smith

THE END

THE 1812 FORMER ARTICLES

The *1812 Former Articles* are a condensed and revised version of the *1660 English General Baptist Confession of Faith*. The Free Will Baptists of the early part of the 1800s saw the need for a revision of the confession of their English General Baptist forefathers to meet the needs of a nineteenth-century

American audience. This confession of faith was used by many Free Will Baptists in the South until well into the twentieth century.

AN ABSTRACT
of the
FORMER ARTICLES OF FAITH
Confessed by the Original
BAPTIST CHURCH
Holding the
Doctrine of General Provision.
With a Proper
CODE OF DISCIPLINE
For the Future Government of the
Church

Newbern
Printed by Salmon Hall
1813
Authorized 1812

PREFACE

Our last general conference met at a meeting house called A. Jones, on little Contentney, Green County, on the 5th of November 1812. The Conference then took into consideration, the general interest of the Gospel, and especially the interest of the Churches they were related unto, and did then represent, judging it expedient to examine and reprint the former confession of faith, put forth by the former Elders and Deacons: the Conference thought it proper likewise to annex a proper code of our discipline; and for the accomplishment of this design Elders James Roach and Jesse Heath were appointed; and they having recourse to all the former Articles of faith and rules of Discipline now extant. Some things stand without variation, and some things with variation and we therefore desire the reader may be pleased to take the pains to peruse the scripture, that the grounds of our faith and practice may be better understood, that this impartial account of our principles and practice may be accompanied with the blessing of God and be beneficial to men, is the hearty prayer of us, your well wishers and servants in the Lord.

James Roach
Jesse Heath

I. We believe that there is but one living, true and eternal God: the Father of whom are all things from everlasting to everlasting, glorious and immutable in all His attributes (1 Corinthians 8:6; Isaiah 11:28).

II. We believe that there is one Lord Jesus Christ, by whom are all things the only begotten Son of God, born of the virgin Mary, whom God freely sent into this world, because of the great love wherewith he loved the world, and Christ as freely gave himself a ransom for all, tasting death for every man; who was buried and rose again the third day and ascended into Heaven, from whence we look for him, the second time in the clouds of Heaven at the last day to judge both quick and dead (1 Timothy 2:5-8; Hebrews 2:9; 1 John 2:2; Revelation 1:7; Acts 24:15).

III. We believe that there is one Holy Ghost the precious gift of the Father, through his dear Son unto the world, who quickeneth and draws sinners home to God (John 26:7, 8; Acts 2:4; Ephesians 4:4-6).

IV. We believe that in the beginning God made man upright and placed him in a state of glory without the least mixture of misery from which he voluntarily by transgression fell, and by that means brought on himself, a miserable and mortal state subject to death (Genesis 2:17; 3:17-19).

V. We believe that God is not willing that any should perish, but that all should come to repentance and the knowledge of the truth, that they might be saved; for which end

Christ hath commanded the Gospel to be preached among all nations, and to every creature (Mark 16:15; Luke 24:47).

VI. We believe that no man shall suffer in hell, for want of a Christ that died for him, but as the scripture has said for denying the Lord that bought them; because they believe not in the name of the only begotten Son of God. Unbelief therefore being the cause why the just and righteous God of Heaven, will condemn the children of men, it follows against all contradiction, that all men at one time or another are found in such a capacity as that through the grace of God, they may be eternally saved. (2 Peter 2:1; 1 John 1:17; Acts 17:30; Mark 6:6; Hebrews 3:10; 1 John 5:10).

VII. We believe the whole Scriptures are infallibly true, and that they are the only ruler of faith and practice.

VIII. We believe in the doctrine of General Provision made of God in Christ, for the benefit of all mankind, who repent and believe the Gospel (Luke 14:16-24; Matthew 28:18-20).

IX. We believe that sinners are drawn to God the Father, by the Holy Ghost, through Christ His Son, and that the Holy Ghost offers His divine aid to all the human family, so as they might all be happy would they give place to His divine teaching; whereas such who do not receive the Divine impressions of the Holy Spirit, shall at a future day, own their condemnation just, and charge themselves with their own damnation, for wilfully rejecting the offers of sovereign grace (Matthew 11:27; John 6:44, 66; Psalm 1:1; Titus 2:11, 12; Jeremiah 22:29).

X. We believe that the Saints shall perservere in grace, and never finally fall away (John 10:27-29).[2]

XI. We believe that God hath before the foundation of the world, chosen or elected unto eternal life, such as believe in Christ; yet confident we are, that the purpose of God according to election was not in the least arising from any foreseen faith or righteousness done by the creature, but only by the mercy, goodness, and compassion, dwelling in God towards the creature, and so it is of him that calleth, Whose purity cannot admit of any unclean person or thing in His presence. Therefore his decree of mercy reaches only the Godly man; whom saith David, the Lord hath set apart for Himself (John 3:16; Romans 9; Psalm 4:3).

XII. We believe that men, not considered simply as men, but ungodly men were of old, ordained to condemnation, considered such who turn the grace of God into lasciviousness, denying the only Lord God, and our Lord Jesus Christ that bought them; and therefore shall bring upon themselves swift destruction: but we observe that they and such the Apostle saith, because they receive not the love of the truth, that they might be saved; therefore the indignation and wrath of God is upon every soul of man that doth evil, living and dying therein; for there is no respect of persons with God (Jude 1:4; 2 Peter 2:1; 2 Thessalonians 2:10-12; Romans 2:9).

XIII. We believe that all children, dying in infancy, having not actually transgressed against the law of God in their own person, are only subject to the first death which was brought on them by the fall of the first Adam, and not that any one of them dying in that state, shall suffer punishment in Hell by guilt of Adam's sin, for of such is the kingdom of God (1 Corinthians 15:22; Matthew 18:2-5; Mark 9:36, 37; Matthew 19:14).

XIV. We believe that good works are the fruits of a saving faith, and that in the use of the means of grace, and not out of the use of those means, eternal life is promised to men (Revelation 22:14, 15; Isaiah 1:19, 20; Matthew 7:7, 8; Jeremiah 6:16; Luke 12:34, 35).

XV. We believe that no man has any warrant in the holy scriptures for justification before God through his own works power or ability which he has in and of himself, only as he by Grace is made able to come to God, through Jesus Christ; believing the righteousness of Jesus Christ to be imputed to all believers for their eternal acceptance with God (Romans 4:24; Jeremiah 22:16).

XVI. We believe that all things are foreseen in the wisdom of God, so that God knoweth whatsoever can or cannot come to pass upon all supposed conditions, yet not as having decreed any person to everlasting death or everlasting life, out of respect or mere choice rather than he hath appointed the Godly unto life, and the ungodly who die in sin unto death (Hebrews 4:13; Proverbs 3:23-31; Matthew 25:31-46).

XVII. We believe as touching Gospel ordinances in believer's baptism, laying on of hands, receiving the sacrament in bread and wine, washing the saints' feet anointing the sick with oil in the name of the Lord, fasting, prayer, singing praises to God and the public ministry of the Word, with every institution of the Lord we shall find in the New Testament (Luke 22:19, 20; John 13:5-17; James 5:14).

XVIII. We believe the Gospel mode of baptism is by immersion, and that believers are the only subjects for baptism (Matthew 3:8, 16; Mark 1:5, 10; Acts 8:38, 39; Romans 6:4; Hebrews 10:22).

XIX. We believe in a general resurrection of the dead and final judgment at the last day (John 5:28, 29; 2 Corinthians 5:10).

XX. We believe the happiness of the righteous is eternal and the torment of the wicked is endless (Matthew 25:46).

NOTES FOR CHAPTER FOUR

[1] Anglican priests, ministers of the Church of England.

[2] This article, which seems to teach eternal security, was deleted in the 1830s. For more information on this article, see the section entitled "America's First Free Will Baptists" in chapter one.

CHAPTER FIVE

Our Treatise

A TREATISE
of the
Faith and Practices
of the
National Association of
Free Will Baptists, Inc.

Adopted by the National Association
November 7, 1935, at Nashville, Tennessee

Revised 1948, 1956, 1958, 1969, 1973,
1974, 1977, 1979, 1981, 1992 and 1996

Published by the Executive Office
of the National Association
of Free Will Baptists, Inc.

PREFACE

The Free Will Baptist denomination is a fellowship of evangelical believers united in extending the witness of Christ and the building of His Church throughout the world. The rise of Free Will Baptists can be traced to the influence of Baptists of Arminian persuasion who settled in the colonies from England.

The denomination sprang up on two fronts at almost the same time. The southern line, or Palmer movement, traces its beginnings to the year 1727 when one Paul Palmer organized a church at Chowan, North Carolina. Palmer had previously ministered in New Jersey and Maryland, having been baptized in a congregation which had moved from Wales to a tract on the Delaware River in northern Pennsylvania.

The northern line, or Randall movement, had its beginnings with a congregation organized by Benjamin Randall June 30, 1780, in New Durham, New Hampshire. Both lines of Free Will Baptists taught the doctrines of free grace, free salvation, and free will, although from the first there was no organizational connection between them.

The northern line expanded more rapidly in the beginning and extended its outreach into the West and Southwest. In 1910-1911 this body of Free Will Baptists merged with the Northern Baptist denomination, taking along more than half its 1,100 churches and all denominational property, including several major colleges. On December 28, 1916, at Pattonsburg, Missouri, representatives of remnant churches in the Randall movement reorganized into the Cooperative General Association of Free Will Baptists.

Free Will Baptists in the southeastern United States, having descended from the Palmer foundation, had often manifested fraternal relationships with Free Will Baptists of the Randall movement in the north and west; but the slavery question and the Civil War prevented formal union between them. The churches in the southern line were organized into various associations and conferences from the beginning, and had finally organized into a General Conference by 1921. These congregations were not affected by the merger of the northern movement with the Northern Baptists.

Now that the remnants of the Randall movement had reorganized into the Cooperative General Association and the Palmer movement had organized into the General Conference, it was inevitable that fusion between these two groups of Free Will Baptists would finally come. In Nashville, Tennessee, on November 5, 1935, representatives of these two groups met and organized the National Association of Free Will Baptists.

This body adopted a treatise which set forth the basic doctrines and described the faith and practice that had characterized Free Will Baptists through the years. Having been revised on several occasions, it serves as a guideline for a denominational fellowship which comprises more than 2,400 churches in 42 states and 14 foreign countries.

The National Offices are located at 5233 Mt. View Road, Antioch, Tennessee 37013-2306. National departments operating here include the Executive Office, Foreign Missions, Home Missions, Retirement and Insurance, Free Will Baptist Foundation, Master's Men and Women Nationally Active For Christ. The mailing address is P.O. Box 5002, Antioch, Tennessee 37011-5002. Free Will Baptist Bible College is located at 3606 West End Avenue, P.O. Box 50117, Nashville, Tennessee 37205. The Sunday School and Church Training Department is located at 114 Bush Road, P.O. Box 17306, Nashville, Tennessee 37217.

PART I
CHURCH COVENANT

Having given ourselves to God, by faith in Christ, and adopted the Word of God as our rule of faith and practice, we now give ourselves to one another by the will of God in this solemn covenant.

We promise, by His grace, to love and obey Him in all things, to avoid all appearance of evil, to abstain from all sinful amusements and unholy conformity to the world, from all sanction of the use and sale of intoxicating beverages, and to "provide things honest in the sight of all men."

We agree faithfully to discharge our obligations in reference to the study of the Scriptures, secret prayer, family devotions, and social worship; and by self-denial, faith, and good works endeavor to "grow in grace and the knowledge of our Lord and Saviour Jesus Christ."

We will not forsake the assembling of ourselves together for church conferences, public worship, and the observance of the ordinances of the Gospel; nor fail to pay according to our ability for the support of the church, of its poor, and all its benevolent work.

We agree to accept Christian admonition and reproof with meekness, and to watch over one another in love, endeavoring to "keep the unity of the Spirit" in the bonds of peace, to be careful of one another's happiness and reputation, and seek to strengthen the weak, encourage the afflicted, admonish the erring, and as far as we are able, promote the success of the church and of the Gospel.

We will everywhere hold Christian principle sacred and Christian obligations and enterprises supreme; counting it our chief business in life to extend the influence of Christ in society, constantly praying and toiling that the kingdom of God may come, and His will be done on earth as it is in heaven.

To this end we agree to labor for the promotion of educational and denominational enterprises, the support of missions, the success of Sunday schools, and evangelistic efforts for the salvation of the world. And may the God of peace sanctify us wholly, and preserve us blameless unto the coming of our Lord Jesus Christ.

PART II
THE FAITH OF FREE WILL BAPTISTS

Chapter I: The Holy Scriptures

These are the Old and the New Testaments; they were written by holy men, inspired by the Holy Spirit,[1] and are God's revealed word to man. They are a sufficient and infallible rule and guide to salvation and all Christian worship and service.[2]

Since the Bible is the Word of God, it is without error in all matters upon which it speaks, whether history, geography, matters relating to science or any other subject.[3]

Chapter II: Being and Attributes of God

The Scriptures teach that there is only one true and living God,[4] who is Spirit,[5] self-existent,[6] eternal,[7] immutable,[8] omnipresent,[9] omniscient,[10] omnipotent,[11] independent,[12] good,[13] wise,[14] holy,[15] just,[16] and merciful,[17] the...Creator,[18] Preserver,[19] and Governor[20] of the Universe; the Redeemer,[21] Saviour,[22] Sanctifier,[23] and Judge[24] of men; and the only proper object of worship.[25]

The mode of His existence, however, is a subject far above the understanding of man[26]–finite beings cannot comprehend Him.[27] There is nothing in the universe that can justly represent Him, for there is none like Him.[28] He is the fountain of all perfection and happiness. He is glorified by the whole creation, and is worthy to be loved and served by all intelligence.[29]

Chapter III: Divine Government and Providence

1. God exercises a providential care and superintendence over all His creatures,[30] and governs the world in wisdom and mercy, according to the testimony of His Word.[31]

2. God has endowed man with power of free choice, and governs him by moral laws and motives; and this power of free choice is the exact measure of man's responsibility.[32]

3. All events are present with God from everlasting to everlasting; but His knowledge of them does not in any sense cause them, nor does He decree all events which He knows will occur.[33]

Chapter IV: Creation, Primitive State of Man, and His Fall

Section I: Creation

1. *Of the World.* God created the world, and all things that it contains, for His own pleasure and glory and the enjoyment of His creatures.[34]

2. *Of the Angels.* The angels were created by God[35] to glorify Him[36] and obey His commandments.[37] Those who have kept their first estate He employs in ministering blessings to the heirs of salvation[38] and in executing His judgments upon the world.[39]

3. *Of Man.* God created man, consisting of a material body and a thinking, rational soul.[40] He was made in the image of God, to glorify his Maker.[41]

Section II: Primitive Man, and His Fall

Our first parents, in their original state, were upright. They naturally preferred and desired to obey their Creator, and had no preference or desire to transgress His will[42] until they were influenced and inclined by the tempter to disobey God's commands. Previous to this, the only tendency of their nature was to do righteousness. In consequence of the first transgression, the state under which the posterity of Adam came into the world is so different from that of Adam that they have not that righteousness and purity which Adam had before the fall; they are not willing to obey God, but are inclined to evil.[43] Hence, none, by virtue of any natural goodness and mere work of their own, can become the children of God,[44] but they are all dependent for salvation upon the redemption effected through the blood of Christ, and upon being created anew unto obedience through the operation of the Spirit;[45] both of which are freely provided for every descendant of Adam.[46]

Chapter V: Of Christ

Section I: His Divinity

Jesus Christ, the Son of God, possesses all divine perfections. As He and the Father are one, He in His divine nature, filled all the offices and performed the works of God to His creatures that have been the subjects of revelation to us. As man, He performed all the duties toward God that we are required to perform, repentance of sin excepted.

His divinity is proved from His titles, His attributes, and His works.

1. *His Titles.* The Bible ascribes to Christ the titles of Saviour,[47] Jehovah,[48] Lord of hosts,[49] the first and the last,[50] God,[51] true God,[52] great God,[53] God over all,[54] mighty God, and the everlasting Father.[55]

2. *His Attributes.* He is eternal,[56] unchangeable,[57] omnipresent,[58] omniscient,[59] omnipotent,[60] holy,[61] and to be worshiped.[62]

3. *His Works.* By Christ the world was created.[63] He preserves[64] and governs[65] it; He has provided redemption for all men[66] and He will be their final Judge.[67]

Section II: The Incarnation of Christ

The Word, which in the beginning was with God and which was God, by whom all things were made, condescended to a state of humiliation in being united with human nature and becoming like us, pollution and sin excepted.[68] In this state, as a subject of the law, He was liable to the infirmities of our nature,[69] was tempted as we are,[70] but lived our example,[71] perfect obedience to the divine requirements.[72] As Christ was made of the seed of David, according to the flesh, He is "the Son of man,"[73] and as the divine existence is the fountain from which He proceeded, and was the only agency by which He was begotten,[74] He is "the Son of God,"[75] being the only begotten of the Father,[76] and the only incarnation of the Divine Being.

Chapter VI: The Atonement and Mediation of Christ

1. *The Atonement.* As sin cannot be pardoned without a sacrifice, and the blood of beasts could never wash away sin, Christ gave Himself a sacrifice for the sins of the world,[77] and thus made salvation possible for all men.[78] He died for us, suffering in our stead, to make known the righteousness of God, that He might be just in justifying sinners who believe in His Son.[79] Through the redemption effected by Christ, salvation is actually enjoyed in this world, and will be enjoyed in the next by all who do not in this life refuse obedience to the known requirements of God.[80] The atonement for sin was necessary.[81] For present and future obedience can no more blot out our past sins than past obedience can remove the guilt of present and future sins. If God pardoned the sins of men without satisfaction for the violation of His law, it would follow that transgression might go on with impunity; government would be abrogated, and the obligation of obedience to God would be, in effect, removed.

2. *Mediation of Christ.* Our Lord not only died for our sins, but He arose for our justification,82 and ascended up to heaven,[83] where, as the only mediator between God and man, He makes intercession for us until He comes again.[84]

3. We believe that all children dying in infancy, having not actually transgressed against the law of God in their own persons, are only subject to the first death, which was brought on by the fall of the first Adam, and not that any one of them dying in that state shall suffer punishment in hell by the guilt of Adam's sin for of such is the Kingdom of God.[85]

Chapter VII: The Holy Spirit

1. The Scriptures ascribe to the Holy Spirit the acts and attributes of an intelligent being. He guides,[86] knows,[87] moves,[88] gives information,[89] commands,[90] forbids[91] sends forth,[92] reproves,[93] and can be sinned against.[94]

2. The attributes of God are ascribed to the Holy Spirit.

3. The works of God are ascribed to the Holy Spirit: creation,[95] inspiration,[96] giving of life,[97] and sanctification.[98]

4. The apostles assert that the Holy Spirit is Lord and God.[99]

From the foregoing the conclusion is that the Holy Spirit is in reality God and one with the Father in all divine perfections. It has also been shown that Jesus Christ is God—one with the Father. Then these three—the Father, Son, and Holy Spirit—are one God.

The truth of this doctrine is also proved from the fact that the Father, the Son, and the Holy Ghost are united in the authority by which believers are baptized; and in the benedictions pronounced by the apostles,[100] which are acts of the highest religious worship.[101]

Chapter VIII: The Gospel Call

The call of the Gospel is co-extensive with the atonement to all men,[102] both by the word and strivings of the Spirit,[103] so that salvation is rendered equally possible to all;[104] and if any fail of eternal life, the fault is wholly his own.[105]

Chapter IX: Repentance

The repentance which the Gospel requires includes a deep conviction, a penitential sorrow, an open confession, a decided hatred, and an entire forsaking of all sin.[106] This repentance God has enjoined on all men; and without it in this life the sinner must perish eternally.[107]

Chapter X: Faith

Saving faith is an assent of the mind to the fundamental truths of revelation,[108] an acceptance of the Gospel, through the influence of the Holy Spirit,[109] and a firm confidence and trust in Christ.[110] The fruit of faith is obedience to the Gospel.[111] The power to believe is the gift of God,[112] but believing is an act of the creature, which is required as a condition of pardon, and without which the sinner cannot obtain salvation.[113] All men are required to believe in Christ, and those who yield obedience to this requirement become the children of God by faith.[114]

Chapter XI: Regeneration

As man is a fallen and sinful being, he must be regenerated in order to obtain salvation.[115] This change is an instantaneous renewal of the heart by the Holy Spirit,[116] whereby the penitent sinner receives new life, becomes a child of God,[117] and is disposed to serve Him.[118] This is called in Scripture being born again,[119] born of the Spirit,[120] being quickened,[121] passing from death unto life,[122] and a partaking of the divine nature.[123]

Chapter XII: Justification and Sanctification

1. *Justification.* Personal justification implies that the person justified has been guilty before God; and, in consideration of the atonement of Christ, accepted by faith, the sinner is pardoned and absolved from the guilt of sin, and restored to the divine favor.[124] Christ's atonement is the foundation of the sinner's redemption, yet, without repentance and faith, it can never give him justification and peace with God.[125]

2. *Sanctification* is the continuing of God's grace by which the Christian may constantly grow in grace and in the knowledge of our Lord Jesus Christ.[126]

Chapter XIII: Perseverance of the Saints

There are strong grounds to hope that the truly regenerate will persevere unto the end, and be saved, through the power of divine grace which is pledged for their support;[127] but their future obedience and final salvation are neither determined nor certain, since through infirmity and manifold temptations they are in danger of falling;[128] and they ought, therefore, to watch and pray lest they make shipwreck of their faith and be lost.[129]

Chapter XIV: The Lord's Day

This is one day in seven, which from the creation of the world God has set apart for sacred rest and holy service.[130] Under the former dispensation, the seventh day of the week, as commemorative of the work of creation, was set apart for the Lord's Day.[131] Under the Gospel, the first day of the week, in commemoration of the resurrection of Christ, and by authority of Christ and the apostles, is observed as the Christian Sabbath.[132] On this day all men are required to refrain from secular labor and devote themselves to the worship and service of God.[133]

Chapter XV: The Church

A Christian Church is an organized body of believers in Christ who statedly assemble to worship God, and who sustain the ordinances of the Gospel according to the Scriptures.[134] Believers in Christ are admitted to this church on giving evidence of faith in Christ, obtaining consent of the body, being baptized, and receiving the right hand of fellowship.[135]

The Church of God, or members of the body of Christ, is the whole body of Christians throughout the whole world, and none but the regenerate are its members.[136]

Chapter XVI: Tithing

Both the Old[137] and New Scriptures[138] teach tithing as God's financial plan for the support of His work.

Chapter XVII: The Gospel Ministry

1. *Qualification of Ministers.* They must possess good, natural and acquired abilities,[139] deep and ardent piety,[140] be especially called of God to the work,[141] and ordained by prayer and the laying on of hands.[142]

2. *Duties of Ministers.* These are to preach the Word,[143] administer the ordinances of the Gospel,[144] visit their people, and otherwise perform the work of faithful ministers.[145]

Chapter XVIII: Ordinances of the Gospel

1. *Christian Baptism.* This is the immersion of believers in water, in the name of the Father, the Son, and the Holy Spirit,[146] in which are represented the burial and resurrection of Christ, the death of Christians to the world, the washing of their souls from the pollution of sin, their rising to newness of life, their engagement to serve God, and their resurrection at the last day.[147]

2. *The Lord's Supper.* This is a commemoration of the death of Christ for our sins in the use of bread which He made the emblem of His broken body, and the cup, the emblem of His shed blood,[148] and by it the believer expresses his love for Christ, his faith and hope in Him, and pledges to Him perpetual fidelity.[149]

It is the privilege and duty of all who have spiritual union with Christ to commemorate His death, and no man has a right to forbid these tokens to the least of His disciples.[150]

3. *Washing the Saints' Feet.* This is a sacred ordinance, which teaches humility and reminds the believer of the necessity of a daily cleansing from all sin. It was instituted by the Lord Jesus Christ, and called an "example" on the night of His betrayal, and in connection with the institution of the Lord's Supper. It is the duty and happy prerogative of every believer to observe this sacred ordinance.[151]

Chapter XIX: Death

As a result of sin, all mankind is subject to the death of the body.[152] The soul does not die with the body, but immediately after death enters into a conscious state of happiness or misery, according to the character here possessed.[153]

Chapter XX: Second Coming of Christ

The Lord Jesus, who ascended on high and sits at the right hand of God, will come again to close the Gospel dispensation, glorify His saints, and judge the world.[154]

Chapter XXI: The Resurrection

The Scriptures teach the resurrection of the bodies of all men, each in its own order; they that have done good will come forth to the resurrection of life, and they that have done evil to the resurrection of damnation.[155]

Chapter XXII: The Judgment and Retribution

1. The Judgment. There will be a judgment, when time and man's probation will close forever.[156] Then all men will be judged according to their works.[157]

2. Retribution. Immediately after the judgment, the righteous will enter into eternal life, and the wicked will go into a state of endless punishment.[158]

APPENDIX TO CHAPTER XIII

Adopted July 1969

1. We believe that salvation is a present possession by faith in the Lord Jesus Christ as Savior and that a person's eternal destiny depends on whether he has this possession. This we hold in distinction from those who teach that salvation depends on human works or merit.

2. We believe that a saved individual may, in freedom of will, cease to trust in Christ for salvation and once again be lost. This we hold in distinction from those who teach that a believer may not again be lost.

3. We believe that any individual living in the practice of sin (whether he be called "backslider" or "sinner") must be judged by that evidence to be lost should he so die in his sins. This we hold in distinction from those who suggest that pernicious doctrine that a man may live in sin as he pleases and still claim Heaven as his eternal home.

4. We believe that any regenerate person who has sinned (again, whether he be called "backslider" or "sinner") and in

whose heart a desire arises to repent may do so and be restored to favor and fellowship with God. This we hold in distinction from those who teach that when a Christian sins he cannot repent and be restored to favor and fellowship with God.[159]

APPENDIX TO CHAPTER I

Adopted July 1979

Free Will Baptists believe in the plenary, verbal inspiration of the Bible. By plenary we mean "full and complete." We hold that all parts of the Bible are inspired and that inspiration extends to all its subjects.[160] By verbal we mean that inspiration extends to the very words of the Scriptures, not just to the thoughts and ideas expressed by human authors.[161]

We believe the Scriptures are infallible and inerrant.[162] The Bible is without error and trustworthy in all its teachings, including cosmogony, geology, astronomy, anthropology, history, chronology, etc., as well as in matters of faith and practice. Being the very Word of God, it is God's final revelation and our absolute authority.[163]

APPENDIX TO CHAPTER VII

Adopted July 1979

Free Will Baptists understand the Bible teaches the following facts: On the Day of Pentecost believers spoke in distinct foreign languages which were readily understood by the nationalities present.[164]

Tongues were given as a special gift to the early church as only one sign which confirms the witness of the Gospel to unbelievers.[165]

While tongues were bestowed by the sovereign will of God on some believers, all did not speak with tongues.[166] When this gift was abused, it became a source of disturbance in the congregational meetings. To eliminate confusion and correct the error, Paul set particular guidelines for the Christian church to follow.[167] The gift of tongues was neither an evidence of the baptism of the Holy Spirit, nor does it bring about sanctification.[168]

We believe that speaking in tongues as a visible sign of the baptism of the Holy Spirit is an erroneous doctrine to be rejected. Any implication of a "second work of grace" has never been tolerated in our fellowship of churches, and will not be permitted.

We teach and preach the fullness of the Holy Spirit and heed the scriptural admonition, "Be filled with the Spirit; Speaking to yourselves in psalms and hymns and spiritual songs, singing and making melody in your heart to the Lord; Giving thanks always for all things unto God and the Father in the name of our Lord Jesus Christ."[169]

NOTES

[1]2 Peter 1:18-21: And this voice which came from heaven we heard, when we were with him in the holy mount. We have also a more sure word of prophecy; whereunto ye do well that ye take heed, as unto a light that shineth in a dark place, until the day dawn, and the day star arise in your hearts: Knowing this first, that no prophecy of the scripture is of any private interpretation. For the prophecy came not in old time by the will of man: but holy men of God spake as they were moved by the Holy Ghost.

2 Timothy 3:16, 17: All scripture is given by inspiration of God, and is profitable for doctrine, for reproof, for correction, for instruction in righteousness: That the man of God may be perfect, throughly furnished unto all good works.

[2]Exodus 4:15: And thou shalt speak unto him, and put words in his mouth: and I will be with thy mouth, and with his mouth, and will teach you what ye shall do.

Psalm 32:8: I will instruct thee and teach thee in the way which thou shalt go: I will guide thee with mine eye.

Hebrews 1:1, 2: God, who at sundry times and in divers manners spake in time past unto the fathers by the prophets, Hath in these last days spoken unto us by his Son, whom he hath appointed heir of all things, by whom also he made the worlds.

[NOTE: The last sentence in Chapter 1, which was added in July 1979, does not represent any change or modification of thought in the doctrine of the Holy Scriptures as it has been historically believed by Free Will Baptists. In view of the fact that some in the theological world have claimed to believe that the Bible is an infallible rule of faith and practice, while at the same time professing to believe that the Bible contains errors which were a part of the original manuscripts, this statement was added to make the position already held by Free Will Baptists unmistakably clear.]

[3]See APPENDIX TO CHAPTER I.

[4]Deuteronomy 6:4: The LORD our God is one LORD. 1 Corinthians 8:4: There is none other God but one. Jeremiah 10:10: But the LORD is the true God, he is the living God. John 7:28; 2 Corinthians 1:19; 1 John 5:20; 1 Timothy 6:17.

[5]John 4:24: God is a Spirit. 2 Corinthians 3:17.

[6]Exodus 3:14: And God said unto Moses, I AM THAT I AM. Psalm 83:18; John 5:26; Revelation 1:4.

[7]Psalm 90:2: From everlasting to everlasting, thou art God. Deuteronomy 33:27; Isaiah 57:15; Romans 1:20; 1 Timothy 1:17.

[8]Malachi 3:6: For I am the LORD, I change not. Numbers 23:19; James 1:17.

[9]1 King 8:27: But will God indeed dwell on the earth? behold, the heaven and heaven of heavens cannot contain thee. Jeremiah 23:24; Psalm 139:7-10; Isaiah 57:15; Acts 17:24.

[10]Acts 15:18: Known unto God are all his works from the beginning of the world. 1 Chronicles 28:9; Psalm 94:9, 10; Acts 1:24.

[11]Revelation 19:6: The Lord God omnipotent reigneth. Job 42:2; Psalm 135:6; Matthew 19:26; Mark 14:36; Luke 18:27.

[12]Ephesians 4:6: One God and Father of all, who is above all. Job 9:12; Isaiah 14:13, 14; Daniel 4:35; Romans 11:33-36.

[13]Psalm 119:68: Thou art good, and doest good. Psalms 25:8; 106:1; 145:9; Matthew 19:17.

[14]Romans 16:27: To God only wise, be glory through Jesus Christ for ever. Daniel 2:20; 1 Timothy 1:17; Jude 25.

[15]Leviticus 19:2: I the LORD your God am holy. Job 6:10.

[16]Deuteronomy 32:4: Just and right is he. Psalms 92:15; 119:137; Zephaniah 3:5.

[17]Ephesians 2:4: God, who is rich in mercy. Exodus 34:6; Nehemiah 9:17; Psalm 100:5.

[18]Genesis 1:1: In the beginning God created the heaven and the earth. Exodus 20:11; Psalm 33:6-9; Colossians 1:16; Hebrews 11:3.

[19]Nehemiah 9:6: Thou preservest them all. Job 7:20; Colossians 1:17; Hebrews 1:3.

[20]Psalm 47:7: God is the King of all the earth. 2 Chronicles 20:6; Psalm 95:3.

[21]Isaiah 47:4: As for our redeemer, the LORD of hosts is his name. Psalm 78:35; Proverbs 23:11; Isaiah 41:14; 59:20; Jeremiah 50:34.

[22]Isaiah 45:21: A just God and a Saviour. Isaiah 43:3-11; 49:26.

[23]Exodus 31:13: I am the LORD that doth sanctify you. 1 Thessalonians 5:23; Jude 1.

[24]Hebrews 12:23: God the Judge of all. Genesis 18:25; Psalm 50:6; 2 Timothy 4:8.

[25]Exodus 34:14: Thou shalt worship no other god. Exodus 20:4, 5; Matthew 4:10; Revelation 19:10.

[26]Job 11:7: Canst thou by searching find out God? Isaiah 40:28.

[27]Romans 11:33: How unsearchable are his judgments, and his ways past finding out! Job 26:14.

[28]Exodus 9:14: There is none like me in all the earth. Exodus 8:10; 1 Chronicles 17:20.

[29]Psalm 19:1, 2: The heavens declare the glory of God; and the firmament sheweth his handywork. Day unto day uttereth speech, and night unto night sheweth knowledge. Psalms 145:10: All thy works shall praise thee. Psalm 150:6: Let every thing that hath breath praise the LORD.

[30]Acts 17:28: In him we live, and move, and have our being. Matthew 10:30: The very hairs of your head are all numbered. Psalm 104:13, 14; Job 14:5; Ephesians 1:11.

[31]Psalm 22:28: For the kingdom is the LORD's: and he is the governor among the nations. Psalm 97:2: Righteousness and judgment are the habitation of his throne. Isaiah 33:22; Exodus 34:6; Job 36:5.

[32]Deuteronomy 30:19: I have set before you life and death, blessing and cursing: therefore choose life, that both thou and thy seed may live. Isaiah 1:18-20; John 5:40; Romans 2:14, 15; Proverbs 1:24-28.

[33]Ezekiel 33:11: As I live, saith the Lord GOD, I have no pleasure in the death of the wicked; but that the wicked turn from his way and live. Acts 15:18; 1 Samuel 2:30; Ezekiel 18:20-25, 31; Jeremiah 44:4.

[34]Revelation 4:11: Thou hast created all things, and for thy pleasure they are and were created. Isaiah 43:7; 1 Timothy 6:17: The living God, who giveth us richly all things to enjoy.

[35]Colossians 1:16: For by him were all things created, that are in heaven, and that are in earth, visible and invisible.

[36]Revelation 7:11: And all the angels stood round about...and fell before the throne on their faces, and worshiped God.

[37]Psalm 103:20: Bless the LORD, ye his angels,...that do his commandments.

[38]Hebrews 1:14: Are they not all ministering spirits, sent forth to minister for them who shall be heirs of salvation? Jude 6.

[39]2 Samuel 24:16: The angel stretched out his hand upon Jerusalem to destroy it. Revelation 16:1.

[40]Genesis 2:7: And the LORD God formed man of the dust of the ground, and breathed into his nostrils the breath of life; and man became a living soul.

[41]Genesis 1:27: So God created man in his own image, in the image of God created he him. 1 Corinthians 6:20.

[42]Ecclesiastes 7:29: God hath made man upright. Ephesians 4:24; Colossians 3:10.

[43]Psalm 51:5: Behold, I was shapen in iniquity; and in sin did my mother conceive me. Romans 8:7: The carnal mind is enmity against God. Ephesians 2:3: And were by nature the children of wrath, even as others. Psalms 58:3; Genesis 8:21; John 3:6; Galatians 5:19-21; Romans 5:12.

[44]John 6:44: No man can come to me, except the Father which hath sent me draw him. 1 Corinthians 2:14: The natural man receiveth not the things of the Spirit of God: for they are foolishness unto him: neither can he know them.

[45]John 3:3: Except a man be born again, he cannot see the kingdom of God. John 3:5; 1:13; Hebrews 12:14: And holiness, without which no man shall see the Lord. Colossians 1:14; Titus 3:5.

[46]See "ATONEMENT," CHAPTER VI

[47]Isaiah 45:21: There is no God else beside me; a just God and a Saviour; there is none beside me. Isaiah 43:10, 11: Beside me there is no Saviour. John 4:42: This is indeed the Christ, the Saviour of the world. Philippians 3:20; 2 Timothy 1:10; Titus 2:13.

[48]Psalm 83:18: Whose name alone is JEHOVAH. Isaiah 40:3: The voice of him that crieth in the wilderness, Prepare ye the way of the LORD (Jehovah). Luke 1:76.

[49]Isaiah 8:13, 14: Sanctify the LORD of hosts himself; and let him be your fear, and let him be your dread. And he shall be for a sanctuary; but for a stone of stumbling and for a rock of offence to both the houses of Israel. 1 Peter 2:4-6; Isaiah 6:5; John 12:41.

[50]Revelation 22:13: I am Alpha and Omega, the beginning and the end, the first and the last. Isaiah 44:6; Revelation 1:1, 11.

[51]1 Timothy 3:16: God was manifest in the flesh. 1 John 3:16; John 1:1; Hebrews 1:8; John 20:28, 29.

[52]1 John 5:20: We are in him that is true, even in his Son Jesus Christ. This is the true God, and eternal life.

[53]Titus 2:13: Looking for that blessed hope, and the glorious appearing of the great God and our Saviour Jesus Christ.

[54]Romans 9:5: Of whom as concerning the flesh Christ came, who is over all, God blessed for ever.

[55]Isaiah 9:6: For unto us a child is born, unto us a son is given: and the government shall be upon his shoulder: and his name shall be called Wonderful, Counselor, The mighty God, The everlasting Father, The Prince of Peace.

[56]Colossians 1:17: And he is before all things. Micah 5:2; Hebrews 1:8.

[57]Hebrews 13:8: Jesus Christ the same yesterday, and to day, and for ever. Hebrews 1:12.

[58]John 3:13: No man hath ascended up to heaven, but he that came down from heaven, even the Son of man which is in heaven. Matthew 18:20; 28:20; Ephesians 1:23.

[59]John 16:30: That thou knowest all things. John 2:24, 25; 21:17; Revelation 2:23.

[60]Colossians 2:8-10: Christ...is the head of all principality and power. Matthew 28:18; Hebrews 1:8; Revelation 1:8.

[61]Acts 3:14: But ye denied the Holy One. Luke 1:35; Hebrews 7:26; Revelation 3:7.

[62]Hebrews 1:6: Let all the angels of God worship him. John 5:23: That all men should honour the Son, even as they honour the Father. Philippians 2:10, 11; Matthew 28:9; Luke 24:52.

[63]Hebrews 1:8, 10: Unto the Son he saith...Thou, Lord, in the beginning hast laid the foundation of the earth; and the heavens are the works of thine hands. John 1:3, 10: All things were made by him. The world was made by him. Colossians 1:16.

[64]Hebrews 1:3: Upholding all things by the word of his power. Colossians 1:17.

[65]Isaiah 9:6: The government shall be upon his shoulder. 1 Peter 3:22; Ephesians 1:21.

[66]Ephesians 1:7: In whom we have redemption through his blood, the forgiveness of sins. Hebrews 9:12; Galatians 3:13; Isaiah 44:6; 1 Peter 1:18; Revelation 5:9.

[67]2 Timothy 4:1: The Lord Jesus Christ, who shall judge the quick and the dead. Matthew 25:31-46; John 5:22.

[68]John 1:14: And the Word was made flesh, and dwelt among us. Philippians 2:6, 7: Who, being in the form of God, thought it not robbery to be equal with God: But made himself of no reputation, and took upon him the form of a servant, and was made in the likeness of men. 2 Corinthians 8:9; Hebrews 4:15.

[69]Hebrews 2:17: Wherefore in all things it behoved him to be made like unto his brethren. Matthew 8:17; 4:2; 8:24; John 11:33, 35; 19:28; Isaiah 53:3; Luke 22:44.

[70]Hebrews 4:15: Was in all points tempted like as we are. Matthew 4:1-11.

[71]1 Peter 2:21: Leaving us an example, that ye should follow his steps. John 13:15; 1 John 2:6.

[72]Isaiah 42:21: He will magnify the law, and make it honourable. Matthew 5:17; 3:15; Galatians 4:4.

[73]Luke 19:10: For the Son of man is come to seek and to save that which was lost.

[74]John 16:27: I came out from God. Matthew 1:18, 20.

[75]Luke 1:35: That holy thing which shall be born of thee shall be called the ~f God. Mark 1:1; John 1:34; 20:31.

[76]John 3:16: God so loved the world, that he gave his only begotten Son. John 1:18.

[77]1 John 2:2: And he is the propitiation for our sins: and not for ours only, but also for the sins of the whole world. Isaiah 53:5; 10:11; Romans 4:25; Matthew 20:28; 1 Peter 3:18; John 1:29; Hebrews 9:26; Romans 5:6, 8.

[78]Titus 2:11: For the grace of God that bringeth salvation hath appeared to all men. Hebrews 2:9: That he by the grace of God should taste death for every man. 1 Timothy 2:6; Isaiah 45:22; 2 Peter 3:9; 2 Corinthians 4:14, 15; 1 Timothy 4:10.

[79]Romans 3:25, 26: Whom God hath set forth to be a propitiation through faith in his blood, to declare his righteousness for the remission of sins that are past, through the forbearance of God; To declare, I say, at this time his righteousness: that he might be just, and the justifier of him which believeth in Jesus. Romans 5:9, 18; Matthew 26:28; Ephesians 1:7; Revelation 5:9; 1 Peter 2:24.

[80]Romans 5:18: Therefore as by the offence of one judgment came upon all men to condemnation; even so by the righteousness of one the free gift came upon all men unto justification of life. Romans 8:1: There is therefore now no condemnation to them which are in Christ Jesus, who walk not after the flesh, but after the Spirit. Mark 16:15; Romans 2:14,15.

[81]Hebrews 9:22: Without shedding of blood is no remission. Ephesians 1:7: In whom we have redemption through his blood, the forgiveness of sins.

[82]Romans 4:25: Who was delivered for our offences, and was raised again for our justification. 1 Corinthians 15:17.

[83]Acts 1:11: This same Jesus, which is taken up from you into heaven. Mark 16:19.

[84]Hebrews 7:25: He ever liveth to make intercession for them. Romans 8:34; Hebrews 9:24.

[85]1 Corinthians 15:22: For as in Adam all die, even so in Christ shall all be made alive.

Matthew 18:2-5: And Jesus called a little child unto him, and set him in the midst of them, And said, Verily I say unto you, Except ye be converted, and become as little children, ye shall not enter into the kingdom of heaven. Whosoever therefore shall humble himself as this little child, the same is greatest in the kingdom of heaven. And whoso shall receive one such little child in my name receiveth me.

Mark 9:36, 37: And he took a child, and set him in the midst of them: and when he had taken him in his arms, he said unto them, Whosoever shall receive one of such children in my name, receiveth me: and whosoever shall receive me, receiveth not me, but him that sent me.

Matthew 19:14: But Jesus said, Suffer little children, and forbid them not, to come unto me: for of such is the kingdom of heaven.

[86]John 16:13: Howbeit when he, the Spirit of truth, is come, he will guide you into all truth.

[87]1 Corinthians 2:11: Even so the things of God knoweth no man, but the Spirit of God.

[88]Genesis 1:2: And the Spirit of God moved upon the face of the waters. Acts 8:39.

[89]Acts 10:19: While Peter thought on the vision, the Spirit said unto him, Behold, three men seek thee. 1 Corinthians 2:13; Acts 21:11; John 14:26.

[90]Acts 13:2: The Holy Ghost said, Separate me Barnabas and Saul for the work whereunto I have called them.

[91]Acts 16:6: And were forbidden of the Holy Ghost to preach the word in Asia.

[92]Acts 13:4: So they, being sent forth by the Holy Ghost, departed unto Seleucia.

[93]John 16:8: And when he is come, he will reprove the world of sin, and of righteousness, and of judgment. Genesis 6:3.

[94]Mark 3:29: But he that shall blaspheme against the Holy Ghost hath never forgiveness. Isaiah 63:10, Acts 7:51; Ephesians 4:30.

[95]Job 33:4: The Spirit of God hath made me. Job 26:13; Psalms 104:30.

[96]2 Peter 1:21: Prophecy came not in old time by the will of man: but holy men of God spake as they were moved by the Holy Ghost.

[97]1 Peter 3:18: Quickened by the Spirit. Romans 8:11.

[98]1 Corinthians 6:11: But ye are sanctified, but ye are justified in the name of the Lord Jesus, and by the Spirit of our God.

[99]Isaiah 6:8, 9: I heard the voice of the Lord,...And he said, Go, and tell this people, Hear ye indeed, but understand not. Acts 28:25, 26: Well spake the Holy Ghost...Go unto this people, and say, Hearing ye shall hear, and shall not understand. Compare John 3:16 with Matthew 1:18.

[100]Matthew 28:19: Go ye therefore, and teach all nations, baptizing them in the name of the Father, and of the Son, and of the Holy Ghost. 2 Corinthians 13:14: The grace of the Lord Jesus Christ, and the love of God, and the communion of the Holy Ghost, be with you all. 1 Peter 1:2.

[101]See APPENDIX TO CHAPTER VII

[102]Mark 16:15: Go ye into all the world, and preach the gospel to every creature. Isaiah 45:22: Look unto me, and be ye saved, all the ends of the earth. Proverbs 8:4; Isaiah 55:1; Revelation 22:17.

[103]Joel 2:28: I will pour out my spirit upon all flesh. John 16:8; John 1:9; Isaiah 55:11; Luke 2:10.

[104]1 Timothy 2:4: Who will have all men to be saved, and to come unto the knowledge of the truth. Acts 10:34: God is no respecter of persons. Ezekiel 33:11; 2 Peter 3:9.

[105]Hosea 13:9: O Israel, thou hast destroyed thyself. Proverbs 1:24-31; Isaiah 65:12; Jeremiah 7:13, 14; Zechariah 7:11-13; John 5:40: And ye will not come to me, that ye might have life. Matthew 23:37.

[106]2 Corinthians 7:10: For godly sorrow worketh repentance to salvation not to be repented of. Psalms 51:17; Proverbs 28:13: He that covereth his sins shall not prosper: but whoso confesseth and forsaketh them shall have mercy. Psalm 32:3,

5; Ezekiel 36:31: Then shall ye remember your own evil ways, and your doings that were not good, and shall lothe yourselves in your own sight for your iniquities and for your abominations. Psalm 51:3, 4; Ezekiel 18:30: Repent, and turn yourselves from all your transgressions; so iniquity shall not be your ruin.

[107] Acts 17:30: But now commandeth all men every where to repent. Luke 13:5: But, except ye repent, ye shall all likewise perish. Acts 3:19.

[108] Hebrews 11:6: He that cometh to God must believe that he is, and that he is a rewarder of them that diligently seek him.

Hebrews 11:1: Faith is the substance of things hoped for, the evidence of things not seen. John 5:46, 47; Romans 10:9.

[109] Romans 10:10: With the heart man believeth unto righteousness. Galatians 5:22: But the fruit of the Spirit is...faith. 1 Corinthians 12:8, 9.

[110] Acts 16:31: Believe on the Lord Jesus Christ, and thou shalt be saved. John 3:16; Romans 4:20-22; Ephesians 3:12.

[111] James 2:17: Faith, if it hath not works, is dead, being alone. Galatians 5:6; 1 Timothy 1:5.

[112] Philippians 1:29: Unto you it is given in the behalf of Christ...to believe on him. 2 Peter 1:1; Ephesians 2:8.

[113] John 3:36: He that believeth on the Son hath everlasting life: and he that believeth not the Son shall not see life; but the wrath of God abideth on him. Mark 16:16; John 8:21, 24; Hebrews 11:6.

[114] John 1:7: That all men through him might believe. Gal 3:26: Ye are all the children of God by faith in Christ Jesus. Acts 10:43; Romans 5:1; John 3:15.

[115] John 3:3: Except a man be born again, he cannot see the kingdom of God. Hebrews 12:14; Revelation 21:27; Galatians 5:19-21.

[116] John 3:5: Except a man be born...of the Spirit, he cannot enter into the kingdom of God. John 1:13; Ezekiel 36:26, 27; Titus 3:5; Ephesians 2:10.

[117] Romans 8:16: The Spirit itself beareth witness with our spirit, that we are the children of God. John 1:12; 5:25; James 1:18; 2 Corinthians 5:17.

[118] Ezekiel 11:19, 20: And I will give them one heart, and I will put a new spirit within you; and I will take the stony heart out of their flesh, and will give them an heart of flesh: That they may walk in my statutes, and keep mine ordinances, and do them. 1 Peter 2:25.

[119] John 3:3: Except a man be born again, he cannot see the kingdom of God.

[120] John 3:6: That which is born of the Spirit is spirit. John 3:5-8; 1 John 4:7; 5:1.

[121] Ephesians 2:1: You hath he quickened, who were dead in trespasses and sins. Psalm 119:50, 93; Ephesians 2:5; Colossians 2:13.

[122] John 5:24: He that heareth my word, and believeth on him that sent me...is passed from death unto life. 1 John 3:14.

[123] 2 Peter 1:4: That by these ye might be partakers of the divine nature. Hebrews 3:14.

[124] Romans 5:1: Therefore being justified by faith, we have peace with God

through our Lord Jesus Christ. Romans 5:16: The free gift is of many offences unto justification. Acts 13:39; Isaiah 53:11.

[125] Acts 3:19: Repent ye therefore, and be converted, that your sins may be blotted out. Hebrews 4:2; 11:6, Romans 9:31, 32; Acts 13:38, 39.

[126] 1 Thessalonians 5:23: And the very God of peace sanctify you wholly; and I pray God your whole spirit and soul and body be preserved blameless unto the coming of our Lord Jesus Christ. 2 Corinthians 7:1; 2 Peter 3:18: Grow in grace, and in the knowledge of our Lord and Saviour Jesus Christ. Hebrews 6:1; 1 John 5:4; Colossians 4:12; Proverbs 4:18; 1 John 1:7,9; 1 Peter 1:16.

Galatians 2:20: I am crucified with Christ: nevertheless I live; yet not I, but Christ liveth in me: and the life which I now live in the flesh I live by the faith of the Son of God, who loved me, and gave himself for me.

[127] Romans 8:38, 39: For I am persuaded, that neither death, nor life, nor angels, nor principalities, nor powers, nor things present, nor things to come, Nor height, nor depth, nor any other creature, shall be able to separate us from the love of God, which is in Christ Jesus our Lord. 1 Corinthians 10:13: God is faithful, who will not suffer you to be tempted above that ye are able; but will with the temptation also make a way to escape, that ye may be able to bear it. 2 Corinthians 12:9: My grace is sufficient for thee. Job 17:9; Matthew 16:18; John 10:27, 28; Philippians 1:6.

[128] 2 Chronicles 15:2: The LORD is with you, while ye be with him; and if ye seek him...but if ye forsake him, he will forsake you. 2 Peter 1:10: Wherefore the rather, brethren, give diligence to make your calling and election sure: for if ye do these things, ye shall never fall. Ezekiel 33:18: When the righteous turneth from his righteousness, and committeth iniquity, he shall even die thereby. John 15:6; 1 Corinthians 10:12; Hebrews 6:4-6; 12:15; 1 Chronicles 28:9; Revelation 2:4; 1 Timothy 1:19; 2 Peter 2:20, 21; 1 Corinthians 9:27; Matthew 24:13; Acts 1:25; Revelation 22:19.

[129] See APPENDIX TO CHAPTER XIII

[130] Genesis 2:3: God blessed the seventh day, and sanctified it. Mark 2:27: The sabbath was made for man. Nehemiah 9:14.

[131] Exodus 20:8-11: Remember the sabbath day, to keep it holy. Six days shalt thou labour, and do all thy work: But the seventh day is the sabbath of the LORD thy God: in it thou shalt not do any work, thou, nor thy son, nor thy daughter, thy manservant, nor thy maidservant, nor thy cattle, nor thy stranger that is within thy gates: For in six days the LORD made heaven and earth, the sea, and all that in them is, and rested the seventh day: wherefore the LORD blessed the sabbath day, and hallowed it.

[132] Luke 24:1-6: Now upon the first day of the week, very early in the morning, they came unto the sepulchre...He is not here, but is risen. Luke 24:33-36; John 20:19, 26; Acts 2:1; Acts 20:7: And upon the first day of the week, when the disciples came together to break bread, Paul preached unto them. 1 Corinthians 16:2; Revelation 1:10; Psalm 118:22-24.

[133] Isaiah 58:13, 14: If thou turn away thy foot from the sabbath, from doing thy pleasure on my holy day; and call the sabbath a delight, the holy of the LORD, honourable; and shalt honour him, not doing thine own ways, nor finding thine

own pleasure, nor speaking thine own words: Then shalt thou delight thyself in the
LORD. Isaiah 56:2; Exodus 20:8-11.

[134] 1 Corinthians 1:2: Unto the church of God which is at Corinth, to them that
are sanctified in Christ Jesus, called to be saints. Acts 2:41, 47; 20:7; 1 Corinthians
16:1, 2; Revelation 1:4.

[135] Ephesians 5:25, 27: Christ also loved the church, and gave himself for
it...that he might present it to himself a glorious church. Ephesians 1:22, 23;
1 Corinthians 12:27, 28; Colossians 1:18, 24; 1 Peter 2:5; John 18:36; John 15:2, 6.

[136] Acts 2:41: Then they that gladly received his word were baptized: and the
same day there were added unto them about three thousand souls. Acts 8:12;
Galatians 3:27.

[137] Genesis 14:20: And he gave him tithes of all. Genesis 28:22: I will surely
give the tenth unto thee. Deuteronomy 14:22: Thou shalt truly tithe. Malachi 3:8-
10.

[138] 1 Corinthians 16:2: Upon the first day of the week let every one of you lay
by him in store, as God hath prospered him. Matthew 23:23; 1 Corinthians 9:9-14;
Hebrews 7:9-17; 2 Corinthians 9:6-8.

[139] 2 Timothy 2:15: Study to shew thyself approved unto God, a workman that
needeth not to be ashamed, rightly dividing the word of truth. 1 Timothy 4:13-15:
Till I come, give attendance to reading, to exhortation, to doctrine. Neglect not the
gift that is in thee...Meditate upon these things; give thyself wholly to them; that
thy profiting may appear to all. Titus 1:9; 2:7, 8; 2 Timothy 1:7; 2:2; 1 Timothy
3:2-7.

[140] Psalm 50:16: But unto the wicked God saith, What hast thou to do to declare
my statutes, or that thou shouldest take my covenant in thy mouth? 2 Timothy 1:8-
11, 14; 2:22; 3:5; Titus 1:5-9; 1 Corinthians 2:12-16.

[141] Acts 20:28: Take heed therefore unto yourselves, and to all the flock, over
the which the Holy Ghost hath made you overseers. Hebrews 5:4; 1 Corinthians
9:16; Acts 13:2.

[142] 1 Timothy 4:14: With the laying on of the hands of the presbytery.
2 Timothy 1:6; Acts 13:3.

[143] Mark 16:15: Go ye into all the world, and preach the gospel to every creature. 2 Timothy 4:2; 2 Corinthians 4:5; Ezekiel 33:7.

[144] Matthew 28:19: Teach all nations, baptizing them. Luke 22:19, 20: This do
in remembrance of me. Acts 20:11; 27:35; 1 Corinthians 10:16; 11:23-28.

[145] Hebrews 13:17: They watch for your souls, as they that must give account.
1 Peter 5:2: Feed the flock of God which is among you, taking the oversight thereof. Acts 20:28; Jeremiah 3:15.

[146] Matthew 28:19: Baptizing (Greek: *immersing*) them in the name of the Father,
and of the Son, and of the Holy Ghost.
   Colossians 2:12: Buried with him in baptism, wherein also ye are risen with
him. Acts 8:36-39; Matthew 3:16; Mark 1:5; John 3:23; Acts 16:32-34; 2:41.

[147] Romans 6:4: Therefore we are buried with him by baptism into death: that
like as Christ was raised up from the dead by the glory of the Father, even so we

also should walk in newness of life. Colossians 3:3; 2:12; Titus 3:5; Galatians 3:27; 1 Corinthians 15:29.

[148] 1 Corinthians 11:23-26: For I have received of the Lord that which also I delivered unto you, That the Lord Jesus the same night in which he was betrayed took bread: And when he had given thanks, he brake it, and said, Take, eat: this is my body, which is broken for you: this do in remembrance of me. After the same manner also he took the cup, when he had supped, saying, This cup is the new testament in my blood: this do ye, as oft as ye drink it, in remembrance of me. For as often as ye eat this bread, and drink this cup, ye do shew the Lord's death till he come. Matthew 26:26-28.

[149] 1 Corinthians 10:16: The cup of blessing which we bless, is it not the communion of the blood of Christ? The bread which we break, is it not the communion of the body of Christ? 1 Corinthians 10:21; 11:27-29.

[150] 1 Corinthians 10:17: For we being many are one bread, and one body: for we are all partakers of that one bread. Matthew 26:27: Drink ye all of it. Romans 14:1, 10; 1 Corinthians 12:12-17; Acts 2:42; 20:7.

[151] John 13:4-8; 1 Timothy 5:1-10.

[152] Romans 5:12: As by one man sin entered into the world, and death by sin; and so death passed upon all men, for that all have sinned. Hebrews 9:27: It is appointed unto men once to die. 1 Corinthians 15:22; Psalm 89:48; Ecclesiastes 8:8.

[153] Ecclesiastes 12:7: Then shall the dust return to the earth as it was: and the spirit shall return unto God who gave it. Philippians 1:23: Having a desire to depart, and to be with Christ; which is far better. Luke 23:43; Matthew 17:3; 22:32; Acts 7:59; Matthew 10:28; 2 Corinthians 5:8; Luke 16:22-26; Revelation 6:9.

[154] Acts 1:11: This same Jesus, which is taken up from you into heaven, shall so come in like manner as ye have seen him go into heaven. Matthew 25:31; 1 Corinthians 15:24-28; 1 Thessalonians 4:15-17; 2 Thessalonians 1:7-10; 2 Peter 3:3-13; Matthew 24:42-44.

[155] John 5:28, 29: The hour is coming, in the which all that are in the graves shall hear his voice, And shall come forth; they that have done good, unto the resurrection of life; and they that have done evil, unto the resurrection of damnation. Acts 24:15; 1 Corinthians 15:22, 23; 2 Timothy 2:18; Philippians 3:21; 1 Corinthians 15:35-44; Daniel 12:2.

[156] Acts 17:31: Because he hath appointed a day, in the which he will judge the world in righteousness. 1 Corinthians 15:24; Revelation 10:6; 22:11; 2 Peter 3:11, 12; Ecclesiastes 9:10.

[157] 2 Corinthians 5:10: For we must all appear before the judgment seat of Christ; that every one may receive the things done in his body, according to that he hath done, whether it be good or bad. Ecclesiastes 12:14: For God shall bring every work into judgment, with every secret thing, whether it be good, or whether it be evil. Matthew 12:36; Revelation 20:12; Romans 2:16.

[158] Matthew 25:46: And these shall go away into everlasting punishment: but the righteous into life eternal. 2 Thessalonians 1:8-10: Taking vengeance on them

that know not God, and that obey not the gospel of our Lord Jesus Christ: Who shall be punished with everlasting destruction from the presence of the Lord, and from the glory of his power; When he shall come to be glorified in his saints. Romans 6:23; 2 Peter 1:11; Mark 3:29; 9:43, 44; Jude 7; Revelation 14:11; 21:7, 8, 27; Matthew 13:41-43; Romans 2:6-10.

[159] 2 Peter 1:4-10: Whereby are given unto us exceeding great and precious promises: that by these ye might be partakers of the divine nature, having escaped the corruption that is in the world through lust. And beside this, giving all diligence, add to your faith virtue; and to virtue knowledge; And to knowledge temperance; and to temperance patience; and to patience godliness; And to godliness brotherly kindness; and to brotherly kindness charity. For if these things be in you, and abound, they make you that ye shall neither be barren nor unfruitful in the knowledge of our Lord Jesus Christ. But he that lacketh these things is blind, and cannot see afar off, and hath forgotten that he was purged from his old sins. Wherefore the rather, brethren, give diligence to make your calling and election sure: for if ye do these things, ye shall never fall.

[160] 2 Timothy 3:16.

[161] 2 Peter 1:21; 1 Corinthians 2:13; 2 Samuel 23:2; Jeremiah 1:9.

[162] John 10:35; Matthew 5:17, 18.

[163] John 17:17; Psalm 119:151, 160.

[164] Acts 2:5, 8, 11.

[165] 1 Corinthians 14:1-40; Hebrews 2:4.

[166] 1 Corinthians 12:10, 30.

[167] 1 Corinthians 14:18, 19, 23, 33.

[168] 1 Corinthians 12:13.

[169] Ephesians 5:18b-20.

PART III
ARTICLES OF FAITH

1. *The Bible.* The Scriptures of the Old and New Testaments were given by inspiration of God, and are our infallible rule of faith and practice.

2. *God.* There is one living and true God, revealed in nature as the Creator, Preserver, and Righteous Governor of the universe; and in the Scriptures as Father, Son, and Holy Ghost; yet as one God, infinitely wise and good, whom all intelligent creatures are supremely to love, adore, and obey.

3.   *Christ.* Christ is God manifest in the flesh; in His divine nature truly God, in His human nature truly man. The mediator between God and man, once crucified, He is now risen and glorified, and is our ever present Saviour and Lord.

4.   *The Holy Spirit.* The Scriptures assign to the Holy Spirit all the attributes of God.

5.   *The Government of God.* God exercises a wise and benevolent providence over all beings and all things by maintaining the constitution and laws of nature. He also performs special acts, not otherwise provided for, as the highest welfare of men requires.

6.   *The Sinfulness of Man.* Man was created innocent, but by disobedience fell into a state of sin and condemnation. His posterity, therefore, inherit a fallen nature of such tendencies that all who come to years of accountability, sin and become guilty before God.

7.   *The Work of Christ.* The Son of God by His incarnation, life, sufferings, death, and resurrection effected for all a redemption from sin that is full and free, and is the ground of salvation by faith.

8.   *The Terms of Salvation.* The conditions of salvation are: (1) Repentance or sincere sorrow for sin and hearty renunciation of it. (2) Faith or the unreserved committal of one's self to Christ as Savior and Lord with purpose to love and obey Him in all things. In the exercise of saving faith, the soul is renewed by the Holy Spirit, freed from the dominion of sin, and becomes a child of God. (3) Continuance of faith and obedience unto death.

9.   *Election.* God determined from the beginning to save all who should comply with the conditions of salvation. Hence by faith in Christ men become His elect.

10.   *Freedom of the Will.* The human will is free and self-controlled, having power to yield to the influence of the truth and the Spirit, or to resist them and perish.

11. *Salvation Free.* God desires the salvation of all, the Gospel invites all, the Holy Spirit strives with all, and whosoever will may come and take of the water of life freely.

12. *Perseverance.* All believers in Christ, who through grace persevere in holiness to the end of life, have promise of eternal salvation.

13. *Gospel Ordinances.* BAPTISM, or the immersion of believers in water, and the LORD'S SUPPER, are the ordinances to be perpetuated under the Gospel. FEET WASHING, an ordinance teaching humility, is of universal obligation, and is to be ministered to all true believers.

14. *Tithing.* God commanded tithes and offerings in the Old Testament; Jesus Christ endorsed it in the Gospel (Matthew 23:23), and the apostle Paul said, "Upon the first day of the week let every one of you lay by him in store, as God hath prospered him" (1 Corinthians 16:2a).

15. *The Christian Sabbath.* The divine law requires that one day in seven be set apart from secular employments and amusements, for rest, worship, holy works, and activities, and for personal communion with God.

16. *Resurrection, Judgment, and Final Retribution.* The Scriptures teach the resurrection of all men at the last day. Those who have done good will come forth to the resurrection of life, and those who have done evil unto the resurrection of damnation; then the wicked will "go away into eternal punishment, but the righteous into eternal life."

PART IV
THE PRACTICES OF FREE WILL BAPTISTS

The following is a description of the organizational practices generally followed in the Free Will Baptist denomination. It is recognized that there is considerably greater variety in actual practice than can be expressed in this section. It is not intended that the following description should require that every organization conform in every detail, so long as there is not variance from the basic principles which underlie these practices. Each organization, including the local churches and the various associations, will define its own practices by usage and/or by a formal constitution and by-laws.

CHAPTER I: The Local Church

SECTION I: Its Authority and Independence

A. The local congregation of believers is the only visible form of the "church" founded by the direct authority of Scripture. Free Will Baptists, therefore, recognize the local church as the sole source of authority possessed and exercised within the visible church.

B. The local church is an independent and self-governing body, with full authority to transact its business, choose its pastor and officers, receive, discipline, and dismiss members, hold free title to all its properties, and conduct all its internal affairs.

SECTION II: Its Relationships

The local Free Will Baptist church bears two important relationships to other churches:

A. Christians within the local church are members of the universal and invisible church, known as the body of Christ.

B. Local churches voluntarily form associations which organize and cooperate as the Free Will Baptist denomination. (See Chapter III: Associations of Churches.)

SECTION III: Its Organization

A. The authority to organize a local church lies within the group of Christians who covenant together, as they believe themselves directed by the Spirit of God, to form a local church.

B. Whenever such a group of Christians wishes to be organized as a regular Free Will Baptist church in fellowship with the denomination, these steps are followed:

1. The Quarterly Meeting or District Association is requested to send a committee to examine the group as to character, doctrine, and fellowship.
2. If the examination proves satisfactory, the formal organization proceeds as follows:
   a. The Bible is presented as the only rule of faith and practice.
   b. The Free Will Baptist Church Covenant is adopted.
   c. A prayer of consecration is offered.
   d. The hand of fellowship is given by the associational committee or its chairman.

C. Occasion often arises when a local church already organized, desires to unite with the denomination. A committee is requested from the Quarterly Meeting or Association for the purpose of examining the church as to its doctrine, character, reputation, fellowship, stability, and organization. The committee, if the examination is satisfactory, makes recommendation to the body which sent it; and the body votes whether to receive the church into fellowship.

Great care should be exercised by associations in examining and receiving into fellowship local churches already organized, especially when those churches have been in fellowship with other associations of churches in either the Free Will Baptist denomination or other denominations.

D. Many local churches find it helpful to adopt a constitution and by-laws; such a document serves as a guide to government and procedure within the congregation. Some Free Will Baptist churches also find it helpful to be legally incorporated.

SECTION IV: Its Officers

One of the primary duties of an organized local church is the election of officers from within its membership. All officers, including the pastor, are elected by majority vote of the congregation. Some of the most usual and important officers are listed below, although there are many others used in various churches.

A. The Pastor, who preaches the Word of God, ministers to the needs of the members, and exercises general leadership within the congregation. It is expected that he will unite with the local church if he is not a member when called. The church should not call a man who is not at least licensed to preach within the denomination. (See further Chapter II: The Minister.)

B. Deacons are ordained—usually by the local church—to minister to the congregation and exercise general spiritual leadership. They assist the pastor in administering the ordinances, and may have to conduct worship services in the pastor's absence. Regular practice insists that deacons be men who meet the qualifications outlined in 1 Timothy 3:8-13.

C. A clerk (secretary) and treasurer, offices which may be combined if desired. Duties include the keeping of careful records of all business and financial affairs of the local church.

D. Trustees, officers elected by many churches to receive and hold title to property owned by the local church, but which may be disposed of only by decision of the church.

SECTION V: Its Meetings

Meetings of the entire congregation of a local church are of two main types:

A. Worship services, which are times set aside by the local church according to the schedule it finds most satisfactory. Included, wherever possible, are services in the morning and evening on the first day of the week, and a mid-week service for prayer and Bible study. Although discouraged as a regular thing, any item of business may be carried on by the congregation at any regularly scheduled worship service.

B. Business meetings (conferences), which are held at regular times scheduled by the congregation.

1. Meetings should be frequent enough to insure that the congregation's authority over its business affairs is not usurped by any person or board. Usually such meetings are held at least once each quarter.

2. All members are obligated to be present, and have a right—regardless of age—to speak and vote, unless otherwise decided by the local church.

3. All matters not specifically delegated to some officer or board by the congregation must be handled by the congregation.

4. The decisive authority of the local church lies in the majority vote of those present and voting at any session where business is legally conducted.

5. Special business meetings may be called for times other than regularly scheduled business or worship sessions, but only in the manner agreed upon by the majority of the congregation.

6. The pastor generally acts as moderator for business meetings.

SECTION VI: Its Ordinances

The Gospel ordinances to be practiced in local Free Will Baptist churches are described in Chapter XVIII of the "Faith" section of the Treatise.

A. Baptism is administered by an ordained minister to the individual as soon as possible after his conversion.

B. Provision should be made for regular observance of the Lord's Supper and washing of the saints' feet by the congregation. Ministers and deacons administer these.

SECTION VII: Its Membership

A. An individual may be received into the fellowship of a local church by decision of the congregation according to its regularly prescribed method. This generally applies to either of two situations:

1. Upon profession of faith in Christ, reception into full fellowship not being final until the convert is baptized by immersion.
2. Upon receipt of a letter of good standing from any church recognized as Christian, with the qualification that the applicant must have been baptized by immersion and satisfied therewith.

B. In no case should an individual be received into membership if there remains any doubt as to the genuineness of his conversion and Christian character. Persons expelled from any sister churches, for example, should not be received into full membership without giving satisfaction to the church from which they have been expelled.

C. Reception into full fellowship should be made final, if possible, by the extending of the hand of fellowship, at least from the pastor and preferably from the congregation.

D. Letters of commendation are granted, concerning members in good standing, to churches making such requests about members desiring to move their membership. The local church should not grant such a letter if there is doubt concerning the profession and character of the member.

SECTION VIII: Its Disciplinary Authority

The local church occasionally finds itself responsible to exercise its solemn right to discipline members. In such cases, the regular procedures of the local church are followed in keeping with the teachings of the Scripture.

A. Cases involving personal offense are to be handled according to Matthew 18:15-17.

B. In some cases, the church may have to effect a "break" in fellowship with a disorderly brother who is yet not an "enemy" (2 Thessalonians 3:6-15).

C. In other cases, the member is expected to submit to the discipline of the church. If the member does not choose to submit, the only course of action open to the church is to withdraw fellowship from the member.

D. In all cases, the member is expected to submit to the discipline of the church. If the member does not choose to submit, the only course of action open to the church is to withdraw fellowship from the member.

E. Withdrawal of fellowship from a member can take place only by majority vote of the congregation (see Section V) and should take place only after every effort is exercised in a humble Christian spirit to restore the member and give him adequate opportunity to be heard.

F. When a member, without providential reason, absents himself from the meetings of the church or refuses to support it for one year, it is considered a violation of the covenant and sufficient reason for dismissal.

G. A member (or minority group of members) dissatisfied with the action of the majority against him, may appeal to the association for a hearing among the sister churches. The nature of the association's powers in such a case is described in Chapter III: Associations of Churches.

H. The actual "trial" of a member, when necessary, should be carried on in the sole presence of the membership and involved parties.

    1. A written notice of the exact charges should be furnished to the accused at least a week in advance.

    2. The pastor, unless personally involved as a witness, should be impartial moderator of the meeting. He should read the charges, without comment.

    3. The pastor should call for volunteer witnesses who wish to sustain the charges by testimony, allowing

the accused, in an orderly way, to question the witnesses.

4. The pastor should allow the accused to speak in his own behalf and ask for witnesses who wish to sustain his position.

5. When both sides are presented, the pastor asks whether there is a motion concerning some type of discipline for the accused. If there is, and it is seconded, the motion is discussed and voted upon.

I. The local church should always stand ready to forgive a genuinely repentant member and restore him to full fellowship in the congregation (2 Corinthians 2:6, 7).

CHAPTER II: The Minister

SECTION I: His Ordination

A. The authority to ordain ministers has its source in the local church.

B. Free Will Baptist churches, in most areas, have traditionally delegated this authority to the associations in which they voluntarily unite themselves. This is done because the local churches desire the assistance of their sister churches and ministers.

C. Ordination procedure varies greatly from one district association to another, depending on the traditions of the various areas. In most cases, something like the following takes place:

1. The candidate must usually be licensed for a period prior to ordination, often at least a year. In some areas, license is issued by the local church directly; in others, it is issued by the association upon the request of the local church.

2. Before ordination, the candidate is examined by a committee of ministers appointed by the association for that purpose.

3. This committee usually makes recommendation directly to the association, which body votes whether to ordain. Usually, a request for ordination must also be received from the local church of which the candidate is a member. (In some areas, the association's "ordination council" makes recommendation back to the local church, which then proceeds to ordain.)

4. The ministers of the association usually administer the actual ordination ceremony when the association has voted approval.

5. The actual ceremony generally includes the "presentation" of the Bible and a formal "charge." In many places, a sermon by a brother minister is preached. The service usually concludes with the "laying on of hands" and a prayer of consecration.

D. Ordination requirements also vary greatly within the Free Will Baptist denomination.

1. Examinations generally include sufficient materials to determine a reasonable acquaintance with the Bible, Christian doctrine, and Free Will Baptist teachings.

2. Some associations require some type of ministerial educational preparation, or at least manifestation of a desire for self-improvement and study.

3. All areas recognize the necessity of a definite conviction on the part of the candidate that he is divinely "called" to the ministry.

4. Some areas have certain specific requirements about special items of conduct, such as, for example, whether a minister can use tobacco. All areas require consistent Christian conduct and character.

5. Many associations require that the candidate already be involved in some specific ministry, usually either as a pastor or evangelist.

E. A minister transferring from one association to another within the denomination generally undergoes the following:

1. He is examined by the local association's ordaining committee, though usually not so closely as the new ordination candidate.
2. He is required to present a letter of good standing from the association of which he was last a member. (Associations should exercise great care in granting such letters of standing; an unqualified letter should not be granted if there are any questions about the minister's reliability.) In general, no association should receive a minister into full ministerial standing who cannot secure a letter of good standing because he has been disfellowshipped or had his credentials revoked or who is in the process of being disciplined by another association. In no case should his credentials be ratified without consultation with the association which disciplined him.
3. His ordination credentials may then be "ratified" by the association upon recommendation of the ordaining council.

F. A minister from another denomination wishing to unite with the Free Will Baptist denomination must first unite with a local Free Will Baptist church and will then be subject to procedure similar to that outlined above in E. He can expect to be examined closely.

SECTION II: His Discipline

A. As in the case of ordination, the authority to discipline a minister has its source in the authority of the local church. Again, however, this is delegated to the association along with the authority to ordain.

B. In most cases, any accusation against a minister that is offered concerning his conduct, character, profession, or doctrine (and which should be considered against his good standing), should be brought to the association by the local church. The only exception that should be made arises when an offense involves a fellow minister (as object or witness) in a situation unknown to the local church. In this case, charges should be preferred by three ministers jointly, with the local church fully apprised of the fact.

C. As with all other matters of church discipline, the minister accused should first be dealt with privately according to the principles outlined in Matthew 18:15-17.

D. If a formal "trial" becomes necessary, it should proceed in the same way as that described for members of a local church in Chapter I, Section VIII, except that here the moderator of the association presides (rather than the local pastor) and the delegates to the association hear the trial (rather than local members). All steps in part H of the Section just referred to should be followed.

E. The association's disciplinary action against the minister can deal solely with his ordination and fellowship in the association as a minister.

1. If an intermediate and temporary act of discipline is needed, the minister may be retained on the roll of ministers but listed as not in full fellowship and denied the right to vote as a standing delegate.

2. The final act of discipline, if labors are not fruitful in bringing satisfactory resolution of the problem, consists in the revoking of the minister's ordination and withdrawal of fellowship from him as a minister in good standing in the association.

3. The association's discipline cannot deal with the minister's relationship to the local church, either as pastor or member. It can make recommendations concerning this to the local church, and the church's fellowship in the association might be endangered if those recommendations were not followed, but no force can be applied.

F. The minister is expected to submit to the decision of the association and relinquish his "credentials" of ordination if they are called for. Civil action is not recommended, however, if he should refuse.

G. The minister who feels he has not been justly treated may, in union with at least one other sustaining minister, appeal to the next broader organization of which his district association is a member (such as the state association) for a hearing among the sister associations. The nature of the broader organization's powers in such a case is described in Chapter III: Associations of Churches.

SECTION III: His Relationships

The minister has unique relationships to many persons. As a divinely-called preacher, he is subject foremost to the Lord and His Word. This relationship qualifies all the others.

A. To his church. Most Free Will Baptist churches recognize their responsibility to support their pastors with such financial means as are available to them.

B. To the association. When the minister becomes pastor of a given local church, it is his responsibility to obtain good standing in the association of which that church is a member if he is not already in good standing therein.

C. To fellow-ministers. Many associations maintain "ministers' conferences," organized for the fellowship and cooperation of the ministers in the area of that association. These conferences should remain subservient to and responsible to the association.

CHAPTER III: Associations of Churches

SECTION I: Their Nature

Free Will Baptist churches, while independent, do not practice isolation. They form associations with one another in several levels of organization described in this chapter. It is to be remembered, however, that these associations are voluntary, both at the beginning and in their continuation. The local church remains at liberty to withdraw from the association it has voluntarily joined.

SECTION II: Their Organizational Structure

There is considerable variety within the denomination as to the exact number and nature of associational organizations.

A. The plan which seems to work best calls for four levels of organization, which can be diagrammed thus:

> Level 1–The Local Church
> Level 2–The District Association
> Level 3–The State Association
> Level 4–The National Association

1. According to this plan, the local churches in a given district form the district association; several (two or more) district associations in a given state form a state association; and the several state associations form the national association. Each of the levels is said to be the broader or larger (not "higher") than the former.

2. In this plan, the district association usually bears a proper name that includes the word Association, although Conference is often used.

3. The district association, in this plan, is the body which deals directly with the local church and would be the first level of appeal from the local church. It is also the body to which the local church delegates its authority to ordain and discipline ministers (see Chapter II: The Minister).

4. In this plan, the district association may meet quarterly. Some district associations cover such larger geographical areas, however, that it is found preferable to subdivide voluntarily into smaller groups for three quarterly meetings between the annual meetings of the entire association each fourth quarter. In this case, these smaller quarterly meetings are mostly devoted to fellowship and inspiration. While the

local churches are expected to report to these smaller quarterly meetings, their main annual reports are
presented directly to the annual meeting of the association.

B. Another plan of structure followed in some areas calls
for five levels of organization, which can be diagrammed
thus:

> Level 1–The Local Church
> Level 2–The Quarterly Meeting
> Level 3–The Yearly Meeting
> Level 4–The State Association
> Level 5–The National Association

This plan works much like the four-level plan outlined
above, except for the fact that the quarterly meeting is given
considerably greater status in the associational structure and
stands between the local church and the yearly meeting
(equivalent to the district association). Here, the churches
form and report only to the quarterly meeting. Quarterly
meetings form and make all reports to the yearly meeting. In
other particulars the two plans are identical.

C. The organizational structure in many areas reflects a
mixture of elements from both these plans, thus adding to the
variety. In all plans, state and national associations meet
annually, and most include representation from the local
churches as well as from the smaller associations composing
them.

SECTION III: Their Purposes

These associations of churches at the various levels are all
organized for cooperation among the churches. These
denominational meetings serve for mutual edification and
inspiration. They also provide opportunity for the churches
to accomplish cooperatively what they might not be able to
do individually.

SECTION IV: Their Relationships

A. The district association (or quarterly meeting) and the local churches.

   1. The association has no authority to interfere in the internal affairs of the local church (see Chapter I, Section I-B).

   2. Once organized, the association of churches is constituted a body distinct from the local churches that compose it, and:

     a. can speak only for itself, not for the churches;

     b. can commit only itself to a course of action, not the churches;

     c. is composed—at any session—of the "delegates" sent from the churches and who can act and vote only as a part of the association itself without the ability to legally commit the churches they represent;

     d. can deal only with the local churches as members of the association, and not with the individual members of the local churches.

   3. The association's only "power" over the local church is limited to dealing with the church's rights as a member of the association:

     a. The association may set whatever requirements it wishes as conditions for the church's "Good standing" in the association although it has no power to force the church to meet those requirements.

     b. The association may, for example, refuse to seat delegates from a local church if there is a breach of fellowship being dealt with.

     c. Ultimately, the most extreme power of the association is to withdraw fellowship from the local church as a member of the association.

   4. An aggrieved minority within a local church may appeal to the association for a hearing among the sister churches, and reasonable appeals ought to be

heard according to the association's regular procedures.

  a. The association may desire, or be requested by the aggrieved minority of the church, to send a committee to meet with the church and investigate the difficulties. In such case, the church is more proper to receive and meet with such a committee, although it is understood it cannot be forced to do so.

  b. If the association agrees with the aggrieved minority, it may exercise all suitable labors to persuade the majority to reconsider. But if persuasion fails, and the matter is serious enough, the association's only recourse is to withdraw fellowship.

5. When a church violates its covenant, or becomes corrupt in doctrine or practice, or discontinues reporting to the association, the association will have to deal with the church in a similar manner. But, again, if advisory and persuasive labors fail, the only recourse for the association is to withdraw fellowship from the church.

If a "trial" of a church becomes necessary, procedures should be followed as nearly identical as possible with those outlined in Chapter I, Section VIII-H.

B. The broader associations, at each successive level, bear exactly the same relationships to the bodies composing them as that defined above between the district association (or quarterly meeting) and the local church.

SECTION V: Their Organization

A. A group of local churches may voluntarily form an association of churches (quarterly meeting or district association, depending on the structure followed in the area, as outlined in Section II) when they feel it helpful to their common cause.

1. If they wish to be in fellowship with the denomination at the time of their organization, they should request the broader association in which they will desire membership (yearly meeting, if a quarterly meeting is being organized; state association, if a district association is being organized) to appoint a committee to assist them in setting the organization in order. This committee can assist in such things as the drafting of a proposed constitution and by-laws for the association before the organizational meeting takes place.

2. The organizational meeting should be set for a date acceptable to all the churches and the assistance committee, and should include at least these items of procedure:

   a. Each church desiring fellowship in the association to be formed should have elected delegates to accompany the minister to the organizational meeting.

   b. Each church should have written a letter stating its purpose to unite in forming the association and naming the delegates that will represent it.

   c. The meeting should begin with the chairman of the assistance committee presiding and reading the letters sent by the churches, followed by the recognition and listing of the delegates assembled.

   d. The assistance committee should examine the delegates as to the character and doctrine of their respective churches, and should examine the constitution and by-laws which are to be presented for adoption by the delegates. Any churches who have previously belonged to other associations should have letters of commendation from those associations.

e. If the examination is satisfactory, the Bible is presented as the only perfect rule of faith and practice.

f. The proposed constitution and by-laws are adopted.

g. The Treatise of the Faith and Practices of Free Will Baptists is adopted.

h. The assistance committee extends the right hand of fellowship to the delegates and leads in a prayer of consecration.

i. Officers for the new association are elected (as provided in the constitution and by-laws) beginning with the moderator, who will preside over the remainder of the meeting.

j. Delegates for the newly formed association are elected to attend the next meeting of and ask for membership in the broader association (from which the assistance committee was sent).

[Note: Other advice concerning the formation of a new organization is given in *Robert's Rule of Order (Revised)*.]

3. A group of churches organized into an association without assistance from some larger association in fellowship with the denomination may request membership in such a broader association at any time. The following steps should be included in this procedure.

a. Delegates are elected to attend the association (yearly meeting or state association, as the case may be) and petition for membership.

b. A letter requesting membership is sent by the delegates, including a statement that the Treatise of the Faith and Practices of Free Will Baptists has been adopted.

c. The delegates are examined by the broader association, as are the constitution and by-laws of the association requesting membership. (If informa-

tion is not complete, the examination may be continued over a specified period.)

   d. When the examination is completed and satisfactory, the delegates are seated and the association
enrolled.

   e. Caution in receiving previously organized associations is urged. The examination should be thorough. It should be clearly determined that the
churches of the association seeking membership
have all been in good standing with any other
associations to which they have belonged, and that
they have departed from those associations in
peace.

  4. Once an association of churches has been organized,
new churches may be received into fellowship at
will, according to the provisions of the constitution
and by-laws of the association, and in keeping with
the practice described in Chapter I, Section III-C.

  B. A group of associations desiring to form a broader association (yearly meeting or state association, as the case may
be), will follow procedure identical to that described above
for churches forming an association.

  C. The constitution and by-laws of the various associations
at any level give detailed provisions for membership, officers,
activities, meetings, and the like. These vary greatly from
place to place, but should not be repugnant to the basic principles underlying the general practices outlined in these
"Practices." The Constitution and By-Laws of the National
Association of Free Will Baptists, Inc. are given in this booklet (Part V) and may serve as a model for any of the smaller
associations.

  D. When a church or association wishes to transfer membership to another association, it should obtain a letter of
good standing.

  E. A church or association which has been expelled by
another association should not be received by another asso-

ciation without first giving satisfaction to the association from which it was expelled.

SECTION VI: Their Business

A. Associations of churches within the denomination have varied ways of conducting business, as provided in their respective constitutions and by-laws. In general the following items are basic:

1. Letters are sent from each local church to each meeting of the association in which it retains membership. The letter reports, as requested by the association, information concerning the state and progress of the church. The letter also names the lay delegates who will officially represent the church.
2. In all associations (and at any level within the denomination), ministers in good standing within the association are standing delegates.
3. The business of the association is decided by majority vote of the standing and lay delegates present and voting at any given session, as provided in the constitution and by-laws of the association.

B. The broader associations (yearly meetings, district associations, state associations, and national association) follow the same principles of business as in the associations composed directly of local churches, except that reports and lay delegates come from the associations composing them rather than directly from the churches (as noted in Section II-C, provision is also made in most of the broader associations for direct lay representation from the local churches).

PART V
CONSTITUTION OF THE NATIONAL ASSOCIATION OF FREE WILL BAPTISTS, INC.

Preamble

From experience we, the members of the Free Will Baptist denomination, being regularly baptized upon a profession of our faith in Jesus Christ and realizing the necessity of a bond of union and fellowship among us; to preserve and maintain correspondence and coordination with us; to unify the work of the various bodies composing the National Association; and to devise and execute measures for the extension of the Kingdom of God in cooperation with the various bodies of the Association, or that may be hereafter represented therein, do therefore ordain this Constitution for our better denominational government.

ARTICLE I: Name

This organization shall be known as the National Association of Free Will Baptists, Inc. of the United States of America.

ARTICLE II: Membership

Section 1. Membership in the National Association is generally based upon affiliation of the several State Associations with the National Association. When a State Association is affiliated with the National Association, according to the process described in the by-laws, its various district associations, local churches, with their members and ministers, are also members of the National Association.

Section 2. Membership in the National Association is similarly open to any district association and its constituency in a state, or area embracing more than one state, which does not have a state association that is affiliated with the National Association and which does not belong to a state association of another state which is affiliated with the National Association.

Section 3. Membership in the National Association is similarly open to a local church and its constituency in a state which has no district or state association that is affiliated with the National Association and that does not belong to an organization in another state which is affiliated with the National Association.

Section 4. Membership in the National Association is similarly open to local churches or associations and their constituencies in any other countries of continental North America.

Section 5. In the above provisions, or in any provisions of the Constitution and By-Laws, an association must be composed of district associations if it will qualify as a "state" association, or the equivalent. Any associations allowed membership which are composed directly of local churches will have the status of a "district" association.

ARTICLE III: Representation

Voting representation in the National Association, at any session, shall be by delegates from the various organizations which hold membership in the National Association according to the provisions of Article II, and upon the payment of fees described in the by-laws. Delegates are of two kinds: standing delegates, who are the ordained ministers, deacons and missionaries in good standing with an affiliated organization, the officers of the National Association, and the members of the various boards, commissions and committees of the National Association; and lay delegates who are elected representatives of the various organizations affiliated with the National Association, according to the provisions of the by-laws.

ARTICLE IV: Officers

The officers of this National Association shall consist of a moderator, an assistant moderator, a clerk, an assistant clerk, and an executive secretary who shall also serve as treasurer, each of whom shall be elected at the close of each regular session, except the executive secretary who shall be elected for an indefinite period.

ARTICLE V: The General Board and Executive Committee

Section 1. Power to act in behalf of and for the National Association from the one regular session to another shall be vested in the General Board of the National Association of Free Will Baptists, Inc.

Section 2. The General Board shall be composed of the general officers of the National Association and the chairmen of all standing boards. The National Association shall also elect one member from each association affiliated directly with the National Association under the provisions of Article II, Sections 1, 2, and 4, with the exception that no state or country will be allowed more than one General Board member. Each association shall be allowed the privilege of making recommendation concerning its representative to the General Board. The president of the Women Nationally Active For Christ shall be an ex-officio member of the General Board.

The terms of office for the elected associational representatives shall be two years, and so arranged that those representing states, countries, or areas of the United States beginning with the letters "A" through "M" shall expire alternately with those representing states, countries, or areas of the Unites States beginning with the letters "N" through "Z".

Section 3. The Executive Committee of the General Board shall be composed of the moderator, assistant moderator, and clerk of the National Association, with six other members to be elected from the General Board by the National Association. Three members shall be elected each year for two-year terms from the General Board members whose terms begin that year. Not more than one elective member shall serve from any state. The outgoing moderator shall serve as an advisory member for one year. The purpose of this committee shall be to serve as the executive arm of the General Board and the National Association. The nature of its work shall be executive and promotional rather than legislative.

ARTICLE VI: Meetings

Section 1. The National Association shall hold its regular meetings annually at the time and place determined by the Association while in session.

Section 2. The General Board shall meet annually, immediately prior to the annual session of the National Association at a time and place announced by the moderator.

Section 3. The Executive Committee shall meet at least semi-annually, one meeting to be held immediately prior to the annual meeting of the General Board, and the others at a time and place determined by the committee.

Section 4. Special meetings of the General Board or Executive Committee shall be called when necessary by the moderator with the written consent of three other members of the Executive Committee. Special meetings of the General Board shall also be called upon the written request of one-fourth of its members. Special meetings of the Executive Committee shall also be called upon the written request of a majority of its members.

ARTICLE VII: Dissolution

In the event of the dissolution of this National Association, any assets of the organization then remaining shall be conveyed to such organizations then existent dedicated to similar objectives to those of this organization selected by the General Board at the time of dissolution, which organization must be exempt under section 501(c)(3) of the Internal Revenue code of 1954 as amended or under successor provisions of the Code as may be in effect at the time of dissolution.

ARTICLE VIII: Amendments

Section 1. This Constitution may be amended or altered at any regular session of the National Association by a two-thirds vote of the members present, provided proposed amendment or alteration be presented in writing to the body one day in advance.

Section 2. The Church Covenant, the Statement of Faith of Free Will Baptists as given in this Treatise may be amended or altered at any regular session of the National Association by a two-thirds vote of the members present and voting, provided proposed amendment or alteration has been presented to the body in writing one annual session in advance.

BY-LAWS

Membership

Section 1. The procedure for becoming a member of the National Association shall be as follows: An organization which is eligible shall present a written application to the Executive Secretary, stating that it has been filed by the majority vote of the body and signed by the officials of the body. The Executive Secretary may make any investigation he feels necessary and shall in turn make recommendations to the General Board. The National Association shall vote upon the recommendation of the General Board.

Section 2. All organizations affiliated directly with the National Association shall be required to adopt the Treatise of the Faith and Practices of Free Will Baptists as adopted by the National Association, and the application for membership must contain a statement to the effect.

Representation

Section 3. It shall be the duty of each body directly affiliated with the National Association to send a letter to every annual session of the Association, reporting its statistics on a

form provided by the National Association. Any body which
fails to do this for two successive sessions may be dismissed
from the Association by a majority vote of members present.

   Section 4. Each affiliated state association, or its equivalent,
shall be entitled to five lay delegates to the National
Association upon payment of the representation fee of twenty-five dollars ($25.00) per church. Each "district" association
affiliated directly with the National Association shall be entitled to three (3) lay delegates upon the payment of a representation fee of twenty-five dollars ($25.00) per church. Each
local church which is affiliated either directly or indirectly,
under any of the provisions for membership is entitled to one
lay delegate, upon the payment of a representation fee of
twenty-five dollars ($25.00).

Duties of Officers

Section 5. The duties of the moderator shall include presiding at the meetings of the National Association, the General
Board, and the Executive Committee; to call special meetings
of the General Board or Executive Committee when the conditions of Article VI, Section 4, of the Constitution are ful-
filled; to appoint such committees as are created without provision for their selection; to announce the time and place for
the meetings of the General Board and Executive
Committee; and in general, to fulfill whatever responsibilities
may be commensurate with his office or delegated to him by
the body.

Section 6. The duties of the assistant moderator shall
include presiding at the request of, or in the absence of, the
moderator and assisting him in such ways as may be necessary.

Section 7. The duties of the clerk shall include the preparation of minutes for the proceedings of all meetings of the
National Association, the General Board, the Executive
Committee; and the handling of such official correspondence
for the Association as he may be directed.

Section 8. The duties of the assistant clerk shall be to act for the clerk at the meetings of the National Association and General Board in his absence or at his request and to assist the clerk in whatever ways may be necessary.

Section 9. The duties of the Executive Secretary shall be:

A. *Administration.* He shall administer the affairs of the executive office and carry out the responsibilities delegated to him by the National Association and the Executive Committee. He shall fulfill all duties commensurate with his office and present such plans and procedures that he feels would be effective in the life of the denomination.

B. *General Promotion.* He shall seek to show through general promotion the correlation and interrelation of all the national ministries. It is expected that he will promote impartially the total program of work as devised by all the departments.

C. *Public Relations.* He shall serve as consultant on general denominational affairs and as official representative when occasion demands. Through personal communication he shall keep close contact with pastors, state organizations and their affiliates. He shall represent the National Association to other bodies when in the interest of the denomination.

D. *Publications.* He shall be responsible for publishing the association's official magazine *Contact,* and to serve as editor-in-chief. He shall direct the production of general promotional materials, pamphlets, audio visuals and books as approved by the Executive Committee.

E. *Stewardship.* He shall provide a program of stewardship education that will produce increased support for the denominational ministries through the Together Way Plan and other methods of proportionate sharing. He is further charged with the responsibility of receiving and disbursing the Together Way funds, and in general to serve as treasurer and business manager of the National Association.

F. *Arranging Annual Convention.* He shall expedite the planning of the National Convention program, enroll all ministers and delegates, print and distribute minutes, and investigate future sites for the annual sessions.

G. *National Offices Management.* It shall be the duty of the Executive Secretary to serve as chairman of the Management Committee of the National Office facilities.

Election of Officers

Section 10. No person shall fill more than one office at the same time, or any office and a place on any standing board, except as he may become a member of the General Board by virtue of his office. No person shall serve on more than one standing board at the same time, except as he may become a member of the General Board by virtue of being chairman of the board of which he is an elected member. No member of the Executive Committee may be a member of any standing board except the General Board.

Section 11. The procedure for the election of officers of the National Association shall be as follows: the nominating committee which is selected at the beginning of the annual session shall present at least one name to the assembly for each vacant office excepting the General Board. Nominations for the General Board shall be made on Wednesday afternoon of the annual session, and nominations for other offices on Wednesday or Thursday.

After the committee's report the floor shall be open for further nominations and the election shall proceed in regular manner.

Section 12. The General Board shall have power to fill irregular vacancies that may occur in its own body, or in any department of the work between sessions of the National Association. When such is necessary, the procedure shall be as follows: The Executive Committee shall serve as a nominating committee and shall circulate ballots by mail to each General Board member with the names of the nominees. These ballots shall be marked by the General Board members, notarized, and returned to the Executive Secretary.

The General Board and Executive Committee

Section 13. It shall be the responsibility of the General Board to make written reports of all its work to each annual session of the National Association, and it shall be responsible to that body for all its actions. Should necessity arise from war, or pestilence or any cause which prevents a regular meeting of the National Association, whether such a condition is of a local or general condition, then the General Board shall be privileged to call and act with full authority in all matters pertaining to the general welfare of the National Association, providing whatever transactions passed shall be by two-thirds vote of the members present, and providing that such transactions shall not conflict with the purpose and edicts of the constitution and by-laws of the National Association.

Section 14. The General Board shall review the annual reports and budgets of all boards at its regular session before these reports are presented to the National Association.

Section 15. The Executive Committee shall make written reports of its work to the General Board and shall be responsible to that body for all its actions. It shall not have power to commit the National Association to any course of action or policy not authorized by the National Association, nor to reverse any action of the National Association. Consequently, its work shall be to implement the policies and plans of the National Association; to publicize and promote the work of the National Association and its various departments; to arrange the agenda and program for the annual meetings of the National Association; to recommend the placement of future National Association sessions; to supervise and transact the business connected with the operation of the office of the Executive Secretary; to make plans and recommendations to the General Board for the advancement of the denomination; and to fulfill whatever other responsibilities may be delegated by the General Board or National Association.

The Executive Committee shall arrange the working contract of the Executive Secretary, who shall assist in carrying out the work of the Executive Committee.

The service of the Executive Secretary may be reviewed by a request from seven members of the General Board. Such services shall be terminated upon a ninety-day notice by either his resignation, a majority vote of the National Association, or the majority vote of the General Board in called session.

Standing Boards

Section 16. In addition to the General Board, the National Association shall perpetuate the following standing boards: The Board of Trustees of Free Will Baptist Bible College, The Board of Foreign Missions, The Board of Home Missions, The Board of Retirement and Insurance, The Master's Men Board, The Board of Sunday School and Church Training, and The Board of Trustees of The Free Will Baptist Foundation.

Section 17. Each of these boards, except the Board of Trustees of the Free Will Baptist Foundation, shall be composed of nine members who are elected by the National Association, according to an arrangement whereby each member has a term of office for six years, and their terms are arranged so that they expire in groups of three biennially. A member can serve no more than two full consecutive terms. The Board of Trustees of the Free Will Baptist Foundation shall consist of the members of the Board of Retirement and Insurance, the Director of Foreign Missions, the Director of Home Missions, the Director of Master's Men, the Director of Sunday School and Church Training, the President of Free Will Baptist Bible College, the Executive Secretary of the Women Nationally Active For Christ, and the Executive Secretary of the National Association.

Section 18. The various standing boards shall plan a program and supervise their operations in their respective fields, and shall be responsible for all their actions to the National Association of Free Will Baptists, Inc. Each board shall operate under its own constitution (or charter) and by-laws, which must be approved by the National Association.

Section 19. Each standing board shall prepare a budget of its proposed financial expenditures at the beginning of each fiscal year and shall present same for approval of the National Association along with an audit made by an independent certified public accountant which audit shall lead to the expression of an unqualified opinion on the financial statements. The auditor's report shall include, where applicable, a balance sheet and income statement and other schedules as may be necessary for a proper presentation of the financial condition and results of operation.

Section 20. The Management Committee shall be composed of the directors of the departments which occupy the National Offices facilities. This committee shall be legal custodians of all property belonging to the National Association, except in the case of the boards of the National Association which are authorized by action of the Association to be incorporated.

Commissions and Committees

Section 21. When the National Association deems it wise, commissions may be established to perform a specific service in a restricted area on a more-or-less permanent basis. The number of members of any commission shall be decided by vote of the National Association, and the members shall be elected by the Association. Terms of office for all members of commissions shall be five years (except when the commission is originally established the member last elected shall serve a one-year term; the next member a two-year term; and so on); and their terms shall be so arranged that only one member's term expires annually. Present commissions include:

A. The Commission for Theological Integrity
  1. The Purpose: The purpose of this Commission shall be:
    a. To alert our people of theological trends that could threaten our theological integrity as a denomination.
    b. To prepare materials that will contribute to the continued preservation of the theological integrity of our denomination.
    c. As the need and opportunity arise to conduct seminars on subjects which are pertinent to the purpose of this Commission.
  2. The Scope: The scope of the responsibility of this Commission shall be to address significant theological concerns such as:
    a. Trends and influences that would threaten orthodox doctrine.
    b. That which would threaten our theological distinctives as a denomination.

It shall not be within the scope of this Commission's responsibility (a) To investigate the theological integrity of any individual, organization or institution in the denomination, or (b) To address points of theology upon which difference of opinion has been permitted in the denomination.
  B. The Historical Commission
  C. The Media Commission
  D. The Music Commission

Section 22. Various committees shall also be constituted, when need arises, by the National Association, General Board, or Executive Committee, to function for a more definite period of time in a specific area. The number of members of any committee shall be determined by the assembly. Committee members shall be appointed by the moderator unless otherwise provided by the action creating the committee; and they shall hold office for the length of time provided, or until their work is completed, or until they are released, or their successors chosen.

Section 23. The following committees shall be used annually in the sessions of the General Board and National Association:

A. The credentials committee, which is identical with the General Board (although the Board may select a smaller committee of its members for this duty if it chooses). This committee has as its duty the examination of all letters to the National Association and the credentials of the various delegates. The committee shall make recommendations to the Association concerning the seating of delegates.

B. The nominating committee, whose duties are provided in Section 11 of the by-laws.

C. The resolutions committee, who shall receive and present worthwhile resolutions to the National Association.

D. The budget committee, who shall make recommendation to the National Association concerning the total denominational budget and the allocation of the Together Way Plan receipts. This committee shall consist of the Executive Secretary and the directors of the various departments which receive moneys through the Together Way Plan of Support.

E. The obituary committee, who will receive names of deceased leaders from state associations and individuals. This committee will give a report to the National Association so that these names can be included in the minutes.

Subsidiary Organizations

Section 24. The Women Nationally Active For Christ shall be recognized as subordinate to the National Association; but it shall organize at its own discretion and have power to create and adopt a constitution and by-laws and maintain complete management of the work for which it is constituted. The scope and character of the work shall conform to the general program and promotional plan of the National Association. It shall report its accomplishments and financial operations annually to the National Association.

Quorum

Section 25. Two-fifths of its members shall constitute a quorum for any meeting of the General Board. Four members shall constitute a quorum for any meeting of the Executive Committee.

Proxy and Voting by Mail

Section 26. No voting shall be done by proxy in meetings of the National Association. Proxy representation shall be accepted for meetings of the General Board and Executive Committee, upon the presentation to the moderator of a statement signed by the member, designating the proxy representative. A proxy for the Executive Committee shall be a member of the General Board.

Section 27. When a ballot of the General Board must be taken by mail, it shall be approved by the Executive Committee and circulated by the Executive Secretary to all members who shall have their vote notarized.

Discipline

Section 28. This National Association shall have the right to settle any questions of discipline, doctrine or practice that may properly come before it from any of the bodies composing said organization of the National Association of Free Will Baptists, Inc., or act upon any appeal that may be made by any body belonging to the National Association. Said appeal shall have been written and properly signed by the constituent body or bodies and filed with the Executive Secretary.

The Executive Secretary shall in turn present it to the Executive Committee who shall make recommendation to the General Board. The General Board shall, at its discretion, hear the appeal and shall make recommendation to the

National Association as to the course of action it deems best. The National Association may, in turn, hear the case by resolving itself into a committee of the whole, from which meeting all but delegates and parties concerned shall be excluded; or it may vote on the report of the General Board without discussion.

Section 29. The decision of the National Association in such matters shall be final; that is, it cannot be appealed, nor can the same issue be raised again except in one of the two following ways: The National Association may vote to reconsider and then refer the matter back to the General Board; or after the vote to reconsider it may again resolve itself into a committee of the whole.

Section 30. Any action which the National Association may take cannot reverse the action of any member body, although it may act in a hortatory and advisory capacity toward that end. Actual disciplinary action upon a member body can deal only with the member's rights as a member of the body; and in this vein the National Association may refuse to seat the delegates from a member body for a session of the Association or may ultimately withdraw fellowship from the member. The only members of the National Association who can be disciplined are those who are affiliated directly according to the membership provisions of Article II of the Constitution. Thus, in the case of those who are affiliated under the provision of Section 1 of that article, only the state associations may be disciplined; in the case of those affiliated under provision of Section 2, only the district associations may be disciplined; and the case of those affiliated under the provisions of Section 3, only the local church may be disciplined.

Honoraria and Reimbursements

Section 31. The moderator and clerk shall receive an honorarium as set by the Executive Committee in the annual convention budget, plus travel expenses to the annual session.

The assistant moderator or assistant clerk shall receive the same benefits in the absence of either the moderator or the clerk from the session of the National Association.

Section 32. When a special meeting of the General Board is called, the National Association shall assume the actual travel expenses of the members or their proxies, including meals and lodging. Automobile mileage shall be paid, not to exceed the amount allowable by the Internal Revenue Service. The same provision shall be made for all meetings of the Executive Committee except for the one which convenes immediately prior to the regular annual meeting of the General Board and National Association. Meals and lodging for the Committee during this meeting shall be provided for the days prior to the beginning of the Convention.

Parliamentary Authority
Section 33. The meetings of the National Association and General Board shall be governed by the rules of parliamentary law as set forth in *Robert's Rules of Order,* except in the case of those rules which are superseded by some rule of these organizations.

Amendments
Section 34. These by-laws may be amended or altered at any regular session of the National Association by a majority vote of the members present, provided proposed amendment or alteration be presented in writing to the body one day in advance.

STANDING RULES
OF THE NATIONAL ASSOCIATION, GENERAL
BOARD, AND EXECUTIVE COMMITTEE

1. Each session of the National Association shall be called into conference by the clerk, or assistant clerk, or in their absence the senior minister in years; and if a quorum is present, charge shall be then taken by the moderator, or assistant moderator, or in their absence the senior minister in years.

2. Each meeting of these bodies shall be opened by reading a portion of the Bible and with prayer, and shall be closed with prayer.

3. All meetings of these bodies shall convene with open doors except when resolved into committees of the whole.

4. Any person not a member of these bodies may be allowed to take part in the discussions by obtaining permission from the moderator.

5. It shall be the duty of all members of these bodies to be present at the time appointed for each meeting, and anyone wishing to retire shall first obtain permission of the moderator.

6. The moderator shall not allow discussions carried on in a spirit which is not Christian or orderly.

7. No member shall be allowed to speak more than ten minutes or more than twice on the same subject in meetings of the National Association and General Board without permission from the moderator.

8. At sessions of the National Association, the moderator shall seat delegates in a body in a designated section of the assembly room at the beginning of each business meeting.

9. At any meeting of the General Board or Executive Committee a member may have his dissenting vote recorded in the minutes by his request.

CHAPTER SIX

The National Association of
Free Will Baptists:
Its Origins and Ministries

THE ORIGIN OF THE NATIONAL ASSOCIATION

The Co-operative General Association of the Southwest and Midwest (founded 1916) was a mixture of those whose background was in the Palmer movement of the South and those who had stayed out of the merger of the northern Freewill Baptists with the Northern Baptist Convention in 1911. The General Conference (founded 1921–also known as the Eastern General Conference) consisted of those Free Will Baptists in the Southeast (the Palmer branch). The General Conference was by far the larger of the two groups.

By 1918 Free Will Baptists east and west had enjoyed enormous growth and success and were exploring possibilities for merging into a national association. The first attempt to merge was made in 1918, when representatives of the Southeast visited the meeting of the Co-operative General Association in Paintsville, Kentucky. These representatives invited the Co-operative General Association to hold its next annual meeting in its own territory of Nashville, Tennessee, but the attempt failed, and after 1919, the two groups went their separate ways.[1]

Two years later, the Free Will Baptists of the Southeast joined together into what came to be known as the General Conference, and soon representatives from the eastern and western segments of Free Will Baptists began to visit each other's conferences. By the end of the 1920s, the dream to merge the two groups again came to life.[2] North Carolina pastor and General Conference moderator R.F. Pittman's sentiments in 1930 were typical of the general mood of the time; he counseled his people to "lay aside selfishness and look beyond our Associations and Conferences, into a National view."[3]

Representatives from the Eastern General Conference and the Co-operative General Association were elected to a joint committee on union which met in 1932. This committee drafted a proposal to be approved by both bodies. By 1934, the two groups were ready to unite.[4] It was decided that both the General Conference and the Co-operative General Association would continue to exist as separate bodies, but they would cooperate in a larger organization, the National Association.

The first meeting of the National Association of Free Will Baptists took place at Cofer's Chapel Free Will Baptist Church in Nashville, Tennessee, on Tuesday evening, November 5, 1935.[5] On Wednesday, November 6, delegates were seated from four state conventions and 14 local associations from such states as Alabama, Florida, North Carolina, Georgia, Mississippi, Oklahoma, Missouri, Texas, Nebraska, Tennessee, Kentucky, West Virginia, and Ohio. In addition to the delegates from these areas, three observers were present from Arkansas, which would join a few years later. The delegates made every effort to ensure equal representation from east of the Mississippi (General Conference) as well as from west of the Mississippi (Co-operative General Association). Thus, of the officers elected by the body of the newly formed association, half were from the east and half were from the west. The new body was led by moderator J.L. Welch, the popular pastor of Cofer's Chapel.[6] On Wednesday evening Thomas H. "Pop" Willey spoke on the subject, "Foreign Mission Work in South America," after which a missions offering was received. This tradition continues to the present: during the annual convention of the National Association,

Wednesday evening is the missions service. The Reverend I. J. Blackwelder was elected Secretary of Foreign Missions (a position he had held in the General Conference). Miss Laura Belle Barnard (who was already a missionary with the General Conference) and Miss Bessie Yeley were officially approved as the first foreign missionaries of the National Association.[7]

In addition to missions, education was at the forefront of the first meeting of the National Association. For several years there had been a joint education committee which consisted of T.B. Melette (president of Zion Bible School in Blakely, Georgia) and J.L. Welch from the General Conference as well as Melvin Bingham, E.E. Morris, and Selph Jones from the Co-operative General Association. At this historic meeting, this committee recommended that the body approve a proposal for a new collegiate level institution to be owned and operated by the National Association and located in Nashville.[8] The delegates accepted the proposal and elected J. L. Welch Secretary of Education, along with five school trustees.[9]

A Treatise Revision Committee was named to frame a statement of doctrine and practice acceptable to both groups. This committee consisted of the Reverend J.C. Griffin (chairman), the Reverend C.B. Thompson, Mr. M.L. Morse, the Reverend W.B. Davenport, Mr. H.E. Post, the Reverend E.E. Morris, the Reverend Ralph Staten (advisory), the Reverend E.B. Joyner, the Reverend M.F. Van Hoose, the Reverend Winford Davis, and the Reverend J.S. Frederick. The newly revised *Treatise* was accepted by the body on Thursday morning, thus making the National Association of Free Will Baptists a reality. The executive committee consisted of the Reverends J.W. Alford (North Carolina), B.F. Brown (Missouri), E.B. Joyner (Florida), C.F. Goen (Texas), and Daniel F. Pelt (Alabama) and was charged with the responsibility of setting a meeting place for the next convention which was to be held in 1938.[10]

The original plan was that the National Association would convene every three years and the two merging bodies–the General Conference and Co-operative General Association– would meet annually. The General conference was renamed the Eastern Association, and the Co-operative General Association was called the Western Association. State and local associations that were affiliated with these bodies would, of course, continue their normal functions. Three years later, at the second meeting of the National Association (1938), the body voted to meet annually. The Eastern and Western Associations ceased to exist. The National Association has convened every year since 1938. After 1938 several state and regional associations affiliated with the National Association.

The National Association has enjoyed steady growth. For example, in 1940, the statistical report of the National Association revealed that there were 1,185 churches with a combined membership of 102,000 individuals.[11] Fifty-five years later, in 1995, the statistical report showed that the National Association had grown substantially, with 2,491 affiliated churches in 29 states, Canada, Mexico, and the U.S. Virgin Islands. The statistical report in 1995 listed 213,716 members. This is a low figure, however, based on the fact that around 160 churches did not report their membership. Interestingly, based on records of how many members have been added and lost over the past several years, Dr. Melvin Worthington, executive secretary of the National Association, has said that the total 1995 membership probably totaled around 270,000.

THE MINISTRIES OF THE NATIONAL ASSOCIATION

Foreign Missions

The Free Will Baptists who came together to form the National Association in 1935 had not had a distinguished record of foreign missions; if for no other reason, they did not have the organizational structure and, as a result, the funds to support missions abroad. The New England Freewill Baptists, who merged with the Northern Baptist Convention in 1911, had been able to support a flourishing foreign mission work in the 1800s, made possible by the large amounts of money which were the result of an efficient organization that spanned several northern states.

First Steps: 1901-1949
The "localism" of the Free Will Baptists of the South and Southwest which had prevented them from joining into a national body prior to 1935 could not produce the cooperative funds that were needed to support missions, but this began to change with the founding of the National Association. Though a Foreign Mission Society existed in the Eastern General Conference of the southeast as early as 1901 (and in 1931 was replaced by a General Secretary for Foreign Missions), a foreign missions program did not take root until the formation of the National Association.

Miss Laura Belle Barnard of Georgia and Miss Bessie Yeley of Ohio were already being supported by Free Will Baptists in the Eastern General Conference and Ohio, Miss Barnard in India and Miss Yeley in Venezuela. Soon after the establishment of the National Association, these two women became its first official missionaries. In 1936 the Reverend Thomas H. Willey, Sr. and his wife Mabel were commissioned by the National Association for mission work in Panama, later transferring to Cuba in 1941. These four great pioneers of modern Free Will Baptist Foreign Missions paved the way for an effective Free Will Baptist response to the Great Commission.[12]

The Board of Foreign Missions as we know it today was not officially begun until 1943, when the National Association approved a denominational constitution and by-laws which established a Board of Foreign Missions. The first chairman-treasurer of the Board, the Reverend Winford Davis, administered the Board from his home until 1950.

A Decade of Expansion: The Fifties

In 1950 the Reverend Raymond Riggs was elected promotional secretary-treasurer of the Foreign Missions Board. In 1953, the office of the Board of Foreign Missions was moved from Riggs' home to the national offices in Nashville, and at this time he became the full-time director of Foreign Missions.[13]

By this time, permanent Free Will Baptist mission works had been established in India, where Laura Belle Barnard had been joined by Miss Volena Wilson, and in Cuba, where the Willeys had established the Cedars of Lebanon Bible Institute in the Province of Pinar del Rio.[14] In 1954, Wesley and Aileen Calvery, "who had been trying unsuccessfully for two years to get into India, were sent to Japan as the first Free Will Baptist missionaries ever to set foot on that Island."[15] Fred and Evelyn Hersey joined the Calverys in Japan in 1956 and were followed in 1958 by Herbert and Geraldine Waid. In 1956 Lonnie and Anita Sparks founded the mission work in Ivory Coast, West Africa, and were soon joined by the Reverend and Mrs. Daniel Merkh and the Reverend and Mrs. Bill Jones. In 1957 the Reverend Dave Franks was appointed to Brazil, to be joined by Ken and Marvis Eagleton the following year. Later, in 1959, Sam and June Wilkinson and Eula Mae Martin were commissioned for ministry in Brazil. Thus by 1960, Free Will Baptists had instituted permanent mission works in five overseas countries.[16]

Free Will Baptist Foreign Missions Comes of Age:
The Sixties and Seventies

In January of 1960, after Riggs's resignation to return to the pastorate, the Reverend Rolla Smith was appointed General Director and served two years in that capacity. Under his leadership the ministry in Panama was reinstituted in 1961 by the families of Tom Willey, Jr., and John Moehlman. The Reverend J. Reford Wilson succeeded Rolla Smith in 1962 as General Director of Free Will Baptist

Foreign Missions and remained in that position for 13 years. These were years of enormous growth, with the total number of adult foreign missionaries increasing from 38 to 94. Wilson's tenure saw the establishment of mission stations in Uruguay (1962), France (1966), and Spain (1973).[17]

The 1960s also witnessed the growth of the stateside foreign mission staff as well as the establishment of a more intense program of mission promotion. Jerry Ballard, who joined the staff in 1960, was responsible for the development of literature and filmstrip resources which spread the work of Free Will Baptist Foreign Missions to its supporters across the country and around the world. Ballard served as the first editor of the now familiar *Heartbeat* magazine, which keeps Free Will Baptists informed about Free Will Baptist ministry around the world. Bill Jones and later Don Robirds continued the work Ballard had started.[18]

Many new missionaries were commissioned in the sixties. Though the Willeys were forced to leave Cuba in 1960 after diplomatic ties between Cuba and the U.S. were severed, they left behind a thriving work which continues to grow to this day. The families of Bill Fulcher and Paul Robinson began the work in Uruguay in 1962, and were subsequently joined by Walter and Marcia Ellison (1965) and Molly Barker, a registered nurse (1966). The mission work in France was begun by the Merkhs, who left Ivory Coast, West Africa, to minister in Nantes, France, beginning in 1966. The mission in Ivory Coast continued to thrive in the 1960s, with the establishment of a medical clinic by Dr. LaVerne Miley, and his wife Lorene in 1962. Expansion also occurred in Japan, where Jim and Olena McClain were added to the staff (1964) to complement the intense training of Japanese Christians for the work of ministry. The work in Panama was expanded in 1964 when the Reverend and Mrs. Estenio Garcia transferred from Cuba to Panama.[19]

The 1970s were a period of continued expansion of global mission among Free Will Baptists. In 1970, a cry went out from the Foreign Missions Department which indicated the unparalleled growth that was occurring in Free Will Baptist foreign missions: "We have more open doors than we can enter. We have an urgent need for more missionaries–Panama, France, Japan, Ivory Coast, and Brazil. We need missionaries now!"[20] In 1971 Spain opened its doors to Free Will Baptists–doors that had been closed by Roman Catholic control for centuries. Dock and Norma Jean Caton, the first missionaries to the new field, were appointed in May of 1972. During the next year they were joined by Lonnie and Anita Sparks, who left a successful work in Ivory Coast to minister in Spain. In 1975 Wilson resigned to become a professor of missions at Hillsdale College of Oklahoma, and Rolla Smith returned to the office. By this time most of the major fields of ministry which are today open to Free Will Baptist Foreign Missions had been established.

Free Will Baptist Foreign Missions Today

R. Eugene Waddell, who had come to the Foreign Missions Department in 1981 as Associate Director, became Director in 1986, when Smith retired. Waddell, who had long served as a Foreign Missions board member and held an advanced degree in missiology, built upon the foundation established in the five decades preceding his tenure. Waddell was assisted by veteran Ivory Coast missionary Jimmy Aldridge, who had become Overseas Secretary in 1984. Under Waddell's tenure, the number of American staff members in all the major mission fields has increased and foreign nationals have continued to assume the leadership of mission works. Emphasis has also been placed on the education of foreign nationals for church ministry; this has been achieved through the establishment of institutes in which nationals may receive instruction in biblical studies, theology, evangelism, pastoral ministry, and other relevant subjects.

Most recently, the Foreign Missions Department has responded to needs in China by sending teachers of English as a second language to China as associate missionaries. These missionaries, of whom Sarah Malone was the first, are sent out jointly with the English Language Institute, China. The most recent development in Free Will Baptist Foreign Mission outreach has been activity in the Former Soviet Union (the Commonwealth of Independent States). In 1996 Leroy and Fay Forlines were sent to the Former Soviet Union to teach Free Will Baptist theology in Russian Baptist educational institutions and churches. The Russian Baptists requested that Forlines' book on systematic theology be translated into Russian for the education of Russian Baptist ministers, who are Arminian Baptists. The book was published in 1996 by "The Bible for Everyone" publishing house in St. Petersburg. At present, the Foreign Missions Department allocates funds and sends short-term missionaries to serve in such ministries as lecturing, conducting pastors' conferences, and church planting in Russia.

The ministries of Free Will Baptist Foreign Missions are supported by the Together Way Plan. As of 1996 Foreign Missions was receiving 23 percent of all undesignated funds contributed through the cooperative plan. Foreign Missions is also supported by designated giving, which consists of general contributions designated to the Foreign Missions Department or to individual missionary accounts. Two national foreign mission offerings are received each year across the denomination: the World Missions Offering, sponsored by the Foreign Mission Department, and the Laura Belle Barnard World Missions Offering, sponsored by Women Nationally Active for Christ.

God has done a great work among Free Will Baptists in taking the gospel to the uttermost parts of the earth. In the first six decades of its existence, the Foreign Missions Department of the National Association of Free Will Baptists has laid the foundation for a vibrant and progressive global ministry in the twenty-first century.

Home Missions

Founding and Early Years

The first Home Missions Board of the National Association of Free Will Baptists was elected in 1938, three years after the founding of the National Association. Its members were the Reverend George Dunbar, the Reverend M.L. Hollis, Mrs. J.E. Frazier, the Reverend Mrs. Lizzie McAdams, and the Reverend J.K. Warkentin.[21] While the Home Missions Board experienced little success in its early years due to lack of funds, Lizzie McAdams and her husband set the pace for future home mission work among Free Will Baptists, organizing churches in Texas, Oklahoma, Kansas, Nebraska, and Missouri.[22]   M.L. Hollis's home missionary activity also served as an impetus for Free Will Baptist Home Missions in the latter half of the twentieth century. During his ministry, Hollis organized 24 Free Will Baptist churches, all in Mississippi and Texas.

Growth and Development

The growth of Home Missions among Free Will Baptists began to occur in the late forties, when the office of Promotional Secretary for Home Missions was established. The first Promotional Secretary, Harry Staires, who was elected in 1947, implemented a program of fund raising which laid the foundation for later efforts. Damon Dodd was elected the first full-time Secretary in 1953. From 1953-1956, Dodd's progressive leadership was the stimulus for the appointment of several "tent-makers" who went out under the Board without compensation. Among these were the Reverend and Mrs. Robert Wilfong (Tampa, Florida), the Reverend and Mrs. George C. Lee, Jr. (Nebraska), and the Reverend and Mrs. Sylvester Crawford (California). In 1955, Miss Bessie Yeley, who had served in Venezuela under the Foreign Missions Board, was appointed for service in the Tampa mission; the Reverend and Mrs. J. J. Postlewaite began ministering in Oregon and Washington; and the Reverend and Mrs. James Timmons became missionaries to Mexico. Damon Dodd resigned as Promotional Secretary (General Director) in 1956, and was succeeded by Homer E. Willis, who served until 1973.

Under Willis's tenure, Free Will Baptists set their sights on New England, and in 1958 the Reverend and Mrs. Mack Owens were appointed as home missionaries to Littleton, New Hampshire. The work of the Owenses led to the organization of churches which eventually joined together to comprise the Northeastern Association of Free Will Baptists.[23] Willis also oversaw the establishment of mission works in Alaska (the Reverend and Mrs. Lee Whaley) and Hawaii (the Reverend and Mrs. Luther Sanders).

The 1960s saw the establishment of mission works in such cities as Arlington, Virginia (Washington, D.C., area–the Reverend and Mrs. Ken Walker. This work was named the Bloss Memorial Free Will Baptist Church, after the Reverend J.B. Bloss, an innovative, early member of the Home Missions Board); Denver, Colorado (the Reverend and Mrs. Roy Thomas); St. Croix, Virgin Islands (the Reverend and Mrs. Larry Powell); and San Juan, Puerto Rico (the Reverend and Mrs. Fred McCoy).[24]

Continuing Ministry

In June 1973, the Reverend Robert L. Shockey, a dynamic minister from Kentucky, took the helm of the Home Missions Department. Shockey had served for five years previously as Associate Director. Roy Thomas assumed this post in 1978, after serving for many years as a successful home missionary and as Associate Director of the Home Missions Department. In 1995, Thomas was succeeded by Trymon Messer, a layman who had enjoyed a successful ministry as a lay-pastor of a growing church and as the Associate Director.

Since 1954, more than 200 families have been commissioned by the Home Missions Department. To date, the

Home Missions Department has placed missionaries in 46 states as well as the District of Columbia, Canada, Mexico, Puerto Rico, and the Virgin Islands. The Home Missions Department is also the endorsing agency for the placing of chaplains in the armed forces to minister to men and women in the service. These chaplains are commissioned officers in the United States armed forces.[25] Other functions of the Home Missions Board have included the publication of the Home Missions periodical, *Mission Grams,* which keeps Free Will Baptists up-to-date on developments in Home Missions, as well as books and pamphlets which engender concern for Home Missions among Free Will Baptists. The present thrusts of the Home Missions Department include the establishment of Free Will Baptist churches in large urban areas which are in desperate need of evangelical churches, as well as cross-cultural ministries in North America.

The Home Missions Department also administers the Church Extension Loan Fund, whereby individuals and churches invest funds, which are in turn loaned to local congregations for church building construction and other needs. The investors earn interest on the money they invest in the loan fund.

The ministries of Free Will Baptist Home Missions are supported by the Together Way Plan. As of 1996, Home Missions was receiving 18 percent of all undesignated funds contributed through the cooperative plan. Home Missions is also supported by designated giving, which consists of general contributions to the Home Missions Department or to individual missionary accounts. Two National Home Mission offerings are received each year across the denomination: the Benjamin Randall Offering, sponsored by the Home Missions Department; and the Lizzie McAdams Offering, sponsored by Women Nationally Active for Christ.

Free Will Baptist Bible College

Free Will Baptist Bible College is the institution of higher learning that is owned and operated by the National Association of Free Will Baptists. It offers bachelor's degree programs in Biblical and ministry studies for the education of ministers, missionaries, and Christian education specialists, as well as programs in such areas as business administration, elementary and secondary education, English, music, music education, physical education, psychology, and sports medicine. The college is fully accredited both regionally, by the Southern Association of Colleges and Schools, and professionally, by the Accrediting Association of Bible Colleges. The college's aim is to prepare "men and women for church-related ministries or for careers that are not church-related but are appropriate for Christians who see their lives as Christian service. In both cases the College is fulfilling the traditional Protestant vision of the sacredness of Divine vocation."[26]

The Desire for a College

Free Will Baptist Bible College arose out of a desire on the part of the people of the National Association to have a national institution of higher education to educate ministers and laypeople. A comprehensive institution had not existed among Free Will Baptists since Eureka College (North Carolina) and Tecumseh College (Oklahoma) had both been destroyed by fire in the late 1920s. Zion Bible School, under the leadership of the esteemed Reverend T.B. Mellette, which educated ministers for 12 years in Blakely, Georgia, closed in 1942 in deference to the Bible College, which opened that year. The need for a centrally-located academic institution was manifested on the part of several early leaders of the National Association, most notably J.C. Griffin and R.B. Spencer of North Carolina (Spencer had served as president of Eureka College in North Carolina from 1925 to 1928); T.B. Mellette and J.R. Davidson of Georgia; Henry Melvin of

Florida, Melvin Bingham of Oklahoma; and John L. Welch, Fannie Polston, Eva Ray, and Mrs. Ed Parker of Tennessee.[27]

Founding and Early Years

As early as 1939, the National Association's Board of Education had decided that Nashville, Tennessee, would be a suitable, central location for a denomination-wide college. Two years later, in 1941, the National Association elected the first board of trustees for the college. This board, made up of the Reverend J.R. Bennett, the Reverend Melvin Bingham, and the Reverend J.R. Davidson, immediately began to search for suitable property to serve the new school. The board unanimously agreed to make a bid for the property and building at 3609 Richland Avenue in Nashville. Their offer fell $1,000 short. Though the owner refused to reduce his price, he did agree to donate $1,000 to the school, enabling the board to purchase the property. Thus the first large donation to Free Will Baptist Bible College came from a Presbyterian layman.[28]

The first students, which arrived in September of 1942, consisted of the following nine individuals: Damon Dodd (Missouri), Sylvia Dodd (Missouri), James Hagin (Georgia), Opal Hiltibidal (Illinois), Rashie Kennedy (North Carolina), Sam Kennedy (North Carolina), Paul Ketteman (Illinois), Marie Thomas (Missouri), and George Waggoner (Illinois). These nine were joined later in the fall semester by Daniel Cronk (Michigan), Chester O'Donnell (Alabama), and Robert Woodard (North Carolina).[29] The first staff of the Bible College included J.R. Davidson, business manager; Miss Laura Belle Barnard, instructor; and Henry Melvin, instructor. The president was the Reverend L.C. Johnson, a bright, young minister from south Georgia.

Growth in the 1940s and 1950s

The college was initially established as a two-year school, and the first four graduates received their diplomas at the end of the 1943-44 school year: Damon Dodd, Sylvia Dodd,

Marie Thomas Hyatt, and George Waggoner. This school year also witnessed an increase in the student enrollment to 34, which represented a significant amount of growth for these wartime years.[30]

Such growth continued through the 1940s. In 1945, the Tennessee Department of Education approved the college for veteran's education under the G. I. Bill; the college was incorporated that same year. By 1950, the college had begun offering the Bachelor of Arts (B.A.) degree. By the 1950-51 school year, the enrollment had climbed from 12 students in 1942 to 100, and the total assets of the college had grown from $15,000 in 1942 to over $60,000. By 1956, the physical plant had grown to a total of six buildings: Richland Hall, Davidson Hall, Music Building, Ennis Hall, Memorial Auditorium, and the President's home. And by 1958, construction was completed on a student lounge and dining hall. By the end of this decade, the student body had surpassed the 200 mark, and the total assets of the college had grown to almost $400,000.[31] This decade also witnessed the accreditation of Free Will Baptist Bible College by the American Association of Bible Colleges (now the Accrediting Association of Bible Colleges) in 1958. The college has maintained recognition from this national professional accrediting organization up to the present.

Expansion in the Sixties and Seventies

The 1960s and 1970s were a time of tremendous growth for the Bible College. In 1964 the board of trustees launched a far-reaching expansion program that resulted in the construction of new buildings on the West End Avenue campus, such as the Academic Building. This program also included the renovation of certain historic Nashville buildings, the most beautiful of which was named Welch Library, in honor of the Reverend and Mrs. John L. Welch. This program of expansion and growth continued into the 1970s, in which was constructed the Cumberland Cafeteria (1971), a gymnasium

(1974), and the Welch Library Annex (1974). This expansion was accompanied by academic progress as well, with the continued development of the college curriculum. By the end of the 1970s, the college offered B.A. and B.S. degrees in such ministry-related fields as Biblical studies, pastoral studies, missions, and Christian education. It also offered degree programs in teacher education, English, music, nursing, and office management.[32]

The 1980s

In 1979 Dr. L.C. Johnson retired as President of the college and was succeeded by Dr. Charles Thigpen, who had served as Academic Dean for over 20 years. During Dr. Thigpen's tenure, the school inaugurated a graduate school which awarded the M.A. degree in the field of pastoral studies. This program was later replaced with the degree of Master of Ministry (M.Min.) which, similar to the standard Doctor of Ministry (D.Min.) programs, could be earned by students through a modular system while students were in ministry. The college continued to prosper under Thigpen's leadership. Dr. Thigpen retired in 1990 after 11 years of strong leadership.

Into the Present

Dr. Thigpen was succeeded by the Reverend Thomas Malone, a prominent pastor and former chairman of the Bible College board of trustees. With Reverend Malone as President and Dr. Robert E. Picirilli as Academic Dean, the college witnessed unprecedented progress in the 1990s. The curriculum was broadened considerably. Major fields such as business administration, physical education, sports medicine, human development and learning, music education, psychology, and youth ministry now complement the already existing majors, while minor fields such as drama and accounting have also been added. In addition to these curricular changes, the college has been granted full, regional accreditation by the Southern Association of Colleges and Schools. Such progress continues to take place within the context of the mission of Free Will Baptist Bible College: "to equip men and women, through Bible-based education, to serve Christ and His Church."[33]

Sunday School and Church Training Service: Randall House Publications

When the National Association of Free Will Baptists was founded in 1935, the Reverend Winford Davis was elected as National Sunday School Secretary. Three years later, the first Sunday School Board of the National Association was elected.[34] From 1940 to 1947, the Sunday school work of the National Association was promoted through a National Free Will Baptist Sunday School Convention, which was a subordinate organization to the National Association.[35] In 1947 the National Association again voted on a Sunday school board, which was chaired by the Reverend John West. The first Promotional Director of the Sunday School Board was the Reverend William Mishler, who took the post in 1954.

For the first 25 years of the National Association's existence, most churches received their Sunday school literature from the Free Will Baptist Press in Ayden, North Carolina, which was affiliated with the North Carolina State Convention. In 1959, after unsuccessful efforts to produce its own curriculum, the National Sunday School Board entered into a contract with the Free Will Baptist Press in North Carolina, whereby the Board would have influence over the Press's publication of the denomination's Sunday school literature. This relationship lasted from 1959 to 1962, during which time the Oklahoma State Association also produced and sold Sunday school curriculum. Because of a controversy between the National Association and the North Carolina State Convention that ended in a parting of the ways, the National Sunday School Department began publishing its own Sunday school literature in 1962, with the full backing of the publishing program in Oklahoma.[36]

That same year, the Reverend Roger Reeds from St. Louis, Missouri, became the first full-time Director of the Sunday School Department, a post he held until 1994. In 1963 Harrold Harrison also began to work for the Sunday School Department as full-time Promotional Secretary. Progress was rapid. By 1965 the Department had introduced a new Sunday school curriculum.[37] By 1966 sales had reached the $200,000 mark, and in 1967 a new Sunday School Department building was constructed at 1134 Murfreesboro Road in Nashville.[38] Growth was so rapid that in 1971, a new, larger property was acquired at 114 Bush Road in Nashville.[39] This facility, since renovated and enlarged, continues to house Randall House Publications and Randall Bookstore. In addition to publishing Sunday school literature, the Sunday School Department, under the name Randall House Publications, began publishing Christian books, pamphlets, and other church educational aids in the early 1970s.

In 1978 the Sunday School Department merged with the Church Training Service (CTS) Department of the National Association. CTS was an outgrowth of what in Free Will Baptist circles had been called Free Will Baptist League,[40] which had been in place by the early 1920s. Numerous people, such as Alice Lupton, J.L. Welch, Henry Melvin, C.F. Bowen, Samuel Johnson, and Ray Turnage were influential in the development of the Free Will Baptist League. In 1964 the National Association changed the name from Free Will Baptist League to Church Training Service. This department was responsible for the present-day youth ministries of the National Association. In 1972 the CTS Department began hosting annual music and arts competitions in conjunction with the annual convention of the National Association. This competition was part of the National Youth Conference (NYC), which has since maintained a vibrant and growing ministry to Free Will Baptist young people. The visionary leader behind the CTS department was Dr. Malcolm Fry, who together with his wife, Mae, labored hard for the success of CTS. After the merger in 1978, CTS, along with the National Youth Conference, came under the auspices of the Sunday School Department.

Steady growth occurred in the 1980s and early 1990s. In 1994, upon the retirement of Dr. Reeds, the Sunday School Board named Dr. Alton Loveless General Director of the Sunday School and Church Training Department. During his tenure Randall House has entered the information age with a presence on the Internet and development of new products utilizing computer technology. At the same time, Dr. Loveless has maintained the scriptural ideals on which the Department was founded. In 1995, the Reverend Keith Fletcher, a former editor at Scripture Press Publications, assumed the position of Editor-in-Chief and began extensive revisions of the Sunday school curriculum on the children's levels. Colorful covers and attractive, new graphics now enhance many products, providing students and teachers effective tools for Christian education. Randall House publishes Sunday school and Church Training literature for all ages. The Sunday school curriculum for teens and adults is based on a through-the-Bible survey approach, while Church Training materials include various topical and practical Christian education programs. Randall House also publishes books, pamphlets, and other Christian supplies which are marketed through Randall Bookstore and numerous Free Will Baptist bookstores throughout the country.

Women Nationally Active for Christ

The Early Twentieth Century

Women Nationally Active for Christ, the women's outreach arm of the National Association of Free Will Baptists, had its roots in local church women's societies at the turn of the century, with the establishment of organizations in such churches as Glennville Church in Glennville, Georgia (1890s), St. Mary's in New Bern, North Carolina (1907), and Cofer's Chapel in Nashville, Tennessee (1907). Women became increasingly active in the support of missions in the early twentieth century. For example, by the time the National Association was established in 1935, the Free Will Baptist women of Missouri could report a membership of 451 ladies.

Before the National Association was founded, the General Conference of the Southeast used such names as Woman's Home Mission, Women's Work, and Ladies' Aid Society, whereas the Cooperative General Association of the West used such titles as "Home Mission" or "Mission." Among the concerns of these Free Will Baptist women of the early twentieth century were missions, education, stewardship, temperance, and orphanages. One of the first women's organization publications was *The Record,* a publication of the Ladies' Aid Society of Cofer's Chapel Church in Nashville, which was introduced in 1908. This began a tradition of publishing among Free Will Baptist women's societies. Women in North Carolina and Tennessee led the way in this field, with the publication of 1,000 woman's organization manuals in 1927.[41]

The two most notable women who promoted women's work and were active in a host of concerns in the early twentieth century were Mrs. Alice E. Lupton of New Bern, North Carolina, and Mrs. Fannie J. Polston of Nashville, Tennessee. Alice Lupton gave the first report on women's activities at the General Conference in 1922 and three years later prompted the establishment of a five-member board of women's activities. Fannie Polston became the Field Secretary in June of 1926. Thus, it was Mrs. Polston who promoted ladies' auxiliaries throughout the denomination and paved the way for the establishment of a national women's organization in 1935.[42]

The Establishment of a National Women's Organization

In June of 1935, a meeting was held at Black Jack Church in North Carolina. This meeting, which preceded the establishment of the National Association of Free Will Baptists, was held in an attempt to unite the women of the East and West into a viable, national women's organization. At this meeting, the following officers were elected: Alice Lupton, North Carolina (President); Mary Ann Welch, Tennessee (First Vice President); Mrs. Sterl Phinney, Texas (Second Vice President); Lizzie McAdams, Texas (Third Vice President); Agnes Frazier, Tennessee (Fourth Vice President); Mrs. J.R. Bennett, North Carolina (Fifth Vice President); Miss Lola Johnson, Georgia (Recording Secretary); Mrs. T.B. Mellette, Georgia (Corresponding Secretary); Mrs. M.H. Mellette, South Carolina (Treasurer); and Fannie Polston (Tennessee), Field Secretary. This group chose the name National Woman's Auxiliary Convention, which was later changed to Woman's National Auxiliary Convention (WNAC).[43] This organization, like its predecessors, would focus on five major areas of concern: Christian education, missions, youth work, stewardship, benevolence, and prayer.[44]

Two of the most influential women in the early years of the National Woman's Auxiliary Convention were Agnes Frazier and Lizzie McAdams. The visionary Frazier served the national organization as, among other things, Editor, Historian, and Executive Secretary. She was responsible for the introduction of the "50,000 Co-Laborer" plan at the convention of the National Association in 1944. Lizzie McAdams established numerous new women's organizations and raised needed money in the early years of the national convention.[45]

The Growth and Development of WNAC

By 1947 the organization sensed the need for a national office. That year Mrs. Huey Gower was named the first Executive Secretary of WNAC with a salary of $50 per month. The first headquarters for WNAC was made possible by Free Will Baptist Bible College, which allowed Executive Secretary Agnes Frazier (who served from 1950-53) and the woman's auxiliary the use of a building on campus in 1952. By May of 1953, the National Association had purchased an office building on Richland Avenue in Nashville. Executive Secretary Gladys Sloan carried on the work of WNAC in this building. Sloan served until 1956, when Mrs. Eunice Edwards moved from Desloge, Missouri, to Nashville to assume the duties of the Executive Secretary. She held this post until 1963, earning a salary of $200 per month. Mrs. Cleo Pursell took the reins of WNAC in 1963 when she was elected Executive Secretary. She oversaw the relocation of the WNAC office into the new national office building at 1134 Murfreesboro Road in Nashville.[46] The WNAC office was maintained in this building until the new national offices were completed in 1991. Under Pursell's leadership, WNAC matured into the progressive organization it is today.

Dr. Mary Ruth Wisehart took the leadership of WNAC in 1985. During her tenure the organization has continued to make progress in ministry to women and Free Will Baptist women's collective ministry to our denomination and to the world. In 1993 the name Woman's National Auxiliary Convention was changed to Women Nationally Active for Christ, still maintaining the familiar initials WNAC. The 1990s witnessed many other good changes in women's work, most notably the increased emphasis on the Christian education of younger women and girls. WNAC continues to publish *Co-Laborer* magazine, of which Suzanne Franks began serving as editor in December 1994. The organization also holds an annual retreat. By 1995, WNAC had member organizations in 28 states and the U.S. Virgin Islands and 724 local churches.

Master's Men

Master's Men is an organization devoted to ministering to Free Will Baptist men. Master's Men "endeavors to relate every man to the work of the church and the work of the church to every man. It is a job of laymen enlistment based on constructive efforts to inform and *activate* every man for whom the local church is responsible."[47] Master's Men's motto is ATTACK: "All Together To Advance Christ's Kingdom." In its focus on equipping laymen for ministry and service, Master's Men has four main goals: to enlist men to serve, to organize men to serve, to train men to serve, and to inspire men to serve.[48] Thus, the organization seeks to carry the message that ministry and service are not reserved for ministers, but are the duty and calling of everyone.

Men's fellowships had long been part of many local Free Will Baptist churches when at the 1955 meeting of the National Association in Huntington, West Virginia, a motion was carried to establish a national men's organization. A three-member committee was elected to begin this men's organization which consisted of W. Stanley Mooneyham, O.T. Dixon, and Luther Gibson. The first few years of the department's existence witnessed the establishing of laymen's breakfasts at the national convention, the publication of *ATTACK* magazine, and the creation of evangelistic educational programs. In 1958 the organization purchased a truck, trailer, and winch for the mission field in Ivory Coast, West Africa. Interest in the work of this men's ministry grew steadily, and by 1964 membership was around the 3,000 mark.[49] That year, the ministry was reorganized as the "National Laymen's Board." A national Laymen's Congress was held in Kansas City with representatives from several states. Beginning in 1967 the board began sponsoring a national Laymen's Day of Prayer.

The year 1969 witnessed the appointment of the first Director of Master's Men, Ray Turnage. Though he served only until 1970, Turnage was successful in chartering 250 local Master's Men chapters and getting Master's Men included as a recipient of Cooperative Plan funds.

Times were difficult for Master's Men during the first half

of the 1970s, since there was no director. However, this decade saw a steady increase in the members and ministries of Master's Men. In 1974, for example, two programs were instituted: Project Tool Shed was set up to provide tools for overseas missionaries, and Project Book Shelf provided them with books. In 1975 the National Master's Men Board voted to hire Loyd Olsan as General Director of Master's Men. He began full-time status in 1978. Under Olsan's leadership, Master's Men continued to expand and began to show signs of maturity and definition as a national department. Olsan faithfully served Master's Men until 1983, when James Vallance was hired to serve as General Director.

James Vallance was a layman from West Virginia who had served on the National Master's Men Board since 1975. He came to the department with a vision as to how Master's Men could continue growing, establishing more chapters in local churches, and fulfilling the purpose for which it was founded. Yet Vallance also wanted to launch out into new areas of ministry for Free Will Baptist men. One such area was the Master's Hands Projects, which were begun in 1984. Under this program, Master's Men members from local churches have come together to build churches and mission facilities in the United States and in nine foreign mission fields. Over 70 such facilities have been constructed since that time. Thus the Master's Hands Projects have saved Free Will Baptists over $3 million in construction costs.

Many of the programs that Master's Men established in the 1980s and early 1990s have become the most defining characteristics of Master's Men as well as their most enduring contribution to the denomination at large. In 1985 the department began a "Decade of Discipleship" (1985-1995), to instill in men the importance of discipleship in the Christian life and the life of the local church. In December 1985 the board voted to begin the LifeMembership program, which has since attracted over 800 LifeMembers. Whereas regular membership dues go to pay Master's Men's day-to-day operating expenses, LifeMember dues, a one-time amount of $200, go into an endowment trust fund and are used for ongoing funding. Thus far, the Master's Men department has earned about $103,000 on the deposits in that trust.

Master's Men sponsors annual conferences as well as Sports Fellowship Ministries, such as the annual Free Will Baptist Softball Tournament in Nashville and an annual golf tournament. The department is also involved in an effort to minister to the Boy Scouts by, among other things, encouraging Free Will Baptist men to become scout leaders.

Master's Men receives 14 percent of all undesignated cooperative funds, just over half of the amount it costs to operate the department and its ministries. Thus the board has investigated ways of providing additional funding for the department. One of these is the Build-A-House campaign, which has the goal of raising $70,000. This amount will then be used in the construction of a residential home, built by Master's Men. The profits from the sale of the house will in turn be used to fund the department. Possibilities for the future include the hope of building housing for retired Free Will Baptist missionaries, ministers, widows, and others on fixed incomes.

The Board of Retirement and Insurance and the Free Will Baptist Foundation

The Board of Retirement and Insurance and the Free Will Baptist Foundation are two departments of the National Association that operate under the same board of trustees and administration. The Board of Retirement and Insurance, headed by Director William Evans, exists primarily to provide retirement income for employees of Free Will Baptist churches and denominational organizations. It also administers life insurance programs for members. The board administers well over 1,000 pension plans and retirement annuity funds for 30 annuitants.

The Board of Retirement and Insurance was founded as

the National Board of Superannuation in 1938. The first Chairman/Treasurer of the Superannuation Board was Mrs. J.E. Simpson, who administered the board along with five other members. During the 1940s the number of insurance and retirement policies increased steadily, and by 1954 the Board was administering a total of 57 "Endowment-at-Age-70" retirement policies. In 1955 they added an "Endowment-at-Age-65" program. In July of that year, the Board requested permission to hire a full-time director. Permission was granted and the Reverend K.V. Shutes was hired. Though Shutes resigned as full-time director in 1957, his wife, Secretary-Treasurer Lora Shutes, remained chief administrator of the board for 14 years.

In 1969 the present Board of Retirement and Insurance replaced the Superannuation Board, taking on the retirement plan of the North Carolina State Association of Free Will Baptists. Herman Hersey was the original director of the Board, and remained so until 1993. At first serving as part-time director of the Board, in 1973 Herman and his wife Vernie Hersey moved to Nashville where he became full-time Director of the Board of Retirement and Insurance. When Hersey began his duties, there were 17 retirement accounts. A year later that figure had risen to 120. In one year funds had risen from $3,600 to $37,000. The growth in assets was steady, and by 1983 pension accounts had topped the $2 million mark.

William Evans, who was hired as Assistant Director of the Board in 1990, became director of the Board after Hersey's retirement in 1993. Under his leadership the Board has adopted more accessible approaches to retirement and insurance for ministers and other denominational employees, attempting to reduce some restrictions that might have made the plan unattractive. There has been a sharp increase in the number of members and assets, and the department has made attempts to build bridges to state associations, initiating plans in some states that would allow funds from state co-operative plans to go to ministers involved in the Board's program.

The Free Will Baptist Foundation operates under the same trustees and administration as the Board of Retirement and Insurance. The Foundation assists individuals, local churches, and other organizations in planned giving. This allows for people and churches to set up trust funds for the perpetual financial support of Free Will Baptist ministries. Thus the Foundation encourages stewardship through gifts by deeds, wills, contracts, trust agreements, and securities. The Foundation also offers consultation in family financial planning and estate planning, including immediate and deferred giving. Through its ministry, the Foundation is attempting to ensure that Free Will Baptist ministries will have endowment funds that will produce income for God's work into the future until Christ returns.

The Executive Office

The Executive Office is administered by Executive Secretary Dr. Melvin Worthington and his staff. The roles of the Executive Office are numerous. It acts as an official liaison with other religious bodies and the federal government. It serves as the public relations arm of the National Association. It administers the Together Way Plan and publishes *Contact* magazine, the National Association's official publication. The Executive Office is also responsible for the annual conventions of the National Association and publishes the minutes, *Digest of Reports,* and the annual *Free Will Baptist Yearbook.* The Office also acts as the promotional office for the programs and ministries of the National Association of Free Will Baptists. The Executive Offices too repetitive publishes and sells *Rejoice: The Free Will Baptist Hymnbook* and *The Rejoice Hymnal for the Church at Worship.*

The head of the Executive Office is the Executive Secretary, whose duties are described in our *Treatise:* administration, general promotion, public relations, publications, stewardship, arranging the annual convention, and management of the national offices. The first Executive Office was begun by Executive Secretary L.R. Ennis between the fourth (1940) and fifth (1941) sessions of the National Association.[50] While it consisted of one part-time employee in 1941, the office now employs six full-time employees.

Perhaps the most important function of the Executive Office is its administration and promotion of the Together Way Plan. This plan is a program whereby denominational giving is promoted through two methods: Cooperative and Designated. The specific elements of the plan are as follows:[51]

1. Each local church will contribute at least 10 percent of its general income for denominational causes—district, state and national—whether cooperatively or by designation.

2. Each local church that does not give this 10 percent cooperatively will designate equitable portions for all denominational agencies.

3. Each state will work toward the goal of retaining 50 percent of this general giving for district and state causes combined and sending 50 percent to national ministries.

4. Each church will give, beyond this 10 percent minimum, appropriate designated offerings for various denominational agencies as needed to assume its fair share of support for those agencies.

The Together Way Plan promotes four special, annual drives to facilitate the giving above the 10 percent minimum. These are as follows:

April: Foreign Missions—"World Missions Offering"
             WNAC—"Laura Belle Barnard World
             Missions Offering"

September: "Rest of the Family Offering"
             Executive Office
             Retirement and Insurance

> Women Nationally Active for Christ
> Master's Men
> Free Will Baptist Foundation
> National Youth Conference
> Commission for Theological Integrity
> Historical Commission
> Music Commission
> Media Commission

November: Home Missions–"Benjamin Randall Offering"
            WNAC–"Lizzie McAdams Offering"

December: Free Will Baptist Bible College–
            "Paul Ketteman Christmas Offering"

Cooperative contributions through the Together Way Plan are divided among the agencies of the National Association. The Cooperative allocations are approved each year at the national convention. In 1996, for example, a budget was approved whereby gifts received through the Together Way Plan were to be allocated to the national ministries on the following basis:[52]

1. Underwrite the Executive Office Administration Budget above designated gifts, not to exceed 55 percent of cooperative gifts.

2. Disburse the balance of cooperative gifts to the following national ministries according to these percentages:

Free Will Baptist Bible College	23.0%
Foreign Missions	23.0%
Home Missions	18.0%
Retirement and Insurance	14.0%
Master's Men	14.0%
Free Will Baptist Foundation	6.0%
Commission for Theological Integrity	0.5%
Historical Commission	0.5%

Music Commission	0.5%
Radio and Television Commission	0.5%
	100.0%

One of the Executive Office's most monumental accomplishments since its creation in 1941 was the purchase of the 30,000 square-foot National Office Building located at 5233 Mt. View Road in Antioch, Tennessee. The Executive Office oversaw the purchase of this property as well as the sale of the former National Office Building property on Murfreesboro Road in Nashville. The new building houses all the National ministries with the exception of Free Will Baptist Bible College and Randall House Publications. It was dedicated on December 3, 1991.

Since its founding, the following Executive Secretaries have served in the Executive Office:

> L.R. Ennis, 1941-1944
> Robert Crawford, 1944-1948
> Ralph Lightsey, 1948-1949
> Damon C. Dodd, 1949-1953
> W. Stanley Mooneyham, 1953-1959
> Billy Melvin, 1959-1967
> Rufus Coffey, 1967-1979
> Melvin Worthington, 1979-

The Executive Office continues to serve the National Association of Free Will Baptists in a vital and indispensable role, being the office which is responsible for the administration and support of the National Association and its ministries.

THE COMMISSIONS OF THE NATIONAL ASSOCIATION

The Commission for Theological Integrity

The Commission for Theological Integrity of the National Association of Free Will Baptists exists for the fulfillment of three basic purposes:

(1) To alert our people of theological trends that could threaten our theological integrity as a denomination, (2) To prepare materials that will contribute to the continued preservation of the theological integrity of the denomination, and (3) As need and opportunity arise, to conduct seminars on subjects which are pertinent to the purpose of the commission.

The Commission was originally begun in 1962 as "The Commission on the Study of Theological Liberalism." The name was changed to "The Commission on Theological Liberalism," which remained the title until the mid-1980s, when it was renamed "The Commission for Theological Integrity." This five-member commission has accomplished several tasks. In addition to the publication of numerous books and pamphlets by such authors as F. Leroy Forlines, Robert E. Picirilli, and J.D. O'Donnell, the commission has held annual workshops on pertinent topics at the national convention. A sampling of the publications of the Commission would include the following: F. Leroy Forlines' *Morals and Orthodoxy* and *Inerrancy and the Scriptures*; Lonnie Skiles' and F. Leroy Forlines' joint work, *Prophets of Prosperity*; Jack Stallings's *Humanism*; Paul F. Hall's *The Battle for Integrity*; Bill M. Jones's *The New Age;* and Harrold Harrison's and F. Leroy Forlines' joint work, *The Charismatic Movement.*

In 1996, an annual Theological Symposium was instituted. The first symposium was held at Free Will Baptist Bible College in October 1996. At these meetings participants read scholarly papers on topics relevant to the denomination's theological integrity. Each paper is followed by a time of questions, discussion, and reflection. Copies of the papers are made available to each person attending. The Commission for Theological Integrity continues to serve in a significant way by encouraging research and writing on theological trends that should be of concern to Free Will Baptists.

The Media Commission

The Media Commission (formerly the Radio and Television Commission) of the National Association of Free Will Baptists was founded in 1983 for the purpose of exploring and implementing ways in which Free Will Baptists could minister through the media of radio and television. The Commission was started as a study commission, but was later given full commission status. In July 1985 the Commission presented an actual broadcast for the national convention body to hear. After that point, the Reverend Tom Malone was the speaker for a weekly broadcast of a half-hour in length.

The plan presented by the Commission was that it would produce the program and would cooperate with local churches or associations, who would provide the funds and make the contacts with local radio stations for broadcast of the program. The Commission produced enough 30-minute programs to have nine months of weekly broadcasts.

Soon, however, the members of the Commission decided it was not feasible to offer 30-minute broadcasts, since it was difficult to find 30-minute time slots at local radio stations. Thus they began producing a 15-minute program with the Reverend Robert Shockey as speaker. The Commission produced 150 of these programs (a three-year supply of weekly broadcasts). Music for these radio programs consists of recordings made by Free Will Baptist musicians. The Media Commission actively seeks new music recordings from Free Will Baptist musicians for inclusion in its programming.

Funding for the Media Commission consists of one-half of one percent of the annual undesignated co-operative funds in addition to any designated funds that might be donated to the

Commission. The Commission has numerous ideas for the future. The most recent project consists of short television spots jointly produced with the Florida State Association of Free Will Baptists. The Commission also anticipates the production of short radio segments of around a minute in length to share the good news of Christ and make the ministry of Free Will Baptists known to local communities.

The Music Commission

In 1987 the Executive Office of the National Association published *Rejoice: The Free Will Baptist Hymn Book*. This book had been produced by a Hymn Book Committee which had been elected by the body of the National Association. The members of the Hymn Book Committee were Vernon Whaley (Chairman), R. Douglas Little (Secretary), W. Blaine Hughes, Leroy Cutler, Bill Gardner, Ted Wilbanks, and Rodney D. Whaley. At the National Convention at Kansas City, Missouri, in July 1988, this committee made two recommendations, among which was the suggestion that the National Association establish a permanent Music Commission. The proposed purposes of this commission were to be the preservation and promotion of Free Will Baptist hymnody, the preparation of the *Rejoice* hymnal for generic use, the institution of music workshops and training seminars, and the publication of choral music and music curriculum. The report, along with its recommendations, passed, and five men were elected to serve on the first music commission: Blaine Hughes (5 years), Vernon Whaley (4 years), Rodney Whaley (3 years), R. Douglas Little (2 years), and Bill Gardner (1 year).

Since its inception, the Music Commission has steadily accomplished its goals. Sales of the 1987 hymnal required a new edition of *Rejoice: The Free Will Baptist Hymn Book,* which was published in 1995. The commission also prepared a generic version for use in non-Free Will Baptist churches entitled *The Rejoice Hymnal for the Church at Worship*. Since then the Music Commission has been in the process of accomplishing numerous goals, among which are the publication of choral song books and the recording of sound tracks of traditional hymns for use in various worship settings.

The Historical Commission

The Historical Commission of the National Association of Free Will Baptists exists to preserve Free Will Baptist historical materials and educate Free Will Baptists on their heritage. The commission was founded in July of 1963 when the National Association convened in Detroit, Michigan. The original commission was made up of Damon Dodd, Bill Hill, and George C. Lee, Jr. The Historical Commission has initiated many projects since its beginning. These projects can be divided into four basic areas:

(1) *Research and Writing.* The commission has worked to produce such publications as *A History of Free Will Baptist State Associations* and *The Fifty-Year Record of the National Association of Free Will Baptists,* both published by Randall House Publications. The Commission members have also been involved in writing articles for the Free Will Baptist Bulletin Service.

(2) *Archival Collection.* One of the most important tasks of the Historical Commission has been to collect and catalogue Free Will Baptist historical materials such as old minutes, books, pamphlets, letters, sermons, and other documents of historical value. The Historical Collection at Welch Library of Free Will Baptist Bible College is the repository for these materials. Free Will Baptists who have old and rare Free Will Baptist materials are encouraged by the Commission to donate these materials to the Collection.

(3) *Sponsorship of Lectures.* The Historical Commission participates in the annual Heritage Week at Free Will Baptist Bible College. This consists of lectures, films, and other events to stimulate and educate students, faculty, staff, and others on various subjects of church history. The Commission

also encourages other colleges to have similar emphases.

(4) *Donations for Historical Enterprises.* The Historical Commission on occasion makes funds available for certain historical preservation projects as well as for research and writing. One example of this work is a $2,500 grant to the historic Ridge Church in New Durham, New Hampshire, associated with the northern Freewill Baptist movement. The Commission has also given grants for projects such as the writing of a graduate thesis relevant to Free Will Baptist history.

NOTES FOR CHAPTER SIX

[1] William F. Davidson, *The Free Will Baptists in America, 1727-1984*, (Nashville: Randall House Publications, 1985), p. 343.

[2] Dodd, p. 118.

[3] William F. Davidson, "The National Association of Free Will Baptists: Fifty Years of God's Faithfulness," in *The Fifty-Year Record of the National Association of Free Will Baptists* (Nashville: Randall House Publications, 1988), p. 5.

[4] Davidson, *The Free Will Baptists in America*, 356-58.

[5] Ibid., 358. Davidson says, "Though formal organization was delayed until additional delegates could be present, this Tuesday evening meeting constituted the first official session of the new National Association of Free Will Baptists."

[6] Ibid., 359.

[7] Damon C. Dodd, *The Free Will Baptist Story* (Nashville: Executive Department of the National Association of Free Will Baptists, 1956) pp. 123-24.

[8] The committee had already seriously investigated purchasing a defunct Methodist college campus in Weaverville, North Carolina, but this venture fell through due to technicalities (Michael R. Pelt, *A History of Original Free Will Baptists* [Mount Olive, North Carolina: Mount Olive College Press, 1996], p. 255).

[9] Dodd, pp. 123-24.

[10] Ibid., 124-25.

[11] This included the members of those churches in North Carolina which severed ties with the National Association in 1962.

[12] "50-Year History of Foreign Missions," in *The Fifty-Year Record*, pp. 54-55.

[13] Davidson, *The Free Will Baptists in America*, p. 388.

[14] "50-Year History of Foreign Missions," pp. 59-60.

[15] Dodd, p. 133.

[16] Davidson, *The Free Will Baptists in America*, pp. 389-90.

[17] Ibid.

[18] "50-Year History of Foreign Missions," p. 57.

[19] Davidson, *The Free Will Baptists in America*, pp. 388-90; "50-Year History of Foreign Missions," p. 66.

[20] Cited in Davidson, *The Free Will Baptists in America*, p. 391.

[21] Pat Thomas, "A Brief History of the Home Missions Department," in *Who's Who Among Free Will Baptists* (Nashville: Randall House Publications, 1978), p. 417.

[22] Ibid.

[23] Davidson, *The Free Will Baptists in America*, p. 393.

[24] Thomas, p. 421.

[25]Ibid., p. 424; *Free Will Baptist Home Missions Directory* (Antioch, Tennessee: Free Will Baptist Home Missions, 1996).

[26]*Free Will Baptist Bible College Catalogue* (1996-1998), p. 7.

[27]"Story of A College: Free Will Baptist Bible College," in *The Fifty-Year Record*, p. 34.

[28]Davidson, *The Free Will Baptists in America*, pp. 395-96.

[29]Dodd, pp. 154-55.

[30]Lonnie Skiles and Mary Ruth Wisehart, "A Brief History of Free Will Baptist Bible College," in *Who's Who Among Free Will Baptists*, p. 475.

[31]Ibid., pp. 476-78.

[32]Ibid., pp. 479-80.

[33]*Free Will Baptist Bible College Catalogue*, 1996, p. 7.

[34]Davidson, *The Free Will Baptists in America*, p. 402.

[35]Roger C. Reeds, "A Brief History of the Sunday School Department," in *Who's Who Among Free Will Baptists*, p. 450.

[36]See chapter eight for more information on this controversy.

[37]Davidson, *The Free Will Baptists in America*, pp. 402-03.

[38]Roger Reeds, "A Brief History of the Sunday School and Church Training Department," in *The Fifty-Year Record*, p. 93-94.

[39]Ibid., 99-100.

[40]This name was suggested by John L. Welch.

[41]"Laborers Together with God: A History of WNAC," in *The Fifty-Year Record*, pp. 103-04.

[42]Ibid., 105.

[43]Ibid., pp. 105-06.

[44]Ibid., pp. 107-12.

[45]Mary R. Wisehart, "A Brief History of the Woman's Auxiliary," in *Who's Who Among Free Will Baptists*, pp. 458-59.

[46]"Laborers Together with God," pp. 112-14.

[47]"A Brief History of the Master's Men," in *Who's Who Among Free Will Baptists*, p. 432.

[48]Ibid.

[49]"Master's Men History," in *The Fifty-Year Record*, pp. 80-81.

[50]*The Fifty-Year Record*, p. 26.

[51]The following is excerpted from a booklet entitled, "The Together Way Plan" (Antioch, Tennessee: National Association of Free Will Baptists, 1994), p. 5.

[52]*The 1998 Free Will Baptist Yearbook*, p. A-245.

CHAPTER SEVEN

Free Will Baptist Ministries on the State and Local Levels

COLLEGES

California Christian College

California Christian College is a Bible college owned and operated by the California State Association of Free Will Baptists. Its primary purpose is the education of ministers and other Christian leaders for Free Will Baptist churches in the western United States. California Christian College is an outgrowth of educational programs begun in 1955 after the California State Association voted to establish a Bible college. The first Board of Christian Education of the California State Association of Free Will Baptists consisted of the Reverend Dean Moore, the Reverend Wade Jernigan, the Reverend Jerry Dudley, the Reverend Wilson Lawless, and the Reverend Ralph Hampton, Sr. This board established a six-week institute, which started in the fall of 1955. These kinds of institutes were held until February of 1958, when a more permanent program of higher education was inaugurated. In this semester, classes met at the Sherwood Forest Free Will Baptist Church in El Sobrante, California. The school, named California Bible Institute, had as its mission the provision of an educational program for Free Will Baptist ministers, teachers, and Christian workers. The institute's first president was the Reverend Dean Moore. Its curriculum consisted of four fields: evangelism (taught by the Reverend Herman F. Hoffman), Bible (taught by the Reverend Bethel H. Robertson), Christian Education (taught by the Reverend

Carl Young), and theology (taught by Dean Moore). This initial program was intended as a post-secondary, two-year program of studies. The institute worked out an agreement whereby graduates of the two-year program could transfer to Free Will Baptist Bible College. The school grew steadily over the next several years. Enrollment during the 1963-64 school year was at 71. In 1965, it was decided that the school should relocate to Fresno. This move had a negative effect on enrollment, with only 26 students registered for the 1965-66 school year. Dean Moore resigned just before the move and was succeeded as president by the Reverend C. Eugene Rogers of Missouri, who served from 1965-68. The Reverend Wade Jernigan was named president in 1968. Under his tenure, the school experienced tremendous growth. The name was changed to California Christian College in 1968. The California Department of Education approved the awarding of the four-year Graduate of Theology degree that same year, and in 1970, the first Bachelor of Science (B.S.) degrees were awarded. During the ten years of Jernigan's administration, the campus was expanded by several buildings and seven acres of land. After his resignation in 1978, Dr. Daniel Parker was elected president.

The 1980s witnessed tough times for California Christian College. Though the enrollment of the college dropped, the Reverend John Smith, a California pastor who was president of the college in the early 1980s, held things together. The administration of the college felt the need for a hiatus for regrouping in 1985-86. Then, in 1986, the Reverend James McAllister succeeded Smith as president. Smith remained as a board member and served several years as chairman of the board. Under the tenure of President McAllister, California Christian College has maintained its emphasis on sound and vibrant Biblical education for Free Will Baptist Christian workers. Though the enrollment is small (the college has maintained a full-time equivalency of between 50 and 100 students), the college maintains a steady flow of effective graduates who use their calling, talents, and education to serve the Lord in California and elsewhere.

Hillsdale Free Will Baptist College

Hillsdale Free Will Baptist College is a four-year college affiliated with the Oklahoma State Association of Free Will Baptists. The college is accredited by the Oklahoma State Regents for Higher Education and is governed by a board with members from Oklahoma, Arkansas, Missouri, Texas, Kansas, and New Mexico. Hillsdale began operations with the name Oklahoma Bible College on February 3, 1959. Though an institution of higher education had been on the minds of Free Will Baptists in Oklahoma for many years, the Reverend John H. West was one of the most important forces behind the idea. West was chairman of the Board of Christian Education of the Oklahoma State Association when the board began serious planning for the opening of the college. In 1959, the board consisted of John West, Wade Jernigan, Melvin Bingham, Weldon Wood, and Marlin Bivins.

In that first semester, the college offered eight semester hours in four courses. The total tuition collected from the 54 students that enrolled was $290. Thirty students finished out the semester. The inaugural faculty at Oklahoma Bible College consisted of the Reverend Roy Bingham (Practical Evangelism), the Reverend Don Payne (English and Pastoral Theology), N.R. Smith (Book of Acts), Bill Sherrill and Mrs. N.R. Smith (both of whom taught Sunday School Administration).

In 1959, at the annual meeting of the Oklahoma State Association, the body voted to relocate the campus to the camp grounds of the Grand River Association in Wagoner, Oklahoma. The hope was that the college would operate there for three semesters until a more suitable site was found. In 1960, the Oklahoma State Association voted to locate the school in Oklahoma City. Property was purchased and the school moved in January 1961. In 1961, the governance of the school changed from the Board of Christian Education of the Oklahoma State Association to a seven-member board of trustees with two members to be elected each year. The first board of trustees included Howard Gwartney, Paul Inbody, Wade Jernigan, J.B. Fletcher, Charles Hinesley, Bob Followill, and John West. That same year, the college, under the direction of its first president, the Reverend Daniel Parker, took a bold step and launched its new junior college curriculum. Parker was succeeded by Don Payne in October of that year.

By the fall of 1962, Oklahoma Bible College had a faculty of five part-time instructors and one full-time president-instructor. Tuition that year was two dollars per credit hour, which made up 20 percent of the college's income. In September of that year, the college purchased its permanent campus near Moore, Oklahoma. By 1964, the college was experiencing tremendous growth, and the Board of Trustees voted to issue $140,000 in first mortgage bonds to finance a building program.

In 1966, the college began steps toward accreditation by the Oklahoma State Regents for Higher Education. That same year, Dr. J.D. O'Donnell was inaugurated president. A $300,000 building program was begun under his tenure. The college continued to experience steady growth, with an enrollment of 70 students in the fall of 1969. During that year, measures were approved to begin construction on an activities building, and the Oklahoma State Association voted to extend trustee board membership so that the board would have one member each from the states of Arkansas, Missouri, Texas, Kansas, New Mexico, and Colorado.

In October of 1970, the State Association voted to change the name of Oklahoma Bible College to Trinity College, owing to the increasing student enrollment in the field of education as well as the effort to include other states in the college's ministry. The Secretary of State of Oklahoma would not approve the measure because there was already an institution of the same name in Oklahoma. In 1971, the name "Hillsdale" was selected by the board of trustees from 27 names that had been suggested to the board. The name was selected in honor of Hillsdale College in Hillsdale, Michigan, which had originated with the northern Freewill Baptists and remained Freewill Baptist until the 1911 merger with the Northern Baptists.

Bill M. Jones was the first president of the school after it changed its name. He took office in August 1971, after Dr. O'Donnell's resignation. Under Jones's administration, the college increased its liberal arts offerings and continued to expand. The Activities Building was completed in February 1972, and by the fall of 1972, enrollment had increased to 115 on-campus students and 40 extension students. The first four-year degree recipients graduated in the spring of 1974. By the fall of 1976, enrollment had reached 188 students. This trend of growth continued into the 1980s.

In 1982, the Reverend Edwin Wade, a Free Will Baptist minister and graduate of Azusa Pacific University in California (B.A., M.A.) became president of Hillsdale. The school continued its development in the 1980s under his leadership. In 1988 Wade resigned and was replaced by the Reverend Jim Shepherd, a Free Will Baptist pastor. Shepherd was the first Hillsdale alumnus to serve as chief executive of the college. In addition to his bachelor's degree from Hillsdale, Shepherd held an M.Div. degree from Southwestern Baptist Theological Seminary. Rev. Carl Cheshier became president of Hillsdale in 1997, after Shepherd returned to the pastorate. Though the 1990s have witnessed some difficulties for Hillsdale, God has blessed them with a strong and committed faculty, staff, and student body.

Hillsdale's mission statement declares that the college is "committed to the intellectual, spiritual, social, moral, and physical development of its students. It seeks to prepare students to serve the Lord Jesus Christ, both in the church and in society at large."[1] The graduates of Hillsdale, who serve in churches and mission fields around the globe as well as in non-ministry related careers, have attested well to the college's commitment to this goal.

Southeastern Free Will Baptist College

Southeastern Free Will Baptist College began operations in the fall of 1983 with an enrollment of 71 students.[2] Southeastern was founded by Free Will Baptist ministers and churches for the primary purpose of educating full-time Christian workers. Its founders were concerned that many in the Free Will Baptist denomination were moving away from fundamentalism toward neo-evangelicalism, and thus they envisioned a college that would embody a more rigorous fundamentalism. The college was initially located in Virginia Beach, Virginia, at Gateway Free Will Baptist Church. The Reverend Randy Cox, pastor of First Free Will Baptist Church in Raleigh, North Carolina, was named part-time president, a post in which he served until 1985.

In May 1985, the board of directors elected Dr. Joe Ange as full-time president of Southeastern. In this same year, the college enjoyed a high enrollment of 170 students. Unable to find land for the college in the Tidewater area of Virginia, in May 1987 the board purchased 61 acres of land in Wendell, North Carolina, just nine miles east of Raleigh. Construction began at the new location in July 1987, and classes began on October 1 of that year.

In 1989, after Joe Ange resigned as president, the board of directors elected the Reverend Billy M. Bevan as the college's third president. Bevan was pastor of Hilltop Free Will Baptist Church in Fuquay-Varina, North Carolina. The board agreed that he should continue to pastor the church while serving as president in a part-time capacity. He served in this position for seven years. On August 1, 1996, he became full-time president of Southeastern and continues to serve in that capacity.

In the early to middle 1990s, the college experienced financial difficulties and a drop in enrollment (89 students in fall 1994), but soon recovered from this slump. As of the fall of 1996, enrollment at the college had reached 152. The college administration is projecting an enrollment of well over 200 by the turn of the century. In 1996, Southeastern embarked upon a building program, with a projected completion date of January 1, 1998. Plans were made for a 21,000 square-feet, multi-purpose building. This facility would house a full-size gymnasium, business offices, offices for the president and promotional director, classrooms, and a conference room.

The college is governed by a twelve-member Board of Directors. As of 1997, this board consisted of the following members: Dr. Dann Patrick, Chairman (North Carolina); Dr. Randy Cox (North Carolina); the Reverend Van Dale Hudson (Mississippi); the Reverend Earl Hendrix (South Carolina); the Reverend Larry Stevens, Secretary (Indiana); Dr. Lorenza Stox (North Carolina); the Reverend Rudolph Outlaw (North Carolina); Dr. Curtis Linton (Oklahoma); the Reverend Larry Haggard (Oklahoma); the Reverend Doug King (North Carolina); the Reverend David Nobles (Virginia); and the Reverend Billy Bevan (North Carolina).

Southeastern offers bachelor's degrees in such fields as Bible, pastoral theology, missions, music, music education, elementary education, secondary education, and business. A recent statement from the college summarizes the educational purpose and mission of Southeastern:

> The purpose of Southeastern Free Will Baptist College is to train young men and women for church-related ministries. While we fully understand and appreciate that all truth is God's truth, it is our purpose to prepare our students for a variety of church related ministries. . . . [We prepare] pastors, associate pastors, evangelists, missionaries, Christian school teachers, youth pastors, bus pastors, church musicians, and Christian business professionals. Students choosing to attend Southeastern Free Will Baptist College do so

because our program is more "ministry oriented" than "career oriented."

In educating men and women for full-time Christian service, Southeastern emphasizes strong local churches, pastoral authority, soul winning, revival, Christian schools, home and foreign missions, high academic standards, and practical application.

Southeastern's commitment is summarized in the following words of President Billy Bevan:

> At Southeastern, we have a commitment to carry out the great commission of our Lord. We want to be personally involved, not in lesson only, but in life, and in telling others about Jesus. But our commitment reaches even deeper than that. Not only do we want to be personally involved, we want to be involved in training an army of young people who will go into the "highways and hedges" of our world to do a work for Jesus.[3]

FAMILY CARE MINISTRIES

Free Will Baptist Children's Home, Eldridge, Alabama

Free Will Baptist Children's Home in Eldridge, Alabama, is a home for children that is licensed for 30 children and is affiliated with the Alabama State Association of Free Will Baptists. The home, under the supervision of the Reverend Levy Corey, is located on a 200-acre plot of land in northwestern Walker County, Alabama. Its agricultural setting allows children to grow up in a wholesome atmosphere and learn a strong work ethic and valuable lessons for life. Free Will Baptist Children's Home began operation in August of 1947.

The purpose of the home is "to provide care for children who are in need of a home because of sexual, physical, or emotional abuse, neglect, tragedy, or death of the parent."[4] The home cares for children from six years of age through high school graduation (though the age of initial admission ranges from age 6 through 14). Court officials, welfare and social agencies, churches, friends, neighbors, and parents, are among those who direct children to the Children's Home. "Our children come from homes broken by separation, divorce, and desertion, or from family distress situations. Boys and girls are accepted simply because they need a good home—because they are innocent victims of circumstances or lack of opportunity."[5]

The Children's Home strives to maintain an atmosphere that is as much like home as possible. Children reside in groups of eight to ten with houseparents in the Manor House, a 19th-century building which is divided into four living units, each with kitchens, living rooms, dining rooms, bedrooms, and bathrooms.

Free Will Baptist Children's Home "is the modern home which teaches the old-fashioned virtues of courage, courtesy, honesty, hard work, and thrift. The children are taught that America is a great nation because it was founded and guided by people who put their trust in God."[6]

Free Will Baptist Family Ministries, Greeneville, Tennessee

Free Will Baptist Family Ministries (FWBFM) is a multi-faceted family care organization which is owned and governed by the Tennessee State Association of Free Will Baptists. The mission of FWBFM is "to meet the individual needs of children and families by seeking to unify and preserve the family *in order to share Christ and instill Christian values.*" The vision of FWBFM is "to be nationally recognized as a model of excellence in *family and child care.*" FWBFM was founded in 1939 as the "Free Will Baptist Orphanage" by Mr. and Mrs. I.L. Stanley. Later the name was changed to "Free Will Baptist Home for Children." In 1994, the Tennessee State Association of Free Will Baptists voted to change the name to "Free Will Baptist Family Ministries." This name change represented the growth and expansion of FWBFM into a more wide-ranging family care organization. Four ministries presently operate under the umbrella of FWBFM.

First is the Trula Cronk Home for Children, the main children's home ministry of FWBFM. Licensed by the Tennessee Department of Human Services as a Residential Child Care Agency, this ministry maintains three homes with eight children each. The home is named for Mrs. Trula Cronk, the first child to be placed in the orphanage in 1939. She later became a pioneering Free Will Baptist missionary to India with her husband, Dan Cronk.

FWBFM also operates The P.A.T.H. Shelter. P.A.T.H. stands for *Protecting Adolescents and Teaching Hope.* This is a "short-term" house on the campus of FWBFM which provides temporary residence (normally up to 30 days) for children who are awaiting a more permanent home environment. Usually, these children come straight from abusive crisis situations.

The Stanley Foster Care Program is named after Mr. and Mrs. I.L. Stanley, the founders. Licensed as a Tennessee child-placing agency, the Stanley Foster Care Program places children from birth to age 18 in Christian foster homes.

FWBFM also operates The Oaks Family Conference Center and Camp. The Oaks is "a biblically based ministry with the purpose of providing adults and youth with an enjoyable environment for developing a stronger relationship with Jesus Christ." This ministry focuses on three basic areas: (1) building functional families, (2) providing programs to build faith and character, and (3) ministering to fellow Christian workers.

An essential part of FWBFM is the Heart Stone Farm, which provides children with work experiences with cattle and sheep. Each child gains experience raising his own animal for competition. This teaches the children a work ethic and gives them valuable experiences on the farm.

In October 1997, Rev. James Kilgore was hired to serve as the Executive Director. Rev. Kilgore is very optimistic about the future of FWBFM. God is continuing to bless this ministry to children and families. In May 1998, FWBFM purchased a home adjacent to the existing property to house 10 to 12 additional children. A capital campaign was also announced with plans for building another P.A.T.H. shelter.[7]

Free Will Baptist Home for Children, Turbeville, South Carolina

Free Will Baptist Home for Children in Turbeville, South Carolina, is a children's home affiliated with the South Carolina State Association of Free Will Baptists. It is located on a 40-acre tract of land in the central South Carolina town of Turbeville. The vision for a children's home in South Carolina was introduced at the Free Will Baptist Sunday School Convention of 1922 in Timmonsville, South Carolina. Yet this vision did not become a reality until October of 1949, when the home first began operation.

The home has since grown from a two-story building to spacious facilities which include a large colonial-style structure with dormitories on either side. The home usually houses over 20 children. "Free Will Baptist Home for Children provides care, support, and training for dependent and needy children. With a marked spiritual emphasis, the Home seeks to meet the needs of the total child, recognizing his physical, educational, social, and emotional needs."[7]

James D. Wilhide, the home's executive director, states, "Our home's most important task is to help a child, hurt by life, once more to find faith and purpose for living." The home accepts children ranging in age from six to seventeen years. Free Will Baptist Home for Children has an annual budget of well over $200,000. Operating funds are contributed not only by Free Will Baptist individuals and churches inside and outside of South Carolina, but also by businesses and other organizations. The staff of the home continues to sense God's blessing on its ministry.

Harvest Free Will Baptist Child Care Ministries, Duffield, Virginia

Harvest Free Will Baptist Child Care Ministries is a children's home in Duffield, Virginia. Harvest began with the burden of Chris Dotson, his brother Newl Dotson, and Teresa Tilson. These three had worked together at the Free Will Baptist Children's Home in Greeneville, Tennessee. In 1992 they began to sense the need for a similar children's home in Southwestern Virginia. The need for child-care ministries in this area was great, due largely to the economic depression that had hit this region. After a survey of social services in this region, they began actively working toward the establishment of a child-care ministry.

The difficulty they faced was the prospect of finding a site for the home and raising enough funds so that they could have at least $70,000 on hand. This was required before they could obtain a license for the home. They were told it would probably be two years before they could obtain a license, but on August 2, 1993, after 11 months, the home was opened.

That initial facility consisted of one house, but over the next three years, God blessed them with additional facilities. There are now two houses: one which is home to 12 boys and another which is the residence of seven girls. Harvest employs, in addition to the three administrators mentioned above, two married couples and two single people as houseparents.

Between its beginning in 1993 and 1997, Harvest had served over 100 children. Their purpose is to provide "a loving Christian and home-like atmosphere for abused, abandoned, and neglected children. Our philosophy is based on a basic belief that a healthy Christian home environment, caring parents, and wholesome family life are fundamental necessities, if not rights, for every child." Most of the children at Harvest have parents, and one of Harvest's goals is to get families back together through evangelism and Christ-centered family counseling programs. Harvest has experienced grand success and senses the blessing of God. Social workers of this region have spoken highly of the caring, family atmosphere that exists at Harvest.

Harvest is constantly looking for areas in which to expand. They presently have 32 acres which they hope to develop. Their eventual goal is to serve 100 children at any one time.

Western Free Will Baptist Rest Home

Western Free Will Baptist Rest Home is a 30-bed rest home owned and operated by the North Carolina State Association of Free Will Baptists. The home is located in the heart of the Blue Ridge Mountains in Candler, North Carolina. Western began operation in 1979, with J.C. Lynn as administrator. He remained in that position until 1988, when he was succeeded by Edwin Hill. Hill was followed by Administrator Jack Ward, who began his duties in 1993. The personal care staff of the rest home consists of CNAs (certified nursing assistants) and nursing assistants.

The home has as its purpose to provide the highest quality medical care and to provide for the spiritual needs of its residents. The home holds church services each Sunday morning and special services during the week. Administrator Jack Ward states, "It is our commitment to make each resident as comfortable as possible. We recognize that every person is different and therefore must be treated as an individual. We pledge to give the best care possible with the resources we have available to us." Western Free Will Baptist Rest Home is licensed by the North Carolina Department of Human Resources Division of Facility Services.

Notes For Chapter Seven

[1] *Hillsdale Free Will Baptist College Catalog,* 1994-96, p. 4.

[2] This synopsis is based largely on an unpublished manuscript from Southeastern Free Will Baptist College entitled, "A Brief Historical Sketch of Southeastern Free Will Baptist College."

[3] Southeastern Free Will Baptist College Catalog, 1993-94, 1994-95, p. 3.

[4] Pamphlet entitled, "Free Will Baptist Children's Home–Eldridge, Alabama."

[5] Ibid.

[6] Ibid.

[7] This information taken from promotional literature published by FWBFM.

[8] Unpublished paper entitled, "Free Will Baptist Home for Children."

CHAPTER EIGHT

Unaffiliated Arminian Baptists in America

THE CONVENTION OF ORIGINAL FREE WILL BAPTISTS

The origin of the Convention of Original Free Will Baptists dates to 1962, when the North Carolina State Convention of Free Will Baptists withdrew from the National Association of Free Will Baptists. There were three basic issues involved in the controversy which led to the withdrawal of the North Carolina State Convention. Two issues—publishing and philosophy of higher education—caused tension between the leadership of the North Carolina State Convention and the National Association. But one issue—church government—was the issue which in the end caused the split.

Free Will Baptist Press in Ayden, North Carolina, had long published Sunday school literature for the denomination. However, in the 1950s tensions began to build between the Sunday School Board of the National Association and the Free Will Baptist Press, each of whom had entered into a contractual agreement in 1956 by which the Sunday School Board would approve curriculum writers and share in the profits from literature sales. This relationship was briefly interrupted but was eventually repaired. Yet controversy over denominational Sunday school publishing had left much discord between many people in the North Carolina State Convention and many others in the National Association.

Controversy intensified as charges were leveled against Mount Olive College, which had been established in 1953 by the North Carolina State Convention. Certain ministers criticized Mount Olive for perceived laxity of doctrinal and Christian-living standards. This aggravated the tension that already existed. The controversy came to a head when one such minister sued the executive committee of the Western Conference of North Carolina over a church polity dispute. The Western Conference eventually declared the minority faction of Edgemont Church in Durham, North Carolina, the true church, entitled to the church property, and so forth. Furthermore, in court proceedings, several North Carolina State Convention leaders had signed an affidavit stating that "connectional" church government was the traditional practice of Free Will Baptists in North Carolina.

These actions were brought up at the 1961 meeting of the National Association, and the body voted to vacate the seats of all National Association board members who had signed the affidavit. Eventually, the Executive Committee requested that the North Carolina State Convention disavow "any and all forms of connectional church government," maintaining that congregationalism was historic Free Will Baptist practice. In a special called conference in March of 1962, the North Carolina State Convention voted to withdraw from the National Association of Free Will Baptists.[1]

Thus the Convention of Original Free Will Baptists was born. The Convention of Original Free Will Baptists (COFWB) has approximately 35,000 members in 249 churches. Most of the churches affiliated with the COFWB are in North Carolina; however, many local churches in such states as South Carolina, Virginia, Georgia, and Florida are affiliated with the COFWB. The COFWB maintains several ministries. The Board of Foreign Missions has mission works in Mexico, the Philippines, India, Nepal, and Eastern Europe; the Board of Home Missions and Church Extension is involved in missions to Vietnamese-American refugees.

Mount Olive College, which was founded by the North Carolina State Convention in 1953, and is located in Mount Olive, North Carolina, has around 1,000 students and is home to the Free Will Baptist Historical Collection, a repository of historical materials from both the southern and northern Free Will Baptist movements. The Free Will Baptist Press of Ayden, North Carolina, continues to serve the COFWB, particularly in the publication of *The Free Will Baptist*, a monthly periodical, in addition to other Sunday school and church publishing ministries.

The COFWB also maintains a children's home; a retirement home; Cragmont Assembly, a retreat center; Camp Vandemere; a retirement program for ministers; and the Church Finance Association. Additionally, the COFWB promotes a Woman's Auxiliary Convention; a Laymen's League; a Sunday School Convention; a League Convention (church training arm); a ministerial association; the Commission on Chaplains; and the Historical Commission. The Carolina Bible Institute, though not owned and operated by the COFWB, is a private Original Free Will Baptist institute founded by the Reverend Floyd Cherry.

OTHER UNAFFILIATED FREE WILL BAPTISTS

Black Free Will Baptist Groups

Most black Free Will Baptists owe their origin to black people of Free Will Baptist sentiments in North Carolina who formed what would become the United American Free Will Baptist denomination in 1867 after the close of the War between the States. However, like their caucasian counterparts, a few black Free Will Baptists could trace their heritage back to the Randall movement, which started ministries among freedmen during the Reconstruction (1865-1877). The black Free Will Baptists of North Carolina formed an "annual meeting" in 1887 and a general conference in 1901. The

United American Free Will Baptists are much like white Free
Will Baptists, with the exception of certain non-Baptistic ele-
ments in church government such as a presiding bishop. The
United American Free Will Baptist Church, the largest
denomination of black Free Will Baptists, has more than
100,000 members in approximately 900 churches, largely in
North Carolina, Georgia, Florida, Louisiana, Mississippi, and
Texas. The headquarters of this denomination are in Kinston,
North Carolina. The church's periodical is called *The Free
Will Baptist Advocate*. The National Association of Free Will
Baptists has made fraternal overtures toward this denomina-
tion, including sending its Executive Secretary to UAFWB
conventions and inviting UAFWB leaders to National
Association conventions.

There are several other groups of black American Free
Will Baptists. The United American Freewill Baptist
Conference (membership unknown) was established in
Tallahassee, Florida, in 1968. Its headquarters are in
Lakeland, Florida. This group is very similar to the United
American Free Will Baptist Church, and little is known about
why the two groups are not united.

Outside of these two groups are smaller scattered associations of black Free Will Baptists in the South as well as in the
Northeast and Midwest. One such group of Free Will Baptists
is called the Unified Freewill Baptists, located in New
England. Unified congregations are made up largely of black
people who have moved from the rural South to urban New
England. Many of these congregations lean toward a pente-
costal-charismatic understanding of Christianity.

Pentecostal Free Will Baptists

The Pentecostal Free Will Baptist Church traces its beginnings to a multi-denominational revival meeting in Dunn,
North Carolina, in 1906, where many Free Will Baptists,
Methodists, Presbyterians, and Baptists gathered to witness
"speaking in tongues, singing in tongues, laughing the holy

laugh," and other manifestations of the new pentecostal movement raging throughout America.[2] G.B. Cashwell was the preacher, and he had just returned from the well known Azusa Street revival in Los Angeles. Among the worshipers at the revival in Dunn was the Reverend H.H. Goff, a Free Will Baptist minister from near Dunn. When he returned from the highly publicized meeting, his children met him at the door saying, "Papa, Papa, have you got the tongues?" He replied that he had not yet added, "but I want it worse than anything in all the world."[3] A few nights later, Goff claimed to have received the gift of unknown tongues. This phenomenon spread like wildfire throughout many churches of all denominations in North Carolina, creating conflict in several Free Will Baptist churches and conferences, especially the Cape Fear Conference. Controversies erupted into splits, and thus was formed the Pentecostal Free Will Baptist Church.[4] Pentecostal Free Will Baptists are much different from mainstream Free Will Baptists due to their emphasis on speaking in tongues and other elements characteristic of the modern pentecostal movement. This group of around 5,000 members maintains a Bible institute and is headquartered in Dunn, North Carolina.

OTHER FREE WILL BAPTISTS THAT ARE UNAFFILIATED WITH THE NATIONAL ASSOCIATION

There are many local associations—and local churches—that are identical to Free Will Baptists in the National Association in belief and practice but which, for one reason or another, wish to remain independent from Free Will Baptist state associations and the National Association. Though it is impossible to record all the local Free Will Baptist associations and churches that remain independent, there are several that are well known.

The Paul Palmer Conference in Southwest Georgia was formed in 1962 as a result of the controversy between the

National Association and the North Carolina State Convention. Though two of its churches maintain official affiliation with the Convention of Original Free Will Baptists, there appears to be no appreciable difference in doctrine or practice between the Palmer Conference and National Association churches in Southwest Georgia. Palmer churches and National Association churches in Southwest Georgia regularly invite ministers from each other's churches to conduct revival meetings, and Free Will Baptists from these two groups regularly fellowship together.

North Carolina is home to four Free Will Baptist associations that are neither affiliated with the National Association nor with the Convention of Original Free Will Baptists: Jack's Creek (a few of these churches are in Tennessee), Mount Mitchell, Western, and French Broad. In the 1970s, these associations together registered 68 churches and 134 ministers.

There is at least one conference in Ohio which is unaffiliated with the National Association. It is called the Ohioana Conference and comprises six churches.

There are evidently three Free Will Baptist associations in Oklahoma which are not affiliated with any larger Free Will Baptist group: Eastern Association, North Grand River Association, and Washita Association. Little is known about these associations.

There are three unaffiliated associations in Tennessee. Eastern Stone and Western Stone are located in the area between Eastern and Middle Tennessee. The Tennessee River Association is located in South Central Tennessee and North Alabama. In the early 1970s, these three associations had a combined membership of over 8,000 with 96 local churches.

The John Thomas Association of Freewill Baptists is the largest association which is unaffiliated with the National Association. John Thomas spans four states, with churches in Virginia, Kentucky, Ohio, and Indiana. In the early 1980s, it recorded 99 congregations with a combined membership of around 7,500.

While there are independent Free Will Baptist congregations in all parts of the United States, it bears mention that a sizeable number of unaffiliated churches exist in southwest Alabama which once were affiliated with the local associations in the Alabama State Association, but have since severed those ties. The same can also be said of North Georgia.

Leaders of National Association-affiliated Free Will Baptists in areas where unaffiliated Free Will Baptist associations exist have built bridges and maintained fraternal relationships with these groups in the hope of gaining official fellowship with them. Some Free Will Baptist associations that were unaffiliated a few decades ago (the Toe River Association of Tennessee, for example) are now affiliated after such overtures.

OTHER ARMINIAN BAPTISTS IN AMERICA

The General Baptists

The General Baptists are very similar to Free Will Baptists. There are almost 900 churches and around 73,000 members in the General Association of General Baptists, headquartered in Poplar Bluff, Missouri. This Arminian Baptist group was begun spontaneously by Benoni Stinson in the 1820s. The General Association was formed in 1870.

The major substantial difference between General Baptists and Free Will Baptists is that, unlike Free Will Baptists, General Baptists believe that the decision whether to practice the ordinance of feet-washing should be left up to the local church or association. Apparently some local associations require that their churches practice the ordinance while other associations leave it as an option.

With churches largely in the Midwest and South, the denomination publishes *The General Baptist Messenger* and operates an accredited college and theological seminary,

Oakland City College, in Oakland City, Indiana. General Baptists are active in home and foreign missions and have around 15,000 members in foreign countries.

Russian-American Baptists

There is a growing number of congregations made up of Russian Baptists who have migrated to the United States. In the mid-1990s, the Baptists of Russia enlisted the help of the National Association of Free Will Baptists, which actively supports missions in Russia. In 1996 the president of the Russian Baptist Union asked leaders of the National Association for Free Will Baptist assistance to several of these congregations. Some of these Russian-Americans now have close contact with American Free Will Baptist churches and ministers.

NOTES FOR CHAPTER EIGHT

[1]This summary is extremely brief due to the nature of this book. It is based on relevant articles in *The Free Will Baptist* and *Contact* magazines published during the years in question. To my knowledge, no histories of this schism have been written from the perspective of the National Association. However, two published sources chronicle this period from the perspective of the Convention of Original Free Will Baptists: Floyd B. Cherry, *An Introduction to Original Free Will Baptists* (Ayden, North Carolina: Free Will Baptist Press, 1989) and Michael R. Pelt, *A History of Original Free Will Baptists* (Mount Olive, North Carolina: Mount Olive College Press, 1996).

[2]Vinson Synan, *The Holiness-Pentecostal Movement in the United States* (Grand Rapids, Michigan: Wm. B. Eerdmans Publishing Company, 1971), p. 124.

[3]Florence Goff, *Tests and Triumphs* (Falcon, North Carolina, 1923), p. 51; quoted in Synan, pp. 124-125.

[4]Synan, pp. 130-131.

Select Bibliography

HISTORY

Baxter, Norman Allen. *History of the Freewill Baptists.* Rochester, New York: American Baptist Historical Society, 1958.

Burgess, Walter H. *John Smyth, the Se-Baptist, Thomas Helwys, and the First Baptist Church in England.* London: James Clarke and Company, 1911.

Cherry, Floyd B. *An Introduction to Original Free Will Baptists.* Ayden, North Carolina: Free Will Baptist Press, 1989.

Davidson, William F. *The Free Will Baptists in America, 1727-1984.* Nashville: Randall House Publications, 1985.

Dodd, Damon C. *The Free Will Baptist Story.* Nashville: Executive Department of the National Association of Free Will Baptists, 1956.

Dorgan, Howard. *Giving Glory to God in Appalachia: Worship Practices in Six Baptist Subdenominations.* Knoxville, Tennessee: University of Tennessee Press, 1987.

Estep, William R. *The Anabaptist Story.* Grand Rapids, Michigan: William B. Eerdmans Publishing Company, 1975.

Burgess, G.A. and J.T. Ward. *Free Baptist Cyclopaedia.* Chicago: Free Baptist Cyclopaedia Company, 1889.

Harrison, Harrold D., ed. *Who's Who Among Free Will Baptists.* Nashville: Randall House Publications, 1978.

Harrison, T.F. and J.M. Barfield. *A History of the Free Will Baptists of North Carolina.* Ayden, North Carolina: Free Will Baptist Press, 1898 [reprinted 1959].

Hasty, Steven. "Did They Survive," *Contact.* July 1988, pp. 12-13.

Hearn, R.K. "Origin of the Free Will Baptist Church of North Carolina," in The Historical Review: *A Journal of Church History Published by the Florida State Association of Free Will Baptists.* Summer 1994, pp. 30-48.

Latch, Ollie. *History of the General Baptists.* Poplar Bluff, Missouri: General Baptist Press, 1954.

Lumpkin, William L. *Baptist Confessions of Faith.* Valley Forge, Pennsylvania: Judson Press, 1959.

McBeth, H. Leon. *The Baptist Heritage: Four Centuries of Baptist Witness.* Nashville: Broadman Press, 1987.

Million, G.W. *History of Free Will Baptists.* Nashville: Board of Publications and Literature, National Association of Free Will Baptists, 1958.

O'Donnell, J.D. *A Survey of Church History.* Nashville: Randall House Publications, 1973.

Owsley, Frank L. *Plain Folk of the Old South.* Baton Rouge, Louisiana: Louisiana State University Press, 1949.

Pelt, Michael R. *A History of Original Free Will Baptists.* Mount Olive, North Carolina: Mount Olive College Press, 1996.

Picirilli, Robert E. *The History of Tennessee Free Will Baptists.* Nashville: Historical Commission of the Tennessee State Association of Free Will Baptists, 1985.

_____, ed. *A History of Free Will Baptist State Associations.* Nashville: Randall House Publications, 1976.

Pinson, James Matthew. *Religious Social Reform in the Antebellum North: Abolition and Temperance Reform among the Northern Freewill Baptists, 1800-1860.* Unpublished M.A. thesis, University of West Florida, 1993.

Smith, Elizabeth. "The Former Articles of Faith of the North Carolina Free Will Baptists," *The Free Will Baptist.* July 27, 1960, pp. 10-11.

Stewart, I.D. *The History of Freewill Baptists for Half a Century.* Dover, New Hampshire: Freewill Baptist Printing Establishment, 1862.

Stevenson, George. "Laker, Benjamin," "Palmer, Paul," "Parker, Joseph," and "Surginer, William," in *Dictionary of North Carolina Biography,* ed. William S. Powell. Chapel Hill, North Carolina: University of North Carolina Press, 1991.

White, B.R. *The English Baptists of the Seventeenth Century.* London: Baptist Historical Society, 1983.

_____. *The English Separatist Tradition: From the Marian Martyrs to the Pilgrim Fathers.* London: Oxford University Press, 1971.

Wisehart, Mary. *The Fifty-Year Record of the National Association of Free Will Baptists.* Nashville: Randall House Publications, 1988.

THEOLOGY

Arminius, Jacobus. *The Works of James Arminius*. The London Edition, translated by James Nichols and William Nichols. Grand Rapids, Michigan: Baker Book House, 1986.

Crowson, Milton. *The Epistle to the Hebrews*. Nashville: Randall House Publications, 1974.

Forlines, F. Leroy. *Biblical Ethics*. Nashville: Randall House Publications, 1973.

_____. *Notes on Ecclesiology*. Nashville: Free Will Baptist Bible College, [n.d.].

_____. *Romans* in the *Randall House Bible Commentary*. Nashville: Randall House Publications, 1987.

_____. *Systematics: A Study of the Christian System of Life and Thought*. Nashville: Randall House Publications, 1975.

Grantham, Thomas. *Christianismus Primitivus, Or the Ancient Christian Religion*. London: Francis Smith, 1678.

Griffith, John. *God's Oracle and Christ's Doctrine, Or, The Six Principles of the Christian Religion*. London: Richard Moon, 1655.

Hyatt, Marie T. *Why the Atonement Was Necessary*. Nashville: Board of Publications and Literature, National Association of Free Will Baptists, 1944.

Jeffrey, William. *The Whole Faith of Man*. [n.p.], England: Printed for G. Dawson, [n.d.].

Loveday, Samuel. *Personal Reprobation Reprobated: Being a Plain Exposition Upon the Ninth Chapter to the Romans*. London: Francis Smith, 1676.

O'Donnell, J.D. *Faith for Today: A Presentation of Free Will Baptist Beliefs*. Nashville: Randall House Publications, 1974.

_____. *Free Will Baptist Doctrines*. Nashville: Randall House Publications, 1974.

Outlaw, W. Stanley. *1 Timothy* in the *Randall House Bible Commentary*. Nashville: Randall House Publications, 1990.

Picirilli, Robert E. *Church Ordinances and Government*. Nashville: Randall House Publications, 1973.

_____. *Perseverance*. Nashville: Randall House Publications, 1973.

St. Claire, E. L. *What Free Will Baptists Believe and Why*. Ayden, North Carolina: Free Will Baptist Printing Company, [n.d.].

Index

– S –

– T –

CPSIA information can be obtained at www.ICGtesting.com
Printed in the USA
LVOW040749111211

258834LV00001B/7/A